ATTACK on TITAN JUNIOR HIGH

5

SAKI NAKAGAWA

Based on "Attack on Titan" by HAJIME ISAYAMA

Contents

TUESDAY, NOVEMBER 3RD

STUDENT ON DUTY: BERTOLT

SIXTIETH PERIOD: LIGHT UP YOUR PASSION

I CAN'T BELIEVE THIS STORY IS FINALLY COMING TO AN END...
EVERYTHING'S READY. THE DRAMA FESTIVAL IS ABOUT TO BEGIN...

PRATTLE
DRIVEL
104th Drama Festival of Attack on Titan Junior High

FIRST, THE "SUREFIRE HIT" SCRIPT THAT JEAN BROUGHT US STUNK WORSE THAN WEEK-OLD DONKEY LEAVINGS.
Attack on History
NOOOOOOOOOOO
RIIIIIIIIIIIIP
I WAS SO SHOCKED THAT I SHREDDED THAT SCRIPT RIGHT IN FRONT OF THAT TITAN SYMPATHIZER AND THEN SET THE SHREDS ON FIRE.

FORTUNATELY, I WROTE A NEW SCRIPT FULL OF HUMAN PRIDE, AND THERE WAS A... GOOD-NATURED DEBATE OVER PARTS.

IN THE END, I OFFERED TO PLAY THE HERO, AND EVERYONE CHEERED. THE OTHER PARTS CAST THEMSELVES.

MY DREAM OF GATHERING A HUGE MOB OF HUMANS, ENRAGED BY TITAN OPPRESSION AND $20 THEATRE COCKTAILS...
Heh...
NOW, THE CURTAIN IS ABOUT TO RISE ON MY (MAKE-BELIEVE) DREAM.

I MEAN, THAT'S ALL I REMEMBER, AT LEAST.
Break a leg, Reiner!
Thanks!

MURMUR
MUTTER
...AND EXECUTING ALL THE TITANS!! (METAPHORICALLY.)
GURGLE
CHATTER
POPCORN
STEP

MY MOB—ER, AUDIENCE IS ALL TITANS?!

SHOCK

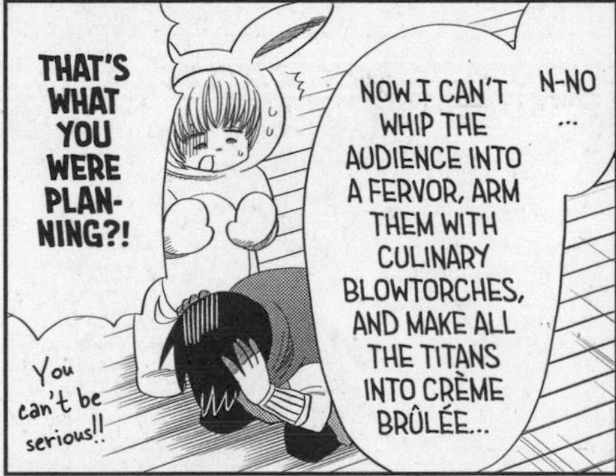

Whaaa?!
ANIMALS SHOULD BE PUNCHED AND NOT HEARD!!
WHAM

HEH HEH...
NICE PUNCH... I GUESS YOU'RE A METHOD ACTOR...
?!

I SEE YOU STILL HAVE PASSION...
...FOR THE STAGE...

SO HORSEY, YOU WERE JUST TRYING TO GIVE ME THE COURAGE TO PUNCH ANYTHING, EVEN THE TITANS...?
So ugly... I must've punched him harder than I thought...
YEAH, SURE, YOU'RE AN EXAMPLE TO US ALL. UH, I MEAN, WHINNY WHINNY.

NOW, IF YOU'LL EXCUSE ME...
...I THINK MY CORNEA MAY BE MISSING...
...

HORSEY... I ADMIT THAT AFTER YOU *JOCKEYED* FOR MY POSITION, I *BRIDLED* AT YOUR ADVICE...
BUT IT BE-*HOOVES* ME TO THANK YOU... I'VE BEEN *SADDLED* WITH GREAT RESPONSIBILITY, AND I WILL CARRY IT OUT... *NEIGH*, I MUST!!
...

HEY... YOU CAN'T DISTRACT ME, TALKING CURTAIN!
I'M GETTING INTO CHARACTER HERE! UH, I MEAN, NEIGH! I WANT OATS!

HEY, YOU. YOU IN THE HORSE GETUP.
GASP

...

SHUT UP! I'M OFFERING YOU A CHANCE TO ESCAPE FROM THAT SWEATY, MUSTY HORSE COSTUME!
WEARING THIS IS LIKE BEING INSIDE CHEESE...
WHAT DO I HAVE TO DO...?

ALL YOU HAVE TO DO IS... MESS UP THIS PLAY FOR ME!!
AH HA HA HA
EREN, YOU SOUND LIKE A GOAT IMITATING WILLIAM SHATNER...
MAYBE YOU NEED TO TRY A MORE... IMPROVISATIONAL STYLE...
ARMIN, ACTING IS ABOUT DOMINATING THE AUDIENCE!
I MEAN, I'LL TRY IT...
SCRIPT

TITANS! HEY! LISTEN! UP YOU PESTS!
I WILL! GET RID OF! YOU!
SCRIPT
GRIN

HENH...
NOW, TITAN, LOOK INTO MY EYES... I WANT YOU TO SEE MY HATE...
heh heh
PANT
PANT
PANT
...AS THE LIFE SEEPS OUT OF YOUR TURGID BODY!
SCRIPT

NEVER MIND! I WAS WRONG! DON'T GO OFF SCRIPT!
I swear I almost peed just now!
ARMIN ...

YOU'RE ALMOST UP...
OH, SORRY!
Hmm...
I WAS JUST RUNNING LINES WITH EREN...
At this rate, he's going to get #punched...

WELL, BREAK A LEG, EREN!!
R-RIGHT!
Don't be yourself!!

THE MOMENT HAS COME...
ACT YOUR HEART OUT, EVERYONE! I'M NOT ON TILL LATER, SO...
CLAMOR
CLAMOR
CLAMOR

I'LL BE BACK HERE, GUNNING PIXY STIX AND GETTING PSYCHED!!
...

HEH
フッ
バーン
BUNNYYY
WE OPEN ON A PASTORAL SCENE OF ANIMALS, LIVING IN PRIMITIVE HARMONY ...
THEY GIVE THANKS TO THE VAGUELY PROTO-GERMANIC FOREST SPIRITS...
...WITH DELICIOUS CANDIED VEGGIES THAT MY MOM MADE BETWEEN SEVEN-AND-SEVENS...
SHINY キラ
SHINY キラ
BUN-BUN IS TRULY GRATEFUL, FOREST GOD...

YOU PROVIDE US WITH SUCH TASTY BOUNTY...
THANK YOU FOR THIS MEAL!!
かぷっ
CHOMP
!!
MUNCH
MUNCH

YOU GUYS!!
WHAT'S GOING ON...?
BLEAAAARGH
YAKYAK
MORE ACTING, LESS WRITHING IN DISGUST!
SHOCK
EREN... I DON'T THINK THOSE WERE THE CANDIED VEGGIES...
THEY LOOKED MORE LIKE WAX TO ME...
WAX?! THE BANE OF HALLOWEEN AND LEG HAIRS?
GUYS, ARE YOU ALL RIGHT?!
TH-THEY'RE WORKING THROUGH IT!
DESE BEGGIES
ARR SO
DELISHUSH...
AS PRESIDENT SHAQSPEAR ONCE SAID, THE SHOW MUST GO ON!

YOU'VE TOUCHED ME IN MY FEELING PLACE...!
DON'T WORRY, EREN, I'VE EATEN MY FAIR SHARE OF WAX FRUIT...
PANT PANT
ACTUALLY, I NOTICED A STRANGER HANGING AROUND A WHILE AGO...
THEY'RE PROBABLY TRYING TO WRECK OUR PLAY...
BUT...

I WON'T GIVE UP THAT EASY!!
I AM A RABBIT!
CARROTS ARE MY LIGHT THAT SHINES ABOVE!! OOOH BABY YEAH!!
MUNCH MUNCH

ARMIN ...!!
TSK
I'M THE PIG! STOP HAMMING IT UP...
AND THIS IS ALL THANKS TO HER!!
TOSS
RIGHT
Y-YES, WHERE IS SHE TODAY...?
HAS SHE WANDERED INTO DEER TRAFFIC AGAIN?
OR IS SHE STRANDED AT A POSSUM DINNER PARTY?!

IT LOOKS LIKE ARMIN MANAGED TO CHOKE DOWN ENOUGH OF THAT SQUISHY ORANGE GLOP THAT THEY'LL MAKE IT TO THE ACT I CLIMAX...
THE ENTRANCE OF PRINCESS KRISTA!!
GASP

EREN... THE WALL...
THE WALL...! HE'S NOT THERE...!!

HUH?

PRIN-CESS!!
YOUR HIGHNESS, WHERE ARE YOU HIDING TODAY!?

AH!
STEP

PRIN-CESS!
THERE YOU ARE!
H-HEY, THAT'S—
わぁぁぁぁぁ

LOVELY AS A SPRING ...
...MOR... ...NING...

HER HIGH-NESS IS SWOLE !!
GAAAAAUUUGH
AND SO THE FIRST HALF OF TEAM EREN'S PLAY CAME TO A MUSCULAR, ODDLY AROUSING CLOSE...

WHERE DID KRISTA GO?!
AND JEAN'S TOTALLY AWOL...
WHAT'S GOING ON?!

THIS 'N' THAT ETC.

HA HA... YOU ALL DESERVE THIS...
AND FOR BEING THE THORN IN MY OATMEAL...

YOU'LL ALL ENDURE ...
STEP

...THE SAME SUFFER-ING AS ME!

AH HA HA HA HA HA HA HA

HITCH ...

DRAMATIC FACE REVEAL

STOP PLAYING WITH THAT FLASHLIGHT AND TELL ME...!!
!
WHY ARE YOU DOING THIS...?!
GUR-GLING FOOL!
AS IF YOU NEED TO ASK...
IT'S ALL THEIR FAULT! THEY ARE THE SAND IN OUR YOGA PANTS!
HAVING SO MUCH FUN PLAYING SEXY MAN PRINCESS ...!
EVEN THOUGH ...
ALL THE WHILE ...!
YES MEANS YES
OUR TEAM HAD TO PUT ON...
ド
SQUISHOOM
GROAAAANH
SQUID MEETS COLOSSUS: A COMIC PARABLE OF PUBERTY AND GRUNTING !!

THE HAM STEAK IN MY LOCKER! THE TACK ON MY SCOLIOSIS PILLOW...!
HITCH...

IT JUST TICKS ME OFF TO SEE THEM HAVING FUN...
THEY'RE THE PEBBLE IN MY ARMPIT HAIR!

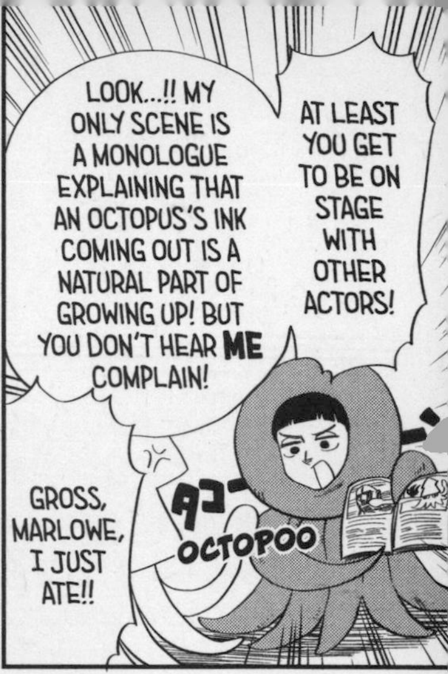
AT LEAST YOU GET TO BE ON STAGE WITH OTHER ACTORS!
LOOK...!! MY ONLY SCENE IS A MONOLOGUE EXPLAINING THAT AN OCTOPUS'S INK COMING OUT IS A NATURAL PART OF GROWING UP! BUT YOU DON'T HEAR ME COMPLAIN!
OCTOPOO
GROSS, MARLOWE, I JUST ATE!!

ONE MORE BOTCHED METAPHOR AND I SWEAR...!!
SPRAY
?!
YOU'RE JUST MAKING THINGS HARD FOR EVERY-ONE OUT OF SELFISHNESS !!

NOW, SAY SORRY !!
BUT...
BUT IT'S SO EM-BARRASS-ING...

I NEVER WANTED TO BE AN AM-OROUS BUT NAIVE SQUID LEARNING A VITAL LESSON ABOUT SEX POSITIVITY...
I WANTED TO PLAY A PRINCESS, TOO...
I WAS JUST SO JEALOUS...

HITCH...
WHY DIDN'T YOU SAY SO FROM THE START...?
YES MEANS YES
OF COURSE WE ALL LONG TO PLAY A PRINCESS WHO OVERCOMES STEREOTYPES AND GENDER NORMS TO BECOME AN OLYMPIC SHOTPUTTER **AND** FIND LOVE...

BUT HITCH... LOOK OVER THERE.
YES MEANS YES
KCHAK
YOU DON'T HAVE ANYTHING TO WORRY ABOUT...

THEIR AUDIENCE...

...IS ALL TITANS...!

YES MEANS YES
AHAHAHAHA-HA YOU'RE TOTALLY RIGHT!
THERE ISN'T A SINGLE HUMAN WATCHING!!

HITCH, SO YOU'RE OKAY PLAYING TENTA-CHAN?
YES...
I CAN FEEL MY SUCKERS RELAXING ALREADY ...

AND YOU'LL SET FREE THE GIRL PLAYING THE PRINCESS?
SHE'S WITH JEAN...
YES MEANS YES

IN THE STUDENT COUNCIL ROOM...
Though even I gotta admit, Reiner made a killer princess...
KRISTAAAA !!
YES MEANS YES

EREN...
OH!
HAVE YOU GUYS SEEN KRISTA...?

YES MEANS YES
Y-YOU TWO...

YOU'RE DRESSED AS A SQUID AND OCTO-PUS?!
THAT'S THE FUNNIEST THING I'VE EVER SEEN!!
AHHAHAHAHAHAHA HEE HEE HA HA HA HA HA
THEY BOTH LIVE IN THE OCEAN AND ARE FOOD, NOT PEOPLE!!

Good God, you're an idiot, Eren...

OH, I ALMOST FORGOT. HAVE YOU SEEN KRISTA ...?
WHEEZE WHEEZE
NO WE HAVEN'T !!

HEY, HITCH!!
DASH

NO ONE GETS AWAY WITH CALLING ME FOOD THAT LIVES IN THE OCEAN...!!
EREN, YOU ARE THE GOAT IN MY RETIREMENT COMMUNITY... AND YOU WILL PAY!!

WHAAAT ?!
ARE YOU SURE, ARMIN...? YOU SAW A SUSPICIOUS FIGURE...?
YES... I ACTUALLY NOTICED SOMEONE WATCHING US REHEARSE...
MAYBE KRISTA WAS KIDNAPPED BY THAT SAME PERSON...
IT'S TIME TO DO WHAT I ALWAYS DO...
...RUN OFF WITH NO PARTICULAR PLAN IN MIND!
DASH
EREN, NO! THINK OF YOUR BRAIN!
NO TO YOU BOTH! **I'LL** TAKE CARE OF IT!
FRIEDA-SENSEI!
YES, IT'S ME, YOUR SAVIOR IN A FLOWER-PRINT FROCK!
FRIEDA-SENSEI!
TELL ME MORE ABOUT THIS FIGURE, ARMIN...
IT LOOKED LIKE...
A SQUID HAVING A TOUGH TIME WITH PUBERTY.
A SQUID ?!

OH GOD NO!
IT'S TIME FOR MY SECRET WEAPON: IMPROV THEATRE.
THAT'S JUST SIXTY KILOGRAMS FROM NOW. WE CAN'T WAIT FOR KRISTA.
LISTEN UP, EVERYONE. THE SECOND ACT STARTS IN ONE MINUTE.
Wasn't there a play with a squid role...?
COME ON...
IT'LL BE OKAY! ARMIN WILL COME UP WITH FUNNY IDEAS, LIKE A PLUMBER IN A... PLACE THAT HAS NO PLUMBERS!
IT'S OUR LAST AND ONLY OPTION!
...LET'S MAKE THIS THE MOST BEARABLE JUNIOR HIGH IMPROV SHOW EVER!

DRAMA! EXTRA COMIC

SQUID MEETS COLOSSUS (SYNOPSIS)

ONCE, THERE WAS A TRIBE OF DELICIOUS SQUID VORE ENTHUSIASTS...
イカガ
HOW 'BOUT IT?
イカガ
HOW 'BOUT IT?
イカガ!?
HOW 'BOUT IT?
THEY SPENT THEIR DAYS LOOKING FOR THAT SPECIAL SOMEONE WHO WOULD WANT TO EAT THEM.
THE SQUIDS WERE OVERJOYED (AT FIRST) WHEN THEY SUDDENLY APPEARED...
SASHIMI... GRILLED... BROILED... AND EVEN SHUMAI...
THE SQUIDS WERE DELICIOUSLY DEVOURED IN EVERY WAY IMAGINABLE...
BUT THEN ONE DAY, A TITAN APPEARED WHO STARTED REPOSTING SQUIDS' ART WITHOUT CREDIT AND ALSO STUFFING THEIR CORPSES WITH RICE BEFORE EATING THEM!
AS YOU KNOW, SQUIDS HATE RICE, SO THEY WERE FURIOUS! THE SQUIDS GOT TOGETHER ON REDDIT AND DECIDED TO TEACH THE TITAN A LESSON ABOUT AFFIRMATIVE CONSENT AND ART SHARING ETIQUETTE!
HAHAHA! SQUIDS POOP IN WATER!!
BWAHAHA!
だははー!!
WHA?!

*Editor's Note: There's a pun on the Japanese word for squid on this page, but I'm not going to explain it to you because translation notes are for feeble-minded people with inspirational wrist tattoos.

SIXTY-FIRST PERIOD: SO WHAT IF THE PRINCESS IS BULKY?
BEEEEEP
104th Attack Junior High Drama Festival
The second half of "Attack on History" is about to begin. Sit down and shut your faces!
FLASH
MURMUR
MURMUR
GWEEGH
OUR POOR PRINCESS! YOU'VE BEEN CURSED BY A... WINDOW WASHER... WHO'S ALSO A... BAKER, OR SOMETHING! YES, AND...
TO BREAK THE CURSE REQUIRES DEFEATING THE TITANS... YES, AND, AND...
BADUMP
BADUMP
BADUMP

...AND THE KISS OF A PRINCE!!

きゃーっ EEEEK

WHA?! WHA?!

BEATING THE TITANS IS FINE, BUT YOU KNOW HOW I FEEL ABOUT OTHER MEN'S SPIT IN MY MOUTH!!

And Reiner, what was that eeking about?!

S-sorry...

IT'S JUST... I DON'T THINK I'M CURSED IN THE SLIGHTEST!

THIS IS OPENING A WINDOW TO A FEMININE SIDE THAT I NEVER KNEW EXISTED! I NEED TO GO TO EUROPE TO THINK!

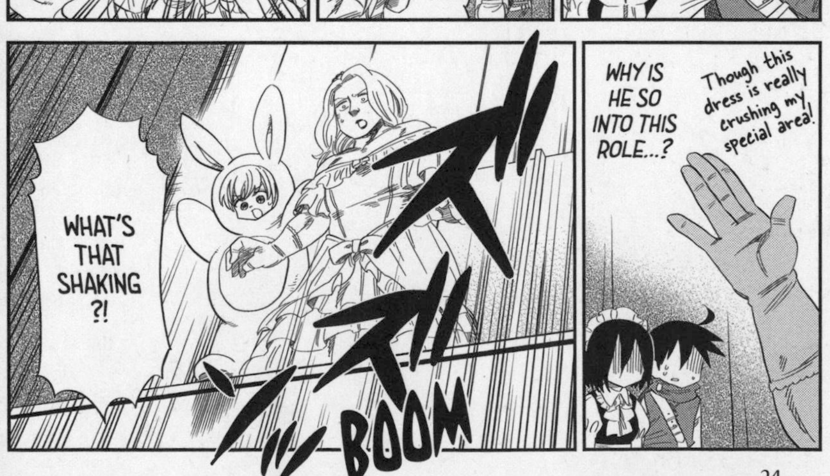

WHY IS HE SO INTO THIS ROLE...?
Though this dress is really crushing my special area!
WHAT'S THAT SHAKING?!
BOOM

PRINCESS! THE QUEEN HAS AWAKENED A TITAN TO KILL YOU!
YES AND, EEK! SOMEONE SAVE ME!!
OOH NOO!
WHAT...?! SHOOT, THERE'S NO WAY AROUND IT!!
GAAAAAH
YOU'LL JUST HAVE TO KILL OFF THE PRINCESS BEFORE I COME ON!!
EREN BELIEVES THAT A MAN'S MOUTH IS HIS CASTLE, AND THE SPIT IS THE BATHROOM OF THE MOUTH.
MEANWHILE...
STUDENT COUNCIL ROOM
AH HA HA HA HA HA
HAHAHAHA
TA DAAA
THAT'S WHAT YOU GET FOR HAVING A REASONABLY NICE TIME IN DRAMA CLASS!!
GRAB
GROAN...
NOW I'LL SWITCH YOUR COSTUME WITH MINE...
...AND WE'LL SEE WHO'S PERCHED ATOP A FETTUCINE BY THE END OF TODAY!!
KABOOOM
KA-BOOM?!

FSHHHHHH
I HAD A HUNCH THIS WAS YOUR DOING... YOU'RE THE ONLY SQUID I COULD THINK OF...
W-WHO THE HECK ARE YOU?! AND YOU KNOW THIS IS A COSTUME, RIGHT?!
STEP
UH, DON'T COME ANY CLOSER OR I'LL INK YOU!
GRAB
FLASH
GAAAAUGH
BLINK
OH...? WHERE ...?
OH HIST— I MEAN KRISTA, YOU'RE ALL RIGHT!
HUG
I SMELL GRILLED SQUID...
DON'T WORRY, IT'S PROBABLY JUST A BRAIN TUMOR...
PSHHHHHH

EVERY-ONE!
I BROUGHT KRISTA BACK!!
WOW! YAY!!

SHE'S READY TO GO! GET HER ON THE STAGE QUICKLY!
WHERE ARE THEY IN THE SCRIPT?!
THE SCRIPT?! UH...!

HEH HEH... I CHANGED THE SCRIPT AND RIGGED THE LOTTERY TO SECURE THE ROLE OF THE PRINCESS FOR HISTORIA.
NOW I GET TO WATCH HER SHINE ON THE STAGE FOR AT LEAST THREE HOURS...
THE THING IS...
EREN, ER, THE PRINCE IS MISSING, SO THE PRINCESS CAN'T GO ON STAGE YET...

HUH...? BUT WHY...?
SOMETHING ABOUT A WINDOW WASHER, AND REINER'S GOING TO FRANCE... ANY-WAY, THE PRINCE HAS TO KISS THE PRINCESS FOR HER TO CHANGE BACK!
GRAAAARGH

WHY DID YOU HAVE TO DO THAT?!
W-WE THOUGHT WE COULD BUY MORE TIME THIS WAY...
JOLT

WHO CARES ABOUT THE STUPID PRINCE ...?

ANYONE, GET OUT THERE AND KISS REINER!
POINT
JUST PLANT A BIG FAT ONE ON THAT SQUARE JAW!
STARTLE

...

L-LET'S STALL UNTIL EREN COMES BACK!
YEAH, I'M SURE EREN IS GONE FOR A REALLY GOOD REASON AND NOT BECAUSE HIS ARM IS STUCK IN A URINAL...

GLARE
LESS JABBER!! MORE SMOOCH-ING!!

IF WE WAIT, KRISTA WILL NEVER GET TO GO ON STAGE...!!
I don't really mind...
FINE... IF YOU WON'T DO IT, THEN...
I WILL !!
PLOP
GALLOP GALLOP GALLOP GALLOP GALLOP GALLOP GALLOP
YANK
STARTLE
WHAAAA?!

FRIEDA-SENSEI AND REINER ARE MAKING SWEET, SENSUAL MEMORIES IN THE GARDEN OF WORDS!!
EEK

EREN... WHERE DID YOU GO...?
WITHOUT YOU, THIS PLAY IS LIKELY...

...GOING TO FALL APART.
NO, MOST DEFINITELY...

10 MINUTES AGO
Eee! Titans are scary!!
GRAAAR

STAGE LEFT
(THAT'S THE RIGHT SIDE OF THE STAGE FOR SOME REASON)

HEY, EREN.
COME OVER HERE.

WHAT IS IT, JEAN?
NEED HELP PEEING IN THE TOILET WITH YOUR UGLY FACE?
GOOD ONE, DUDE.
NO, JUST COME LOOK AT MY SWEET POG COLLECTION.
HEY, WHAT HAPPENED TO YOUR HORSE COSTUME ...?
I-IT'S FINE! I DON'T HAVE ANY MORE LINES, ANYWAY!
SO, WHAT ARE POGS, ANYWAY...? SOME KIND OF CHEESY TREAT?
EREN...
GRAB
WHACK
JEAN...

HM...
SPLAT

THIS IS ALL YOUR FAULT, YOU KNOW. YOU REFUSED TO HAND OVER THE LEAD ROLE TO ME...
...EVEN THOUGH I USED MY SPECIAL NASAL WHINING VOICE...
YANK
SO THIS COSTUME BELONGS TO ME NOW!

!!
GRAB
HEY!!
I SAID, I'M TAKING YOUR CLOTHES OFF!
TREMBLE
TREMBLE
TREMBLE
TREMBLE

WHAT'D YOU DO THAT FOR?!
GLARE
Y-YOU'RE BACK ON YOUR FEET ALREADY ...?!
...!
THAT KARATE CHOP WAS LIKE BEING HIT WITH A FLOPPY HOT DOG! NOW WHY?!

DO YOU CARE ABOUT THIS ROLE SO MUCH..
THAT YOU'D KISS REINER FOR IT...?

OH, THAT'S RIGHT. THE PRINCE WILL HAVE TO KISS REINER...!

I CAN'T...!
THUNK

E-EREN, WHAT ABOUT YOU...?
CAN YOU—

JUST THIS ONCE... YES.
HEH

I'M PREPARED OVERCOME MY SPIT PHOBIA, OPEN THE DOORS TO THE PALACE OF MY MOUTH...

...AND ALLOW REINER IN...

...TO THE THRONE ROOM OF MY TONGUE!

YOU WIN, EREN...
YOU... ARE A TRUE PROFES-SIONAL!!

ON STAGE
GRAAAARGH
LIKE I WAS SAYING EARLIER... R-REINER AND...
EEEEEK
FRIEDA-SENSEI!
HE...
...KISSED THE HORSE FACE...
GRRRRIIIIIND

YES AND, UH—
SMOKE BOMB!!
EEEK
COUGH
モク
HACK
モク
GUHAGH
モク
DRAG
ずる
DRAG
ずる
HURK
モク
HORK
モク
BWEGH
モク
I...
UM...
Make up something
YAAAY!
THE CURSE IS LIFTED, AND I FEEL FRESH AS A NEW STICK OF SPEAR-MINT GUM!!

GLANCE
くいくい WAVE
HOLD ON, EVERYONE! YES AND WE'RE NOT OUT OF THE WOODS YET!
オオオ ARGH
GRAAAAAAAAAA ウォオオォ
YES AND WE HAVEN'T BEATEN THE TITANS YET!
きゃーっ!! EEEEK!!

Pssst.
EREN ISN'T BACK YET... IF HE DOESN'T GET TO GO ON STAGE WE'LL NEVER HEAR THE END OF IT...
WE HAVE TO GIVE HIM SOMETHING TO DO!
STEP

COME ON, EREN!!

H-HURRY...!

STILL...

SHOOT... WHY DO YOU KEEP YOUR POGS SO FAR AWAY, JEAN...?!

PANT

PANT

PANT

PANT

HEY, GUYS!!

I'LL GET TO BEAT UP THE TITANS!!

FINAL-LY...I'LL FINALLY BE ON STAGE...

GET READY TO BE SLAPPED WITH MY HANDS!!

HEY, TITANS!!

DASH

EREN!

And so every last titan was killed...

And peace returned to this small nation in the forest...

NOW EVERY-ONE CLAP FOR KRISTA! NOW!!
CLAP
パチパチ
CLAP
CLAP
CLAP

ぷんぷーん
GRRRRRR

I'M NOT VERY HAPPY, EITHER...

OH, DEAR. SEEMS THA SOME IN TH AUDIENCE AREN'T VER HAPPY WITH T WAY THE PLA WENT...
Rub
I WAS JUST WORKING HARD TO MAKE EVERYONE LOVE KRISTA— I MEAN, EVERYONE IN THE SHOW, EQUALLY...

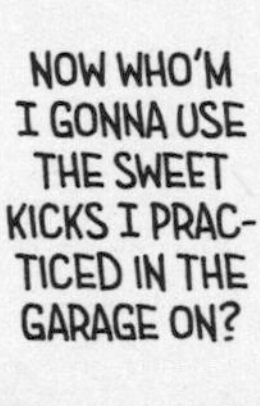

WHY...? WHY ARE THE TITANS ALREADY BEATEN...?
NOW WHO'M I GONNA USE THE SWEET KICKS I PRAC-TICED IN THE GARAGE ON?

YOU'VE LEFT ME NO CHOICE...
KCHAK

OH NO—
THAT PLAS-TIC SWORD WOULD LEAVE A SMALL SCRATCH ON MY SKIN...!

?!
LEAP

I'M GOING TO SMASH UP SOME REAL TITANS INSTEAD!!
RPAPAPAAAAAA
AAAAAUGH
NOOOO
Eren, you idiot!
YAAAAH
EREN WAS QUICKLY SUBDUED.
IT TOOK DAYS TO GET THE STENCH OF TITAN DROOL OUT OF HIS DOUBLET.
WHY DID I EXPECT HE'D EVER LEARN...
GAAAAUGH
...

THIS SCRIPT... IT'S JUST LIKE THAT TIME BEFORE...
YES.
ALSO...

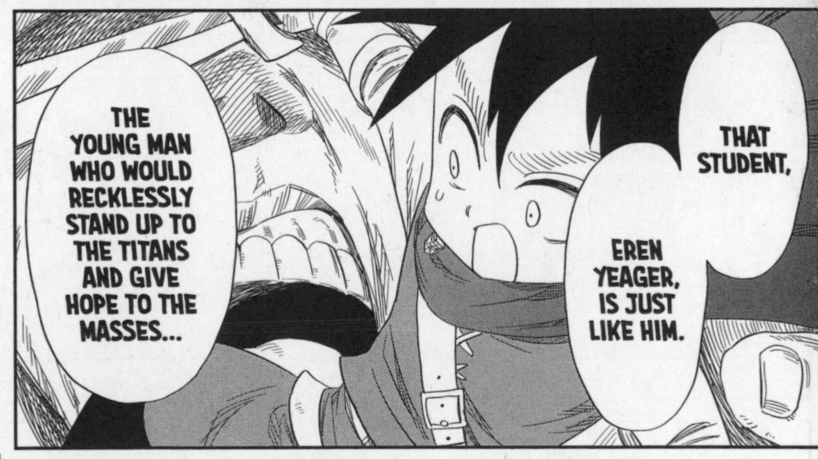
THAT STUDENT, EREN YEAGER, IS JUST LIKE HIM.
THE YOUNG MAN WHO WOULD RECKLESSLY STAND UP TO THE TITANS AND GIVE HOPE TO THE MASSES...

COULD IT BE...
THAT HISTORY WILL REPEAT ITSELF...?

AAAHA-HAHA! YOU GRINNING FREAK SHOWS!
LET ME DOWN SO I CAN HATE CRIME YOU!
DANGLE
AHAHAHAHAHAHA
UMM...
THEN AGAIN, MAYBE NOT...

GLOOOM

HA HA...
TOO BAD THAT THE DRAMA FESTIVAL HAD TO BE CANCELLED...
OH, THAT'S OKAY. I DON'T THINK WE COULD HAVE WON ANYWAY.

BESIDES... WE ALL GAINED SOMETHING IMPORTANT TODAY.

I GUESS WE GOT SOME FUN MEMORIES OUT OF IT...
EREN... YOU MUST BE THE MOST FRUSTRATED OF ALL OF US FOR NOT GETTING TO DO ANYTHING ON STAGE...
I GUESS HE GREW UP A LITTLE...
LOOK, YOU GUYS...
I RIPPED OUT A TITAN'S EYELASHES AND FLOSSED MY TEETH WITH THEM!!
THIS IS A HUGE ACHIEVEMENT FOR HUMANITY!!
TADAAA
GROSS, AND WHO CARES?!
DRAMA FESTIVAL ARC: FIN

BONUS STORY: IT'S ONLY PUBERTY

ATTACK JUNIOR HIGH FIRST-YEAR STUDENT EREN YEAGER.
HE LOVES CHEESE MEATLOAF SO MUCH THAT HE'D EVEN FIGHT THE TITANS FOR IT... THOUGH HE'D REALLY DO THAT ANYWAY.
I READ AN ARTICLE ABOUT SOMETHING CALLED "OMEGA-3." I WONDER IF THIS'LL GIVE ME TELEKINESIS OR SOMETHING.

EREN... IS THAT YOUR LUNCH FOR TODAY?
YEAH? WHY?

IT'S A LUNCH BOX WITH MACKEREL COOKED IN MISO.
MACRACKLIN'
...
SO IT'S NOT CHEESE MEATLOAF FOR ONCE.
MEAT... LOAF...?

WELL, SURE, I LIKE THEM...
...BUT IF I ATE THEM EVERY DAY THEY WOULDN'T TASTE AS SWEET!
HUH?!
BUT I THOUGHT YOU SAID YOU EAT CHEESE MEATLOAF THREE TIMES A DAY! IT'S, LIKE, YOUR ONLY REAL CHARACTER TRAIT!
Aside from racism.
HUH...?
I NEVER SAID THAT...
WHAT'S WRONG WITH YOUR FACE?!

ACCORDING TO MY RECORDS...
EREN HAS BEEN ACTING FUNNY SINCE 1:58 AM ON OCTOBER 4.
1:58 AM ON OCTOBER 4?!
RIGHT AROUND 2ND-AND-A-HALFTH DINNERTIME?

THAT NIGHT...
HE SUDDENLY STARTED SAYING, "I'M NOT MAD ABOUT THE MEATLOAF, I'M MAD THAT THEY ATE MY WHOLE LUNCH..."
WHAT DID THAT MEAN...?
...WELL,
IT MEANS JUST WHAT IT SOUNDS LIKE...!!
HUH?

THERE'S BEEN LIKE A THOUSAND PAGES OF THIS MANGA...

...AND I'M TIRED OF NOT HAVING ANY DEVELOPMENT BEYOND "CHEESE MEATLOAF GUY"!

(And racism.)

THERE'S EVEN BEEN AN ANIME, FOR CRYING OUT LOUD!!

... WHAT ARE YOU TALKING ABOUT...?
SO, AS USUAL, I'VE DECIDED TO WILDLY OVERREACT...
...AND NEVER EAT CHEESE MEATLOAF EVER AGAIN!

...EXCEPT FOR ONCE A DAY.
WILL EREN STOP BEING KNOWN AS THE CHEESE MEATLOAF GUY?
WILL HE KEEP EATING FISH? IS ANYONE STILL READING THIS AFTER THIS VOLUME GOT DELAYED LIKE FIVE TIMES?
FISHYLISHISH

THE NEXT DAY!!
STEAM
じゅわわ
うんうん
GROAN GROAN
HE WAS FINE ONLY YESTER-DAY...
IS EREN GOING TO BE OKAY?!
I'VE SEEN THIS BE-FORE! IT'S...
...CHEESE-LOAF FEVER.
OH, GOOD LORD.
WHEN YOU EAT AS MUCH CHEESELOAF AS EREN DID, THE BODY BECOMES DEPENDENT. HE'S MORE LOAF NOW THAN MAN. IF HE IS TO SURVIVE...
EREN...
...HE MUST EAT MEATLOAF WITH CHEESE AT LEAST THREE TIMES A DAY!!
WHAAAAT!!?
GROAN
WOW, ALL THOSE QUESTIONS SURE WERE ANSWERED FAST. ANYWAY, ONLY 20 CHAPTERS LEFT TO GO...
HEY! WAIT! COME BACK! THE NEXT ONE HAS ERWIN IN IT!

FACULTY ROOM
AND SO...
BLAH BLAH BLAH...
SKCH SKCH
AND YADDA YADDA YADDA AND THEN WE SUGGESTED IT TO THE STUDENTS. AS A RESULT...
月別3年成績
I SUCCEEDED IN BRINGING UP ACADEMIC ACHIEVEMENT FOR THE WHOLE GRADE 25% COMPARED TO LAST MONTH.
4 5 6 7 10
WOW
*LAZY TENURED ASSOCIATION
*SPIRIT-BREAKING APTITUDE TESTS
THIS IS AMAZING AND REVOLUTIONARY!
HE'S HANDSOME, SMART AND HAS TWO INTACT ARMS!
BRAVO!!
WOW... EVER SINCE ERWIN-SENSEI TOOK OVER THE GRADE, THE SCORES FOR OUR SBATS* HAVE BEEN GETTING HIGHER AND HIGHER!
I HEAR HE'S POPULAR WITH THE PARENTS AND THE LTA,* TOO.
AMAZING! JUST TWO YEARS AGO, THE PARENTS WERE READY TO SEAR US LIKE PRAWNS...
THUD
Hm?
GURGGLURGL...
ズウウウウウウン...
HUH!?
うおう!?
SIXTY-SECOND PERIOD: STRESS IS THE CAUSE OF COUNTLESS ILLS

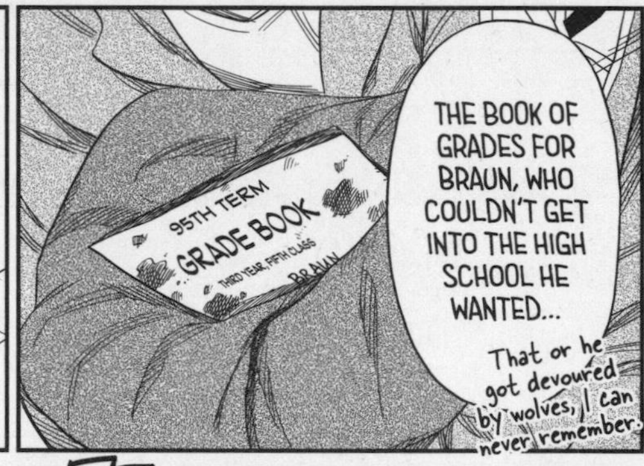

ごほんっ AHEM

WELL, ANOTHER DAY OF TEACHIN' THOSE DUMB BRATS WITH SOME TOUGH LOVE!!

GATUNK ガッ

SLAAAAAAAAM

SLIDE

...

HE PUTS ON THAT TOUGH ACT... BUT HE'S REALLY CHANGED SINCE THEY KICKED HIM OFF THAT GRADE TWO YEARS AGO...
TRAGIC...
HE WAS SUCH A MAN'S MAN... WITH A BIG, LOUD MAN VOICE, AND A CALM, STRONG MAN STRUT...

...AND THAT HEAD OF MAN HAIR... MAN.

Taken in front of Wall Maria Third Year

Oh, that's me!

Wow, you look like a twit!

BWAHAHAHAHAHAHA

...

PANT
PANT
HEH HEH... MAN, I'M TOTALLY HOOKED ON THIS STUFF...
SAVOR IT, GELGAR.
IT WAS REALLY HARD TO GET MY HANDS ON THIS BATCH...
PANT
PANT
ZLURP ...
BUT THIS STUFF'S JUST AMAZING, EVERY SINGLE TIME...! JUST OUT OF THIS WORLD...
THIS...
IF THAT HAPPENS, I'M TAKING YOU DOWN WITH ME. YOU'RE THE ONE THAT GOT ME STARTED ON THIS STUFF...
HEH HEH... HEY, YOU WERE THE ONE WHO SAID YOU WANTED TO TRY IT!
BUT WE CAN'T TAKE TOO LONG. WHAT IF SOMEONE SEES US?
WE'D GET EXPELLED FOR SURE.
OH-YEAH!!
くはーっ!!
ICE CREAM IN A CONTAINER THAT KINDA LOOKS LIKE A BOOB !!
SHHHUCK
Boiiing

ブチーんっ
WHAM
YOU CLODS!! HIDING TO EAT THESE STUPID THINGS...
SPLURT
ぴゅ〜
YOUR PUN-ISHMENT WILL BE... "STUPID NICK-NAMES"!!
うわーんっ
NOOOOO

SOB
Hi, my name is URINE ON FACE.
SOB
Hi, my name is I AM A JACKASS.
SOB SOB SOBSOB
Hmph

LOOK! ONE OF THE TWELVE PUNISH-MENTS OF HELL, "STUPID NICKNAMES"!!
AND THEY'VE GOTTEN WAY MEANER AND LESS CREATIVE LATELY, TOO!!
OH NO, THE DEMON LOOKED AT US...!
LET'S GET OUTTA HERE!!
IT'S BEEN TWO YEARS SINCE I LEFT MY POSITION AS THE TEACHER IN CHARGE OF THIRD YEARS...

I HAD COMPLETE CONFIDENCE IN MY ABILITIES AS AN INSTRUCTOR.
BUT MANY PARENTS CRITICIZED MY METHODS AS "OUTDATED," "INEFFECTIVE," OR "ASSAULT."

IT DIDN'T HELP THAT THE STUDENTS' GRADES WEREN'T VERY GOOD...

IT HAD BEEN THREE YEARS SINCE MY HAIR STARTED TO— I MEAN SINCE I BECAME HEAD OF THE GRADE.
ERWIN, THE ONLY TEACHER WHOSE STUDENTS' GRADES HAD BEEN ON THE RISE, WAS PROMOTED TO REPLACE ME...

EVER SINCE THEN... THE STUDENTS' GRADES HAVE IMPROVED ALONG WITH THE SCHOOL'S REPUTATION AND LEGAL SITUATION.
HOWEVER...
I CAN'T HELP BUT FEEL...
THAT THE BEHAVIOR OF THE STUDENTS HAS ONLY GOTTEN WORSE...!!
FWOOOO
OOOO

パコーンッ
THWAACK

AAAAH! I' SO SORRY!!

...BRING ME THE JACKANAPE WHO HIT ME WITH THIS BALL !!
KEITH-SENSEI ...?!

I-IT WAS HIM!! OLUO BOZADO FROM SECOND YEAR!! IT WAS ALSO HIS DASTARDLY SCHEME TO PLAY VOLLEYBALL IN THE FIRST PLACE!!
DAMN YOU!! YOU DARE BETRAY ME?!

ガッ
GRAB

ゴチーンッ
WHAAAM

THIS KIND OF THING NEVER HAPPENED WHEN I WAS IN CHARGE...!
THESE SPROUTS HAVE GONE COMPLETELY TO SEED SINCE HE TOOK OVER...!

I'M SO SORRY!!
THERE'S NO MISTAKE ABOUT IT...
DRAG ずる ずる DRAG

I HAVE NO CHOICE...
...BUT TO LEAD THIS SCHOOL ONCE AGAIN...
I got it!
I got it!

ポコーン
THWAAACK!!
AAAUGH!!
I'M SO SORRY, MICKEY MOUSE!!

ゴチーン
WHAAAM

THIS SCHOOL IS LOST!
I HAVE TO SHOW THEM THE WAY OR THEY'LL NEVER SEE...
Reaaady!
I'M CERTAIN OF IT NOW...
Waah! Mickey is mean to children!

HEH...
IF THEY THINK THE SAME GAG IS GOING TO WORK TIME AND TIME AG...
ポテーン
PLOP
DODGE

SPLIT
THWOP

EEK! WHO DID THAT HIT?! I'M SO SORRY!!

OH NO!!

WH-WHAT HAVE I DONE...?
ALL BECAUSE MY HAND SLIPPED A LITTLE... THIS IS TOO TERRIBLE...!!

MY POOR, BROKEN POTATO!! CPR! DOES ANYONE KNOW CPR?!
NOOOOO!!
SPLIT

THWACK-BOOM—!!

I CAN'T UNDERSTAND IT...
WHAT KIND OF PERSON WOULD JUST IGNORE SOMEONE INJURED ON THE GROUND...?

THAT STARVING GIRL I MAIMED...
...HAS PUSHED ME OVER THE EDGE.
THIS IS ALL BECAUSE ERWIN IS TOO SOFT ON THE STUDENTS!!
YAY!
WEE
I HAVE TO GET RID OF HIM AND BRING THE MISERY OF THE OLD DAYS BACK TO MODERN CHILDHOOD!!

I HAVE TO RESTORE THEM AS SOON AS POSSIBLE..
LAW AND ORDER... MY HAIR- I MEAN THE PRIDE OF THE SCHOOL!
UM...

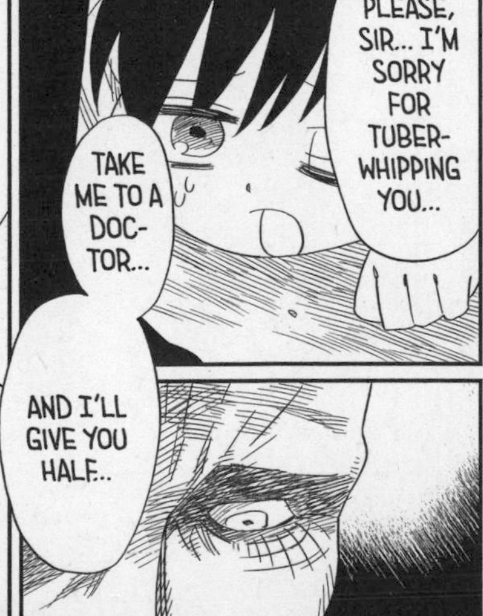
PLEASE, SIR... I'M SORRY FOR TUBER-WHIPPING YOU...
TAKE ME TO A DOCTOR...
AND I'LL GIVE YOU HALF...

OF A HALF OF A HALF...
...of the potato.
IT'S MOSTLY COOKED...

RUSTLE...

STEP

WHAT'S THIS ALL ABOUT, KEITH-SENSEI...?
CHALLENGE BY KEITH
DID YOU JUST CALL ME OUT IN A NOTE? ARE WE CHIL-DREN IN THE FIFTIES?
ERWIN...

PUT UP YOUR DUKES AND YOUR PERFECT BLOND LOCKS AND FIGHT ME FOR THE GRADE!!
TADAAAA

I HURT MY SHOULDER THE OTHER DAY AND LEVI SAID I SHOULD TAKE IT EASY...
DON'T TRY TO RUN AWAY FROM THIS, ERWIN!

YOU MUST SEE IT. SINCE YOU TOOK OVER THE GRADE...
THE STUDENTS HAVE RUN WILD. STRIKING PEOPLE WITH ROOT VEGETA-BLES, WEARING SHIRTS WITH THOSE SHOULDER WINDOWS...

LET'S DUEL, THEN...
NOW, UN-SHEATH YOUR... WHAT ARE YOU DOING?

YES... IT'S TO BE A HEAD-BUTT DUEL!!
SPARKLE

OH GOD, MY SHOUL-DER IS FLARING UP...
SO YOU ADMIT DEFEAT, ERWIN?

NO, I'LL TAKE YOU ON...
BUT I WOULD NEVER WILLINGLY ENDANGER COUNT PREN-DERGAST.
...THAT'S MY HAIR'S NAME.

Speaking of which...

WHAT?! WHAT IS IT?!
WHAT WERE YOU LOOKING AT?!
WAS IT MY HEAD? STOP IT RIGHT NOW!

SORRY, IT'S SO SHINY... DO YOU WAX IT?
HELL NO!!
YOU'RE JUST SCARED BECAUSE YOU DON'T THINK YOU CAN BEAT ME. ISN'T THAT IT?
FINE. I'LL LET **YOU** PICK OUR CONTEST.
OH? ARE YOU SURE?

WELL, IN THAT CASE...
WHAT WILL YOU CHALLENGE ME WITH...?
I MAY BE OLD, BUT I'M A GYM TEACHER.
IT ISN'T JUST MY HEAD THAT COULD TAKE YOU ON!!
THEN LET'S START...
BY COMPETING WITH THE PERCENTAGE OF STUDENTS...
TADAA
...WHO PASSED THEIR CLASSES WHEN YOU AND I WERE IN CHARGE!
Keith
2%
Erwin
73%
THUD
WH-WHAT IS WITH THIS GUY...? HE CAME STRAIGHT AT ME WITH HIS RECORD ON THE JOB...!
ERWIN... ARE YOU TRYING TO RIP MY PRIDE TO SHREDS?

THEN THE PERCENTAGE OF TIME THEY SPENT WEARING PANTS.
Erwin 98%
Keith 9%
GAH
HOW OFTEN THEY THREW AWAY THEIR CREAMED BROCCOLI.
Erwin 3%
Keith 72%
GUH
THE PERCENTAGE OF FLAT TIRES AND WEDGIES IN THE HALLS.
Erwin 5%
Keith 89%
HURGH
AND THE FINISHING BLOW...
...THE PERCENTAGE OF STUDENTS WITH SMILES ON THEIR FACES!!
Keith 1%
99%
GAAAAAAAH
TADAAAA
THESE ARE DAMNED LIES...!
WHO CARRIES AROUND PIE CHARTS ON COMPARATIVE JOB PERFORMANCE?!
WHEN I WAS IN CHARGE, I KNOW...
STUDENTS LOVE THE RIGID ENFORCEMENT OF ABSOLUTE AUTHORITY!

...!
THE STUDENTS WERE SMILING...
STRAIN...
ERWIN... SINCE YOU HAVE FACTS ON YOUR SIDE, I MUST RE-SORT INSTEAD TO MACHO PHYSICAL VIOLENCE!
NOW, IF YOU CALL YOUR-SELF A MAN, EXTEND YOUR SANDY SCALP... AND LET US BUTT HEADS!
WHAT THE ?!
LUUUNGE
WOOP

THWACK
ポコーン
NO... THIS IS THE SAME BALL... AND THE SAME GAG!
GAAAUGH!!
うわあああ
AAAAAAAUGH
あああ
KIDS!!
WE HIT A TITAN WITH A BALL!

WE'LL SETTLE THIS LATER! WE HAVE TO GO, SENSEI!
Tsk ...
BWAAAAAAAAAUGH
BLECHECHECH EEK SE-SE-SE-SE-SE-SENSEEEEEEEI!
O-OLUO...
GRAB
KEITH-SEN-SEI, PLEASE GO HELP THE OTHER STUDENTS WITHOUT TRAUMATIZING THEM.
TREMBLE TREMBLE
TREMBLE TREMBLE
HAH!
A LITTLE MILD MENTAL TRAUMA BUILDS CHARACTER!
AND...
AFTER I'VE SAVED EVERY-ONE–
DASH
PREPARE YOUR HEAD FOR A BUTT!

MY STARCHY DEAREST!!
DROP
EEEEEK
ROLL
GRAB
I GUESS THIS IS IT... MY DAYS OF SHOT-GUNNING SURGE MIXED WITH MAPLE SYRUP ARE OVER...
LOOKS LIKE I'VE FILLED MY LAST FRIED TWINKIE WITH CANNED CHEESE...
GASP
I'LL NEVER REALIZE MY DREAM...
...OF BECOMING A GUINEA PIG AT THE HORMEL FOOD SCIENCE LAB...

KABOOOOOOM
POP

Y-YOU'RE THAT MAN FROM EARLIER...
...

WITH A HEAD LIKE WAXY DONUT FROST-ING!!
SNAP

RUMBLE
RUMBLE
RUMBLE
RUMBLE
MBLE
RUMBLE
RUMBLE
RUMBLE
FLING
KABOOOOOOOOM

TURN
GASP
TH-THANK YOU SO MUCH FOR SAVING ME!!
THE POTATO'S A LITTLE SPITTY, BUT YOU CAN STILL HAVE...
NOT INTERESTED.
WHAT? YOU DON'T WANT A POTATO? WHAT ARE YOU, A VEGETARIAN?
POTATO GIRL...
YOU REALLY HAD ME WORRIED!!
WHAAAAAAM
WHANG!!
AND YOU...
WHANG
AND YOU, TOO!!
BWEEEH
OOWWWW
UGH, STOP CRYING!!
WAAAAAAAAH

I CAN'T BELIEVE HOW SOFT THESE TWERPS ARE...
THEY NEED A GOOD CLEAN LESSON, LIKE A BEATING OR GETTING LOCKED IN A SHED...
MY DEAR LITTLE ONES!
WAAAAAAH
わあぁあ
あぁぁ
I'M SO GLAD YOU'RE OKAY.
THE BLOND FOOL...!
CAN'T HE SEE THEY'RE MANIPULATING HIM WITH THEIR LARGE EYES AND HIGH-PITCHED VOICES...?!

LOOK AT THE CONNIVING LITTLE...
I'll never drop a potato ever again...
I guess I need to practice. I was aiming for the window!

SHOOOOM
YOU WIN, ERWIN...
SPLAT

アハハハ
AHAHAHA
AND NO ONE HAD TO HIT THEM...!
HA
THEY REALLY ARE SMILING...
NOW I KNOW WHAT I WAS LACKING...
ERWIN... I'M GOING TO LEAVE THIS SCHOOL IN YOUR...!
KEITH-SENSEI.
THANK YOU.
I LEARNED SOMETHING TODAY, TOO.
HUH?
I CAN BE A LITTLE TOO SOFT ON THE KIDS SOME-TIMES... BUT YOU'RE DIFFERENT...
YOU ALWAYS TEACH WITH PASSION. WHICH IS WHY...
...
...ALL YOUR HAIR FELL OUT, CUE BALL!
ぺちーんっ
SLAAAP
SHUT UP, YOU GOODY-GOODY !!

FULL OF HAIR! EXTRA COMIC.
THE BARREN LAND
KACHAK
CREAK
THERE'S NO ONE HERE...
GOOD...
HAHA
CLINICAL HAIR GROWTH TREATMENT
ATTACK ON FOLLICLES
HAHA
HEH...
I CAN'T HAVE ANYONE CATCH ME...
DOING A THING LIKE THIS...
KLAK
KLAK
HUFFFFF
THIS ONE'LL WILL WORK FOR SURE...!
I HAD TO SELL MY FAVORITE PORCELAIN DOG FIGURINE TO BUY IT... SORRY, POODIDDLE...
TWIST
TWIST

ザバ
SPLASH!!
ペカーッ
SPARKLE
OH WOW! THE 25-METER POOL, WHICH IS 82.02 AMERICAN FEET, IS SPOTLESS!
MR. LEVI SURE IS GREAT!
I'VE GOT AN IDEA!
MR. LEVI LIKES CLEANING SO MUCH! LET'S TELL HIM ABOUT ALL THE DIRTY SPOTS SO HE CAN CLEAN THEM!
ぽんっ
CLAP
HE'LL LOVE THAT!
MR. LEVI!!
メチャクチャーッ
MESSY
THE SPORTS SUPPLY SHED IS IN TATTERS!
WON'T YOU CLEAN IT FOR US?!
...
OH, FINE...
おおーっ
WOW
WOOSH
EXTRA STORY–FORECAST: EXPLOSION

MR. LEVI!!
SHOOM
TSK...
WOW
おぉーっ
THE BOYS' LOCKER ROOM SMELLS LIKE BUTT YOGURT!!
ゴチャッ
CLUTTER
...
MR. LEVI, SOMEONE THREW UP RAW POTATO IN THE CLASSROOM!
SWEEP
BERTOLT'S BUNK BED IS ALL CRUSTY FOR SOME REASON!
SPARKLE
OLUO'S LACTOSE INTOLERANCE HAS LED TO A CRIME AGAINST HUMANITY IN THE BATHROOM!!
SQUEAK
SQUEAK
5 HOURS LATER
WOW, THE WHOLE SCHOOL IS SPARKLING!
SEE? ALL OF MY IDEAS ARE THE BEST IDEAS!
NOW LET'S GET A LOOK AT MR. LEVI'S HAPPY, SATISFIED FACE...
RUMBLE RUMBLE RUMBLE
RUMBLE RUMBLE RUMBLE

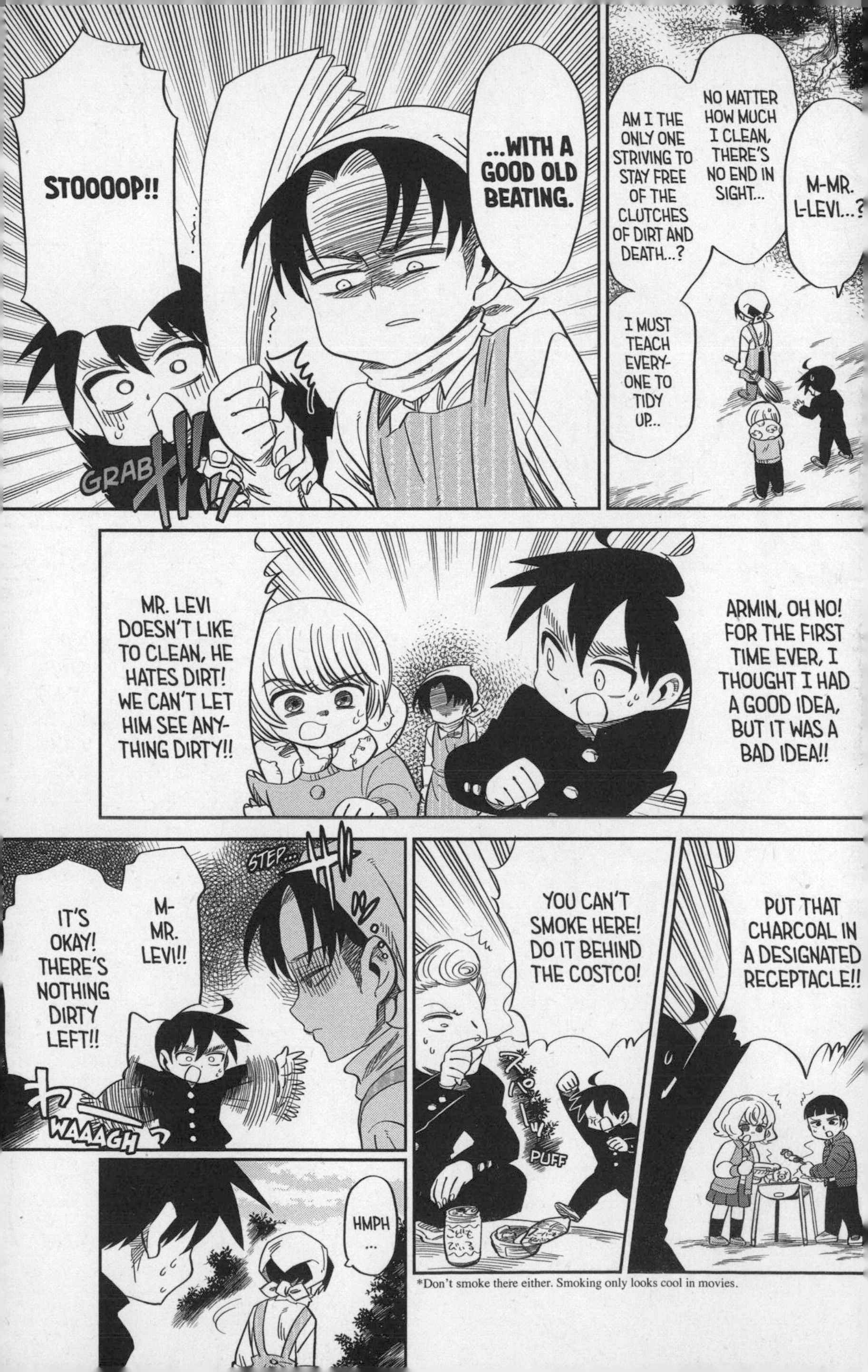

M-MR. L-LEVI...?
NO MATTER HOW MUCH I CLEAN, THERE'S NO END IN SIGHT...
AM I THE ONLY ONE STRIVING TO STAY FREE OF THE CLUTCHES OF DIRT AND DEATH...?
I MUST TEACH EVERY-ONE TO TIDY UP...
...WITH A GOOD OLD BEATING.
STOOOOP!!
GRAB

ARMIN, OH NO! FOR THE FIRST TIME EVER, I THOUGHT I HAD A GOOD IDEA, BUT IT WAS A BAD IDEA!!
MR. LEVI DOESN'T LIKE TO CLEAN, HE HATES DIRT! WE CAN'T LET HIM SEE ANY-THING DIRTY!!

PUT THAT CHARCOAL IN A DESIGNATED RECEPTACLE!!
YOU CAN'T SMOKE HERE! DO IT BEHIND THE COSTCO!
PUFF

*Don't smoke there either. Smoking only looks cool in movies.

STEP...
M-MR. LEVI!!
IT'S OKAY! THERE'S NOTHING DIRTY LEFT!!
WAAAGH

HMPH ...

I-I GUESS WE GOT OUT OF THAT...
PHEW
WE SHOULD BE IN THE CLEAR FOR TODAY.
UNLESS THERE WERE TO BE A LARGE GROUP OF PEOPLE ENGAGED IN A STEREOTYPICAL NOISY STUDENT PARTY WITH LITTERING, UMBRELLAS, AND NUDITY...
AHAHAHAHAHA
BUT OF COURSE NO ONE WOULD...

JANGLE
JONGLE
WOOT WOOT
BWAHAHAHAHAHA
OH NO!!

THWOP
LEVI, BALLS LOVE YOUR HEAD!

GAAAAAUGH
KABOOOM
KEEP YOUR SCHOOL CLEAN!

SIXTY-THIRD PERIOD: ON A RAINY DAY, PLAY WITH YOUR FRIENDS

HEY, IT'S THE FIRST TIME WE'VE BEEN IN COLOR IN THE FRONT OF THE MAGAZINE IN FOUR YEARS!

And we're on the front cover, too!

GEE, YOU'D REALLY BE IM-PRESSED RIGHT NOW...

...IF YOU WERE READING THE JAPANESE MAGAZINE AND NOT THE AMERICAN VERSION!

IT'S SUPER OBVIOUS WHENEVER THEY MAKE A COLOR PAGE INTO BLACK AND WHITE... BUT THEY DON'T CARE. CHEAP BASTARDS.

I WONDER WHAT COOL STUFF WE'RE GONNA GET TO DO IN THIS CHAPTER.

WE'RE NOT EVEN IN IT!!
Sorry!
IT'S TIME TO CHECK IN ON THESE GUYS WHO'VE BEEN DEAD IN THE MAIN SERIES FOR YEARS!

This typhoon will grow stronger as it moves past this lump over toward this circle...
FRANCE
MIKE'S HOUSE
CLEVELAND
And it looks like there's some lazy art retouching over here, so be careful.

I DON'T KNOW WHERE THIS IS, BUT LET'S SEND THE KIDS HOME JUST IN CASE.
DING DONG DING
Dear students, storm's a-comin'. Head straight home now, y'all hear?
WHOOSH
If ya little varmints stay in the school...

ROAAAAAR

...ye landlubbers won't be able to get home!! Arr!

Wait, why am I a pirate now—?

...HE HAD IT IN HIS MOUTH!

AHAHA HAHA HAHA HAHA HA

GWEH HEHEHE HEHEHE HEHE HE

Anyway, the important thing is—

...OH GOD, OLUO IS PEEING EVERYWHERE!

AHAHA HAHA HAHA HA

Get outta here right now or—

OH, SHUT UP ALREADY.

FLICK

ANYWAY, THE NEXT DAY LEVI AND ERWIN--

AHA HA HAHA HA HAHA HA

BWA HA HA HA HA HA HA HA HA HA

MANY HOURS LATER ...

OH, SO FUNNY...

I ALMOST DIED LAUGHING AT THE PART WHERE OLUO BIT HIS TONGUE AND NEARLY KILLED HIMSELF...

アヒー WHEEZE

アヒー WHEEZE

WHAT TIME IS IT ANYWAY?

LET'S SEE...

I lost track.

AHA HA

ゴオオオオオ ROOOOOAR

10:30...

AT NIGHT...

ROOOOOAR
OH NO... I'M NOT GETTING ANY SIGNAL...
YOU'RE KIDDING...
SOMEONE ATE ALL THE EMERGENCY RATIONS...
OH NO...
THANKS! SASHA
RATIONS
TH-THEN THAT MEANS WE CAN'T GET HOME...
NOOOO
GET IT TOGETHER, GUYS!!
LOOK! A THIN GREEN PLASTIC PONCHO!!
WE CAN GO OUT-SIDE IN THIS!!
OOH!!

WHY AM I AS WELL-PREPARED AS I AM HANDSOME, YOU ASK?
BECAUSE MY MOMMY TOLD ME TO PACK IT-- I MEAN...
AS A MEMBER OF THE SURVEY CLUB, IT'S JUST COMMON SENSE TO BE THIS PREPARED!
SO YOU'LL BRAVE THE STORM FOR US WITHOUT PISSING YOURSELF AGAIN, OLUO?!
HEH... OF COURSE I WILL.
LEAVE IT TO ME.
Be careful!

I'M OFF TO DIG UP THE TOASTER PASTRIES I BURIED LAST YEAR!
POUUUR
SPLISH
SPLASH

POUUUR
10 MINUTES LATER
IT'S NO GOOD... NOT EVEN THE LIMITED-EDITION PUMPKIN PIE ONES WERE--
WHAM
YOU IDIOT!!

NEVER MIND! I'LL GO!
GRAB
PETRA, WAIT!
GASP
SLIDE
THE HALL IS...

SPLAAAAASH

SPLISH
チャプ
SPLISH
チャプ
SPLISH
チャプ

THE HALLWAY IS FLOODED!!
WHY DIDN'T YOU LEAD WITH THAT?!
WHACK

SQUEEZE
ぎゅるーっ

I'M SORRY, EVERY-ONE...

HONESTLY, I KNEW IT WAS GETTING LATE...
BUT I'M THE TYPE WHO KEEPS BRINGING UP NEW TOPICS OF CONVERSATION WAY PAST THE POINT WHEN I SHOULD'VE GONE HOME...
D-DON'T BE SILLY, PETRA ...!!

"STRANG-EST PLAC-ES WE'VE FOUND ERWIN'S PANTS" WAS MY IDEA...
AND MY IMPRESSION OF OLUO'S DEAD MOM GOT A LIT-TLE OUT OF CONTROL...

BUT I'VE LEARNED ONE THING...
...FROM WATCHING A LOT OF TV.

BEING STUCK IN SCHOOL DURING A STORM IS NO BIGGIE.
IT'LL BE A BEAUTIFUL MEMORY WE LOOK BACK ON WHEN WE'RE OLDER...
ND HAVE HING TO K ABOUT EPT OUR MORIES M HIGH HOOL.

NOW ALL WE HAVE TO DO UNTIL MORNING...

...IS WASTE TIME AS UNPRODUCTIVELY AS POSSIBLE.

ELD...!! GUNTHER...!!

WE'VE GOT PLAYING CARDS, AND UNO, TOO!

WE'LL HAVE NO PROBLEM KILLING TIME WITH THESE!

YAAAY

THEN WHAT SHOULD WE PLAY FIRST?

POKER

OF COURSE!

UNO

TADAA

Y-YEAH, I REALLY WANT TO PLAY BOTH...
ELD... WOULDN'T IT BE WISER TO PLAY CARDS FIRST? UNO IS PRETTY DULL...
THAT'S EXACTLY WHY WE SHOULD PLAY UNO FIRST! MY PLAN IS TO PLAY IT UNTIL WE CAN'T STAND IT ANYMORE, AND THEN SWITCH TO POKER...

IT ONLY TAKES ME 7.3 SECONDS TO GET BORED OF UNO!!
OUT WITH IT, YOU BASTARD! YOU JUST WANT TO PLAY UNO!
GRAB
WHAT?! WELL, POKER'S ALL LUCK ANYWAY!!
PLUS, ERWIN-SENSEI SAYS IT OPENS A DOGGY DOOR IN YOUR HEART FOR THE DEVIL TO GET IN!!

LIES!! POKER IS ALL ABOUT SKILL! THAT'S WHY IT'S ON ESPN7!
WELL, UNO IS THE FAST, FUN FAMILY GAME FOR EVERYONE!

NOOO
JUST LET IT GO!!
I'LL STOP THEM!!
GAAAAH
RAAAAH

YOU'RE ALL STUPID!!
GASP

WHY DO BOYS ALWAYS SPEND MORE TIME AR-GUING...

...OVER WHICH **ACTIVITY** TO DO...

...WHEN YOU COULD WASTE TIME PERFECT-LY WELL MOCKING CELEBRI-TIES' HAIR-STYLES?

PETRA ...

SORRY, WE...

I JUST BRING UNO WITH ME WHEREVER I GO BECAUSE I'M SCARED OF RELATING DIRECTLY TO PEOPLE...

AND I SPENT MY DAD'S MORTGAGE PAYMENT ON MOBILE POKER...

...I THINK I HAVE A REAL PROBLEM!

YES, YOU BOTH SUCK...

...SO IF YOU MUST HAVE AN ACTIVITY...

WIPE

I SEN-TENCE YOU...

..TO BUILD HOUSE OF ARDS UNTIL MORNING!!

AHAHAHA HAHAHA
アハハハハハ

A HOUSE OF CARDS... I GET IT...!!
CARDS AND UNO CAN'T HOLD A CAN-DLE TO IT...
LEADER PETRA'S PUNISH-MENT SURE IS HARSH ...!!

YES! THERE'S ONE LAYER!
GOOD STACKING, PETRA!

GIGGLE
キャッ
GIGGLE
キャッ
Can we do it?
AHAHAHAHAHAHA
アハハハハハハ

NOW, MY TURN...
BADUMP
ドキ
BADUMP
ドキ
BADUMP
ドキ

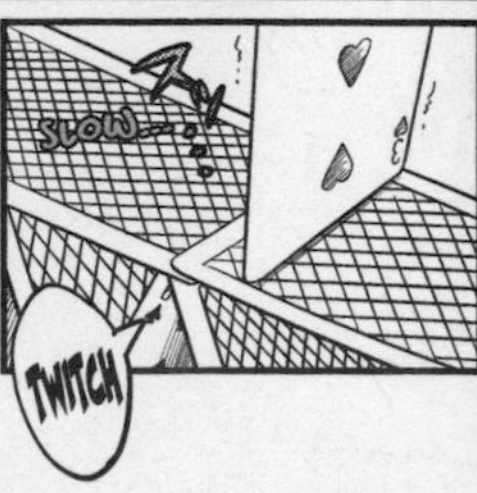
SLOW...
TWITCH

FLOP

AHA HAHAHA. OH, DON'T WORRY ABOUT IT.
WE'VE GOT PLENTY OF TIME.
ぽんっ TAP
ポッ PHEW
WE'LL JUST START OVER!

WE GOT TWO LEVELS!!
おおーっ WOAH

ドキドキ BADUMP
MY TURN ...
MAN, I'M NERVOUS ...
ドキドキ BADUMP
FOOOOO

DON'T BREATHE... DON'T EVEN FART...
W-WOW, THIS IS PRETTY HARD...
HAHA-HAHA-HAHA-HA...
TWITCH

ドシャ FLOP
...

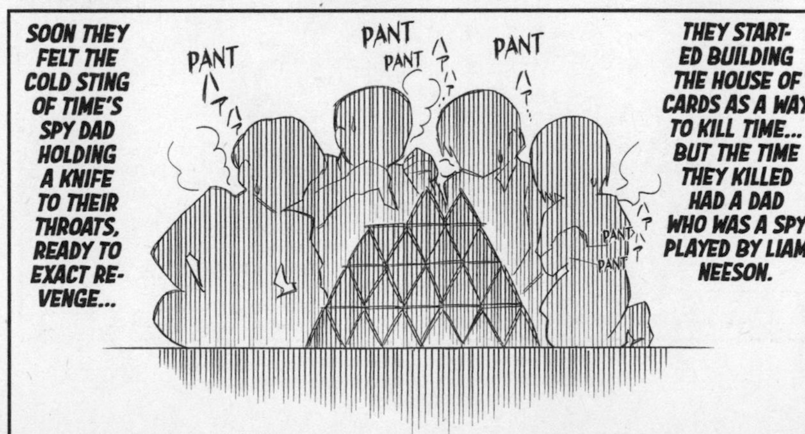
THEY STARTED BUILDING THE HOUSE OF CARDS AS A WAY TO KILL TIME... BUT THE TIME THEY KILLED HAD A DAD WHO WAS A SPY PLAYED BY LIAM NEESON.
PANT
PANT
PANT
PANT
PANT
PANT
SOON THEY FELT THE COLD STING OF TIME'S SPY DAD HOLDING A KNIFE TO THEIR THROATS, READY TO EXACT REVENGE...

BUT THEN, FIVE HOURS INTO THEIR 105TH ATTEMPT--
W-
WE DID IT!
AHHHHHH
YEAAA
FINISHED!
THAT WAS ROUGH...I NEVER KNEW PLAYING CARDS COULD GIVE YOU PAPER CUTS...
I KNOW... MY HANDS LOOK LIKE ED-WARD JAMES OLMOS'S FACE...
I STILL DON'T KNOW WHY YOU NEEDED TO SLASH MY FACE AND CHANT "QUEEN OF CUTS"...
I GUESS THEY'RE BADGES OF HONOR...
HAHA, WE...
GRIP
WE WASTED PRECIOUS HOURS ON SOME-THING POINT-LESS...
ACHIEVEMENT UNLOCKED!!
YEAAAAAAAAAH
PLASH

SPLASH

A LEAK?!
HEY, LOOK...!

TRICKLE
SPLASH

NOO! WE HA-VEN'T EVEN MOVED THE NENDOROIDS INTO THE CARD MAN-SION YET!
WE'VE GOT TO FIX THE CEILING!!

CAREFUL

HOLD ON...

WHAM
WHAM
WHAM
WHAM
LURCH

...UH...
C-
CAN'T YOU POUND IT IN A LITTLE MORE DELICATELY?!
TAP TAP TAP TAP TAP TAP
MY ARM HURTS ...
DO YOUR BEST!
ALL DONE!
THANKS!
Good job!
That was impressive.
I'M SO GLAD... THE HOUSE IS SAFE...
SPLISH
ぴちょん SPLISH
ぴちょん SPLISH
SPLISH ぴちょん
ぴちょん SPLASH
ぴちょん SPLISH
SPLASH ぴちょん SPLASH
ぴちょん SPLASH
ぴちょん SPLASH

PHEW
ふーっ
WHEEZE
WHEEZE
ゼエ
ゼエ
PANT
PANT
ハァ
ハァ

IT'S ALL RIGHT NOW.
...

WHY DID WE BOTHER?
LIFE IS BUT AN EFFERVESCENT DREAM.
GONE IN AN INSTANT LIKE FOAM OFF THE SEA. THIS HOUSE OF CARDS IS THE SAME...
HUH?

YOU'RE WRONG! IT'LL LAST FOREVER!
WE FIXED ALL THE LEAKS...
RATTLE
RATTLE
RATTLE
WHAM
ガタ
HUH ?!
I-IT CAN'T BE...
WILL A GUST BE OUR UNDOING...!

STRAIN...

IT'S ALL OVER...

AFTER THE FOUR OF US WORKED SO HARD TOGETH-ER...!

O--

OLUO!!

WE'VE GOT THIS!
ELD! GUNTHER!
WELL, WE'RE STILL REPAIRING THE DAM- AGE...
IT'S ONE HELL OF A TYPHOON.
THE TWO OF US HAVE TO HOLD IT DOWN OR IT'LL BLOW AWAY!
THEN I'LL HELP, TOO!
NO, PETRA, WAIT.
WE'RE ACTUALLY DOWN TO OUR LAST NAIL.
CAN YOU BRING MORE FROM THE STORE- ROOM?
THAT'S A PIECE OF CAKE!
I'LL BE RIGHT BACK!
RIGHT!

WE STARTED OUT SO FAR APART...
WE NEARLY BROKE OUT INTO SECTARIAN VIOLENCE OVER POKER OR UNO...
THEN I SECRETLY WANTED TO POISON EVERYONE WHEN WE WERE BUILDING THE HOUSE...
BUT WE GREW TO LOVE THE HOUSE...
...AND NOW WE'RE ALL DOING OUR BEST TOGETHER TO PROTECT IT!!
NOW IT'S MY TURN...
...TO HELP THE OTHERS, AND SAVE THE HOUSE!!
WHAP
GASP
DON'T OPEN THE DOOR!!
W-WAIT, PETRA... DON'T!
HUH?
SLIDE

WHY NOT...?
SLIDE
SLIIIDE
OH!!
SPLASH
I FORGOT ABOUT THE FLOOD FROM 16 PAGES AGO!
SPLASH
SPLASH
SPLAAAASH

BLOOP
PLOP
...
SPLISH
SPLISH

...
WHAT HAVE I DONE ...?
YOU GUYS, I'M SO SORRY...
MY MOTHER WAS RIGHT! I AM A WASTE OF AN OVUM!!
WAAAAH
HAHA... IT'S OKAY, PETRA...
LOOK OVER THERE.

THE MORROW HAS COME.

THIS SUNRISE IS LIKE A BEAUTIFUL, COQUETTISH SMILE...

THE STORM PASSED ...

...AND SO THE TIME MURDERERS GOT AWAY WITH THEIR DASTARDLY CRIME.

THIS MANGA IS FINALLY TURNING INTO AN ANIME...*
進撃!巨人中学校
まさかのアニメ化!
*TWO YEARS AG
THEY SAID WHEN IT STARTED THAT IT WOULD BE LUCKY TO LAST 3 VOLUMES.
IT'S THANKS TO OUR INCREDIBLY PATIENT READERS THAT IT'S GOTTEN THIS FAR...
Emotional...
WHAT ARE YOU TALKING ABOUT, KUKLO?
*SERIOUSLY, WE KNOW THIS WAS SUPPOSED TO BE OUT TWO YEARS AGO
BUT I LIVE IN A TREE...
SO I CAN'T WATCH THIS ON CRUNCHY-BUN...
SIGH
OH, RIGHT...
DING
OH!
I KNOW...
*WE KNOW, WE KNOW, THE BLURAYS ARE OUT NOW AND EVERYTHING
YOU CAN COME OVER TO OUR PLACE TO WATCH!
WE'VE GOT A HUGE THEATER, AND YOU CAN WATCH ON A SCREEN THIS BIG!
WHAT? REALLY?!
SCRATCH SCRATCH SCRATCH SCRATCH SCRATCH
EXTRA STORY: LET THEM EAT POPCORN

TADAAAA
UM... HOW DO I SET UP THE CRUNCHY-BUN APP...?
WHAT WAS MY APP STORE PASSWORD AGAIN? WHAT'S A SPECIAL CHARACTER?
DIT
DIT
WHAT ARE YOU DOING, SHARLE?
OH, XAVI!
UM... CAN YOU TEACH ME HOW TO PROGRAM THE TV?
I can't figure it out at all!
IS THERE SOMETHING YOU WANT TO WATCH THAT BADLY?
I WANTED TO WATCH IT WITH KUKLO...
UH-HUH!
HMPH
OUT OF THE QUESTION!
I'LL NEVER ALLOW THAT VILE BOUNDER IN THIS HOUSE!
IF YOU LET HIM INSIDE...
YOUR BREAKFAST PORTION WILL BE REDUCED...
SIZE
Down!
...FROM A QUARTER LOAF TO ONE FIFTH!
SHOCK

HE THREATENED MY CARBS. I'M SO SORRY, KUKLO...
IT'S OKAY...
FOOD IS MORE IMPORTANT THAN FRIENDS. I KNOW THIS.

SO YOUR BROTHER SAID HE WOULD STARVE YOU TO DEATH IF YOU LET ME IN...?
SWEAT
SWEAT
SWEAT
SWEAT
SWEAT
SWEAT
SWEAT
UM, UH-HUH...

BUT... IT REALLY IS FINE, SHARLE...

TO ME, BEING IN SHARLE'S THOUGHTS IS BETTER THAN DELICIOUS CAKE.
KUKLO...!

UM... EVEN IF YOU CAN'T WATCH AT MY PLACE...
I DID THINK OF A WAY THAT WE CAN WATCH TOGETHER!

THAT'S THE THIN BOARD THAT CAN BE A TELEVISION OR A PEDOMETER OR EVEN A TELEPHONE...!!
THAT'S RIGHT. WITH THAT, I COULD WATCH ANIME ANYWHERE!

OF COURSE... I DO NOT NEED THE BIG SCREEN AT ALL...
THE IMPORTANT THING IS TO ENJOY WATCHING IT TOGETHER...
OH, HELLO?

There is no 4DX version of Attack on Titan Junior High

64TH PERIOD: A BOY AND HIS ERASERS

WHISPER WHISPER WHISPER WHISPER WHISPER
ヒ ヒ ヒ ヒ ヒ
WHISPER

WHISPER ヒソ
WHISPER ヒソ
WHISPER ヒソ
WHISPER ヒソ
WHISPER ヒソ
WHISPER ヒソ
The Old Man and the Sea

SWIFF

THEY'VE GOT NO ONE TO BLAME FOR THIS BUT THEM-SELVES... WHISPER-ING THEIR SECRETS...

I BET THEY'RE SAYING I'LL EAVES-DROP ON THEM AND FIND OUT EVERYTHING!!

Meatloaf with cheese...

No... potato...

DIT DIT BZZZZZ

So about Armin...

What should we do with him...

One week from now, right?

I KNEW IT!!

WHAT'RE THEY GOING TO DO TO ME?!

That's right... Armin's...

... surprise birthday party!!

YEEAAAAAAAH!!

AHHH-HHHHH, I'M SO SORRY, GUYS!

We need to cook four chickens right?
And some vodka. Er, non-alcoholic vodka.
I don't think that's a thing!
AWW GUYS, YOU DIDN'T HAVE TO...
Well, that's all for the preparations.
A SURPRISE PARTY, REALLY? I'M SO HAPPY!!
All that leaves is...
...the presents!!
HUH? PRESENTS? I DON'T NEED PRESENTS!
What to get him?
WELL, I MIGHT WANT A NEW CLOAK, MAYBE? MAYBE ONE THAT GLOWS WHEN ORCS ARE NEAR? A REAL FLUFFY ONE...!
Well, for Armin...
Oh, good idea!
IF IT'S FROM YOU GUYS, I DON'T CARE WHAT...
Then his present will be...
ガターン
WHAM
ONE HUNDRED NOVELTY ERASERS!
NO, WAIT, I CARE!!
TADAAAA
BIGNOMO

1-4
CHATTER
ざわ
ざわ
CHATTER
HEY, TIME TO GO HOME, ARMIN.
O-OKAY.
WHY DID THEY DECIDE ON ERASERS...?

AND A HUNDRED OF THEM...? WHAT, WAS THERE A BACK-TO-LAME-SCHOOL SALE?
HOW COULD THEY NOT NOTICE MY ALMOST FETISHISTIC LOVE OF FUTONS...?
OH!

HEY, LOOK AT THIS.
REMEMBER THESE, ARMIN?
YOU USED TO REALLY LIKE THESE.
ERASERS SHAPED LIKE FOOD!
OH, RIGHT!
ちょこーんっ
CUTE

I REMEMBER EVERYONE USED TO HAVE THEM!
RIGHT! IF YOU HAD A LOT OF THEM, IT WAS LIKE A STATUS SYMBOL!
THAT TAKES ME BACK! SOME OF US USED TO EAT THEM BY MISTAKE!
Uh, that was just you, Eren.
AHAHAHAHAHAHA
OH, GOOD
YUP, I WAS RIGHT!
IS THAT WHY?!
FLASH
SURE, I PRETENDED TO LIKE THEM... BUT I WAS JUST GOING ALONG WITH THE TREND...
How many do you have, Armin?
Uh, this one is a carrot? I also have an eggplant and a cucumber...
Oh, there's a theme there...
LOOK AT ME AS I AM NOW!

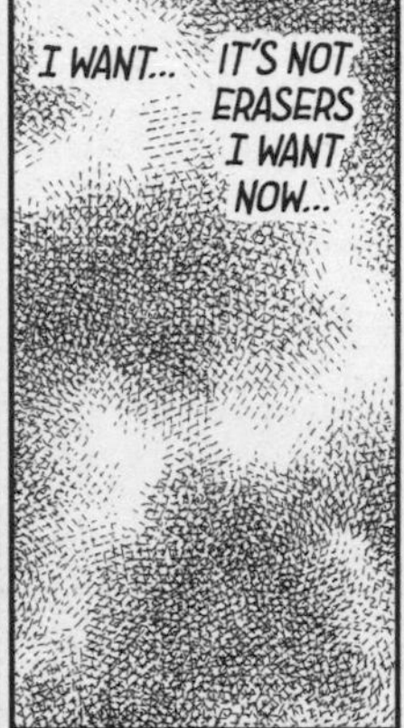
IT'S NOT ERASERS I WANT NOW...
I WANT...

A FLUFFY KITTY FUTON WITH IMMUNITY TO FIRE AND A SNAPPY PERSONALITY!!
ONE THAT WILL GRAB ME AND PULL ME OUT OF DANGER WHEN THE BAD GUY SNEAKS UP ON ME!
COMFORTERRR

GIVING SOMEONE A HUNDRED ERASERS IS A WASTE OF ERASERS, ANYWAY!!
Hey, Armin!
DON'T THEY KNOW THERE ARE PEOPLE IN FAERÛN WHO DON'T EVEN HAVE PENCILS?!

CHATTER
CHATTER
1-4
DID EVERYONE GO CHECK OUT THE ERASERS IN STOCK?
I SAW SOME GOOD ONES!
OKAY, TODAY WE HAVE TO DECIDE WHICH ONES...
AHCHO-FUTON!!

OR-AT-LEAST!

HACK COM-FORT-ER!

AH-CHO-FU-TO

AHEM COM-FORTER AHEM

AH-CHOO

SNIFFFFFFLE

ARMIN, ARE YOU OKAY?!

THAT WAS SOME SERIOUS SNEEZ-ING!!

Y-YEAH...

I'M FI...

AHCHO-NOERAS-ERS!!

ARE YOU REALLY OKAY?!

IS IT JUST ME, OR DOES IT SEEM LIKE...

THERE'S A MESSAGE HERE...?

A COMFY FUTON!!

GASP

PFFFFT

A-ARMIN, YOUR FUTON THING...
IT'S RAGGED AND COVERED IN SNOT!!
ボロローン
TATTERS
OH!!
THAT'S WHY YOU CAUGHT A COLD!
YOU NEED A NEW, UN-SNOTTED ONE!
Y-YEAH... BUT...
I ONLY HAVE JUST THIS ONE...
I DON'T HAVE ANY MONEY SO I CAN'T GET ANOTHER ONE.
I SEE...
THEN WE'VE GOT NO CHOICE...
HEY, GUYS!
TURNS OUT THAT ARMIN...
WHAT?!
I-I DID IT! THERE CAN BE NO MISTAKING IT NOW...
THAT DOESN'T SOUND GOOD...
THEN WHY DON'T WE DO THIS?!
MY PRESENT WILL BE A GREAT NEW CLOAK NOW FOR SURE!!
ARMIN!!

HAVE YOUR GRANDFATHER BUY YOU A NEW ONE.
TAP

I TRIED TO MAKE IT AS OBVIOUS AS POSSIBLE...
JUST HOW OBLIVIOUS ARE YOU, EREN...?

I'LL HAVE TO TRY A DIFFERENT STRATEGY...
ARMIN!!

CAN I BORROW AN ERASER?!
YOU USUALLY BRING TWO, DON'T YOU?
OH, SURE.
TAKE THIS...
GASP
OH, I KNOW!

EREN... SORRY,
BUT I CAN'T LET YOU BORROW MY ERASER.
WHAT?!
B-BUT WHY?!

YOU WANT TO KNOW WHY...?
IT'S BECAUSE ...
ゴク...
GULP

PFFFFFFFF

I HAVE TRANSFORMED MYSELF INTO A PEN NERD!

CHECK THIS SWEET TITANIUM ROLLERBALL I BACKED ON KICKSTARTER!

WH-WHAT?!

WHAT DO YOU DO ON TESTS?!

You can't fix things.

I HAVE THE RIGHT ANSWER ALWAYS BECAUSE OF MY SMARTNESS!

SHOCK
SO...
I CAN'T BORROW AN ERASER...?
UH. YUP. THAT'S RIGHT...

I SEE...
TEETER...
YOU DON'T USE ERASERS ANYMORE...

EREN... YOU LOOK SO LONELY...
DID YOU NEED AN ERASER THAT BADLY...?

HEY GUYS ...
LISTEN UP...
NO, THAT'S NOT IT...!!

HE'S GOING TO CHANGE MY PRESENT... EREN'S MADE UP HIS MIND!
YOU FINALLY REALIZED... I FINALLY GOT IT THROUGH YOUR THICKASS SKULL...
FOR ARMIN'S PRESENT...

WE'VE GOT TO CUT OUT EVERYTHING REMOTELY PRACTICAL...

ONLY NOVELTY ERASERS THAT WILL FALL APART IMMEDIATELY IF YOU TRY TO ERASE SOMETHING WITH THEM!!

GOT IT

BUT WHY?!

IS HE TAKING MONEY FROM THE ERASER LOBBY?!

ARMIN CONTINUED TO MAKE EVERY EFFORT TO CHANGE EREN'S MIND...

HE GAVE A THOROUGH PRESENTATION ON THE WONDERS OF A GOOD FUTON.
HE WATCHED "BOB ROSS PAINTS NEIGHBORS' FUTONS THROUGH A TELESCOPE."
Just look at this!
So fluffy! It's so fluffy!
AND HE EVEN PUT UP VIDEOS ON THE INTERNET ABOUT SELLING COMFORTERS...

HOW-EVER ...
1–4
GUYS, TOMORROW'S THE BIG DAY... ARMIN'S BIRTHDAY...
LET'S GO BUY ERASERS AFTER SCHOOL!!
おーっ!! YEAH
Eren... inside voice.

I CAN'T BELIEVE... NO, I CAN BELIEVE THIS IS HAPPEN-ING!!
うわぁぁぁぁん WAAAAAH
LET'S GET GOING!
OH.

SORRY, ARMIN.
WE'RE HEADING HOME NOW, SO YOU'LL HAVE TO WALK ALONE TODAY...
N-NO YOU CAN'T!!
I'M GOING WITH YOU!!
ぎゅ SQUEEEZE
WHA?!

Whisper...
SORRY, GUYS...
YOU'LL HAVE TO GO BUY THEM WITHOUT ME...
I WANT TO WALK HOME WITH ALL OF YOU!!
WHAAAT?

I HAVE TO DO SOME-THING BEFORE WE GET HOME...
THINK! IS THERE SOME KIND OF FUTON STORE NEAR THE OFFICE SUPPLY PLACE...?
HEY GUYS! LOOK!

TADAAAA
JUST SO MANY ERASERS
ATTACK ON STATIONERY
VARIOUS ERASERS
A STATIONERY STORE!!
!!

WHISPER
WHISPER
WHAT SHOULD WE DO? SHOULD WE JUST BUY THEM NOW?
SOMEONE KEEP AN EYE ON ARMIN.
?!

ARMIN, LET'S GO LOOK AT THE PEN SECTION...
NOOOOO!!

I WANT TO LOOK WHERE EVERYONE ELSE IS LOOKING ...!!

HEY, WE CAN'T BUY THEM LIKE THIS...
WHISPER WHISPER WHISPER
DO YOU THINK HE'S CAUGHT ON?
NO, THAT'S IMPOSSI-BLE!
My plan is perfect!
HUFF
HUFF

THIS IS THE ONLY STATIONERY STORE ON THE WAY HOME! IF I CAN GET THEM OUT OF HERE SOMEHOW...
I'LL BE FREE OF THE ERASERS...!!
GWEHEHEHEHEHEHEHE
HEY GUYS, LOOK!
Hm?

IT'S AN ERASER CART!!
Get yer erasers here!
Erase all your regrets!
ROLL ROLL ROLL
WHAT ON EARTH?!
ROLL ROLL ROLL
TADAAAA

EXCUSE ME! I'D LIKE TO TAKE A LOOK!
HUH?!
OH?!
LET'S SEE, THIS... AND THIS...

AHHHHHH! WHAT DO I DO? I'M NOT AN EXTRAPLANAR, DISEMBODIED, FLOATING HEAD... I CAN'T POINT MY EYESTALKS IN DIFFERENT DIRECTIONS!
BUT IF I GO OVER THERE, THEY'LL BUY ERASERS AT THE OTHER ONE... THIS WAY... THAT WAY... ERASERS... GUH...!

I'LL TAKE 50 OF THESE...
WHAAAAM

HUH?

OUT COLD!!

ARMIN!

PSHHH
HE'S BURNING UP!
ARMIN... YOU'VE GOT A FEVER...
PSHHHHH
THIS DOESN'T LOOK GOOD!
WE'VE GOT TO GET HIM HOME RIGHT AWAY!

ARMIN'S FUTON...
IT'S STILL IN TATTERS...
HUH?!

ARMIN

...

DO YOU REMEMBER ALL THIS...
...FUTON... MERCHANDISE BEING HERE?
AMAZING COMFORTERS OF 2016
COMFORTERS

THIS IS A PILE OF FLY-ERS. IS HE SUPPLYING A COLLEGE DORM?
THE ONE HE'S USING IS IN ROUGH SHAPE.
I THOUGHT WE TOLD HIM TO ASK HIS GRANDFATHER FOR A NEW ONE...

COULD IT BE THAT HE WANTS A NEW ONE...
...BUT HE'S TOO ATTACHED TO THIS ONE TO LET IT GO?
THAT COULD BE...
BUT IF HE DOESN'T GET A NEW ONE, HIS COLD WILL NEVER GET...
I KNOW!!

IF WE GET HIM A COMFORTER,
DON'T YOU THINK ARMIN WILL USE IT?!

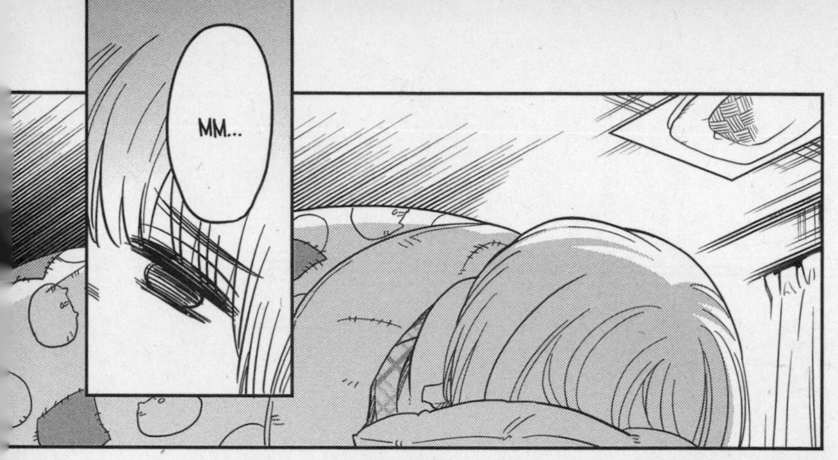
MM...

squirm...
HUH...?
I...

AHCHOO-TON!
ブシシー
BSHHHT

11 3 16:50
OH RIGHT... I COLLAPSED... AND SLEPT TILL THE NEXT DAY...
I SHOULD BE HAVING MY BIRTHDAY PARTY HERE NOW...
ぐすっ...
SOB...

I SUPPOSE I'M GOING TO SPEND TODAY AS LONELY AS A TOPAZ DRAGON...
THEN AGAIN, IT'S MY OWN FAULT...
THEY WERE TRYING TO BUY ME A PRESENT AND I TRIED TO STOP THEM...

I'M COLD...
AND ALL ALONE...

I DON'T CARE ABOUT PRESENTS ANYMORE...
I JUST WANT TO SEE MY FRIENDS...
ぐずっ
SNIFFLE

WHAAM
ビクゥッ
JOLT

YOU IDIOT! THERE'S A SICK KID HERE! CAN'T YOU OPEN IT MORE QUIETLY?!
YOU'RE BEING LOUD, TOO, YOU IDIOT!

HEY THERE, ARMIN.

SFC

WAAAAAH
WAAAH!
YOU GUYS CAME!!
あああん
WHOA!
YOU SEEM TO HAVE YOUR ENERGY BACK.

ARMIN...
I'M SORRY...

FLING
WHAAAAA?!
CUT
HUH?!
WHAT'RE YOU DO...
NOW NOW, JUST WATCH.
THIS WELL-WORN FUTON...
AND NEW COTTON!
SEWING STRING!
A ZIPPER!
AND NEW CLOTH THAT ALL OF US PICKED TOGETHER!
Comforter Cotton
AND...
OPEN
MIKASA'S TECHNIQUE!!
HURL

WHOOSH
WHOOSH
WHOOSH
WHOOSH
THUMP
BWIP
SNIP
WHIP
WHIP
WHIP
WHIP
WHIP
FLUFF
ARMIN...

WON'T YOU...
...ACCEPT OUR PRESENT TO YOU?

I'M GOING TO CHERISH IT ALL MY LIFE!
Happy Birthday
HAPPY BIRTHDAY!

IT'S FALL.
THE SCHOOL YEAR'S ALMOST OVER. EVEN THE FIRST-YEARS, USUALLY GOOFING OFF LIKE IDIOTS, GET TERRIFIED INTO PLACIDLY READING IN THE LIBRARY.
Shut up, you little freaks
Tasty Potato
YES... READING GRACE-FULLY.
GATUNK
WHAT THE HELL?!
100 YEARS OF HISTO OF ATT JUNIOR HIGH, VOL.
EREN, THIS IS THE LIBRARY...
THIS IS NO TIME TO WORRY ABOUT SOCIAL NORMS!! HERE, TAKE A LOOK AT THIS!

SIXTY-FIFTH PERIOD: HISTORY REPEATS ITSELF

IT WAS THE YEAR XITY X. AFTER DECIDING TO SHARE SCHOOL WITH THE TITANS, THE HUMAN STUDENTS FOUND THEMSELVES IN A SERIOUS PREDICAMENT.
THE TITANS HAD BEGUN STEALING THEIR LUNCH BOXES FROM THEM, SO THEY HAD TO LIVE THEIR LIVES WITHOUT LUNCH...!!

THESE GROWING CHILDREN DES-PERATELY NEEDED NUTRIENTS, LIKE SELENIUM, AND OATMEAL.
BUT THE TEACHERS LOOKED THE OTHER WAY...
AND SO, ONE STUDENT TOOK A STAND!!

IN THE END, HE SUCCEEDED IN RECLAIMING ONE LUNCH BOX!

IT WOULD GO DOWN AS ONE OF THE MOST SIGNIFICANT EVENTS IN THE HISTORY OF ATTACK JUNIOR HIGH...

...

UH-HUH... SO?

IDIOT! THE PROBLEM IS THE NEXT PART!!

YES, THAT HE WAS...
LOOK AT THIS...
THIS GREAT DEED OF THE STUDENT...AND THE CHARACTER OF THE YOUNG MAN HIMSELF WILL SURELY BE RETOLD BY FUTURE GENERATIONS--
HUH...?
TURN...
But the teachers looked
And one student took a stand—!!
In the end, he succeeded in reclaiming one lunch box!
This event would go down as one of the most significant in the history of
Attack on Titan Junior High—
This great deed of the student…And the charact of the young man him-
self will surely be retold by future generations—
Yes, that he was…
and
student.
THE END
IT'S BEEN EATEN BY WORMS !!
Only that part!

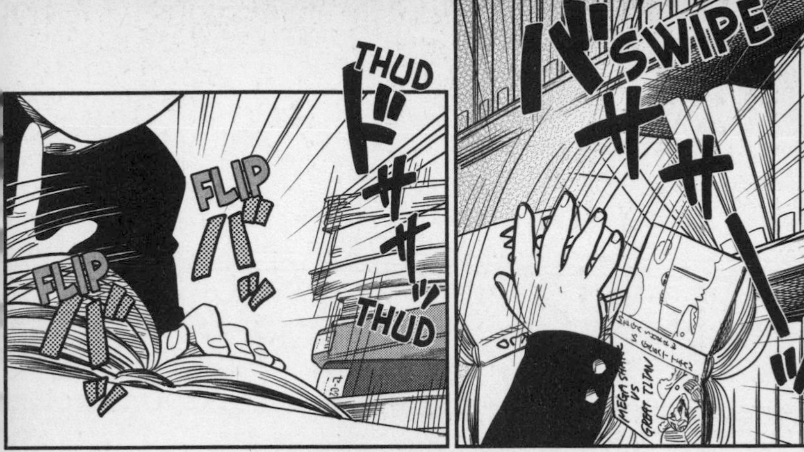
SWIPE
THUD
THUD
FLIP
FLIP

WHAT KIND OF A PERSON WAS HE...? I HAVE TO KNOW...!!
FLIP
I BET IT'LL LEAD TO A HINT ON ERAD-ICATING THE TITANS!
Guri and Titan

HEY, EREN...
DON'T STOP ME!
I'M NOT LEAVING THIS SPOT UNTIL I GET TO THE BOTTOM OF THIS MYSTERY!!
NO, IT'S THAT...
IF YOU DON'T STOP SQUAWKING IN THE LIBRARY...
STEP

RUMBLE RUMBLE
RUMBLE
RUMBLE
RUMBLE
WHAT'S THIS...?
KYOJIN CHELIN

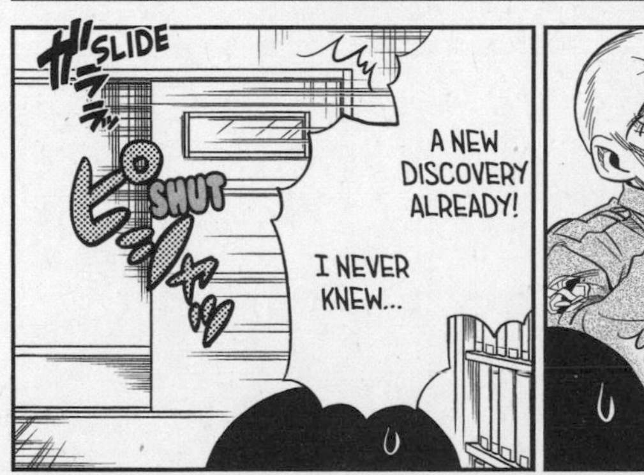
SLIDE
SHUT
A NEW DISCOVERY ALREADY!
I NEVER KNEW...

GATUNK
A- AMAZING...!
KYOJIN CHELIN

WHAAAAAM
...THAT THERE'D BE A GOOD CHEESE MEATLOAF RESTAURANT SO CLOSE...
AAAAAAAAUGH

EREN...

ドォォォオオオン SHOOOOOOM

I HAVEN'T USED THAT MOVE IN 7 YEARS......

...!
THIS IS...!
100 YEARS OF HISTORY OF ATTACK

HEY...
WHERE'D YOU GET YOUR GRUBBY HANDS ON THIS?!
YANK
WELL...
HE WANTED TO KNOW ABOUT THE PART THAT WAS EATEN BY BUGS...
I'M SORRY... I'LL BE SURE TO TEACH HIM HOW TO BEHAVE IN A LIBRARY...
...

HEY, YOU THERE... DO YOU STILL HAVE EAR-DRUMS...?

STOP LOOKING INTO THIS.

THE AT-HOME PARENT-TEACHER MEETING FROM HELL!
SHOOOCK
PULL
WHAAAAAT?!

GAAAH! LEAVE MY PARENTS OUT OF THIS!!
I'M NOT GOING TO SMASH YOUR PARENTS!!
IF YOU HAVE TO SMASH SOMEONE, HIT ME!!
HEH... I KNEW THAT THIS WOULD BE THE BEST WAY TO PUNISH A KID LIKE YOU...

UH, SIR, IT'S ABOUT YOUR SON...
HIS BEHAVIOR AT SCHOOL IS QUITE, ER, UN-SUITABLE.
WHAT?! I-I'M SO SORRY...
THAT'S WHY I CAME HERE TO TALK TO YOU TODAY.
COULD I HAVE A FEW MINUTES OF YOUR TIME?
Y-YES...
HMM ...?
THEN LET'S GO INSIDE...
NO, PLEASE HOLD ON...
U-UM...

ARE YOU...
KEITH...?

OH...
IS...

IS THAT YOU...?
GRISHA...?

HUH...
DAD, SO YOU KNOW KEITH-SENSEI FROM WAY BACK...?
FROM MY BRUISES, I KNOW YOU HAVE AT LEAST ONE COMMON INTEREST! HAHA!
HUH?
AHAHAHAHAHA
HOW DID WE MEET ...?
I MET KEITH WHEN I WAS ON MY DAILY WALK IN THE FOREST...
REALLY ?!
HEY, THIS ISN'T THE TIME FOR THAT...

AND THEN WE WENT TO A BAR TOGETHER, AND THAT'S WHERE I MET YOUR MOM...
SMASH
K-KEITH?!
I CAME HERE TODAY TO TALK ABOUT YOUR SON!!
BLEED
BLEED
BLEED
BLEED
BLEED

HE THINKS HIMSELF THE EQUAL OF THAT STUDENT FROM BACK THEN!
AND THE SENSITIVITY TRAINING DID NOTHING TO STOP HIM FROM TALKING ABOUT ERADICATING EVERY LAST TITAN FROM THE SCHOOL!

WHAT...?

EVERY LAST ONE IN THE SCHOOL ...?
WHO KNOWS HOW MANY YEARS THAT WOULD TAKE...?

YOU'D NEVER GRADUATE JUNIOR HIGH SCHOOL!

YES, GENO-CIDE IS VERY TIME-CONSUM— THAT'S NOT THE ISSUE HERE!!

YOU KNOW ALL TOO WELL...
ABOUT THAT STUDENT ...

EREN...
NO ORDINARY STUDENT COULD BECOME LIKE HIM.
WHAT? DAD KNOWS SOMETHING ABOUT HIM, TOO...?!

I DON'T CARE ONE BIT, DAD!!
I'D... I'D DO ANYTHING TO ERADICATE THE TITANS!!
EREN...
I SEE...
IT SEEMS THAT YOUR DETERMINATION IS REAL...
HOWEVER...
IT MEANS NOTHING IF YOU DON'T HAVE THE ABILITY TO BACK IT UP!!
GUH
SLAM

SLIDE

KEITH... HEAD-BUTTING MY CHILD IS MY JOB...

Guh ...

WELL, YOU MAY NOT WANT TO HEAR THIS, BUT...

...IF HE'S GOING TO SUFFER, THE SOONER THE BETTER.
YOU KNOW WHAT WOULD HAPPEN IF HE TRIED TO DO THE SAME THING AS THAT STUDENT...
OW OW OW OW OW

DAD, THAT MEDICINE OUCHIES MY BOOBOO !!
OUCH
RUB RUB

IT'S HEALED!!
JUST LIKE THAT?!
ぜんかーいっ
FULL POWER
GLARE
キッ
KEITH... KEITH-SENSEI!
THEN LET'S HAVE A REMATCH !!
IF I WIN, YOU HAVE TO TELL ME ALL ABOUT HIM!
びしーっ
POINT
VERY WELL...
BUT IF YOU WANT TO DEFEAT ME...
YOU MAY HAVE TO RADUATE FROM NIOR HIGH UNDRED IMES...
GRAAAAAAAAH

WHEN OTHERS ARE TALK-ING...

...YOU SHOULD KNOW...

GRAB

...NOT TO INTER-RUPT!!

WHAAAAAM

FLAIL
AAAAGH
FLAIL
THIS TIME DID YOU LEARN YOUR LESSON, YOU RECKLESS BRAT?

YOU'LL NEVER BE ABLE TO DEFEAT THE TITANS...
PAT
PAT
It stings

I'M HEALED!!
JUMP
WHAT, REALLY?!

RUB
THWACK
RUB
RUB
SLAM

OKAY, NO MORE OF THAT!!

HOW ARE YOU HEALING ANY AND ALL DAMAGE?!
WHAT ARE YOU, A WIZARD?! I THOUGHT YOU WERE JUST A DOCTOR!!
W-WELL ...
GAAAH

TOSS
EREN!
OKAY...!
SQUEEZE
DON'T WORRY, DAD... I'M SURE I CAN WIN...
AND IT'S BECAUSE ...
MY SPRY FORM CAN FIGHT AT FULL POWER...
...WHILE KEITH-SENSEI'S WORN SKELETON SPENT A BUNCH OF HIS STRENGTH IN ALL THOSE ATTACKS!!
HAHAHAHAHAHAHA
AH-HAH!
GRIIIND
YOU'RE COMPLETELY RIGHT, YOU STUPID FAMILY!
HAHA... WOW...
I'M SO EXCITED THAT I'M SHAKING...
NOW I CAN GET ONE STEP CLOSER...
...TO MAKING MY DREAM COME TRUE...!!

...
SO YOU REALLY GENUINELY WANT TO ERADICATE THE TITANS...
...THAT STUDENT HAD THE SAME HANGUPS...
BUT...
YOU CAN NEVER BE LIKE HIM!!
DASH
...AND I'LL TELL YOU WHY...
WHAAAAA

IF YOU CAN'T DEFEAT ME...
...YOU CAN NEVER BE LIKE HIM...
THUD
HE WAS FREAKISHLY STRONG IN A FIGHT...
HE WAS ONLY AVERAGE IN SCHOOLWORK OR SPORTS...
...BUT HE WAS PEERLESS IN A FIGHT !!
PANT
PANT
AAAUUUGH

YOU STILL GET UP AND FIGHT, EREN YEAGER...
HOWEVER...
I ALREADY KNOW WHERE YOU'LL...
SWIFT...
TEETER...
WHAM

SLUMP
JUST... AS YOU SAID...
THE DAMAGE PREVENTED ME FROM MOVING MY AS I WANTED TO...
THAT WAS A GOOD BLOW, EREN YEAGER.
STILL...
THANKS!
GRISHA... WHY DON'T YOU...
TELL HIM ABOUT THAT STUDENT...?

ALL RIGHT...
I WILL..

EREN...
HE WAS...

HE WAS...
GULP
...
WHAT? YOU CAN'T REMEMBER?
WHISPER
YOU IDIOT! HE WAS... UH...
WELL, YOU KNOW ...

HE REALLY WAS QUITE AVERAGE AT SPORTS AND SCHOOL-WORK...
HE HAD FEWER FRIENDS THAN AVERAGE...
AND HE WAS GOOD IN A FIGHT, BUT ONLY IN HIS GRADE...
THERE WASN'T ANY-THING ELSE THAT REALLY STOOD OUT ABOUT HIM...
UHHHH, I CAN'T REMEMBER HIS FACE THAT WELL, EITHER...
UHHHH
うーん
I CAN'T EVEN REMEMBER HIS NAME...
OH, BUT I DO REMEM-BER THIS.
THE REASON HE CAME TO HATE THE TITANS WAS BECAUSE THEY ATE HIS FAVORITE FOOD, A CHEESE-BURGER...
OH... HUH...
THEY'RE THE SAME...
STOP IT!!

WAAAAAAAH

ATTACK ON TITAN

AW, MAN!! I WAS HOPING FOR SOME SUPER COOL STORIES!!

AFTER ALL THAT BUILDUP, YOU CAN'T THINK OF ANY-THING?

UH, EREN, TAKE THIS AS A CON-SOLATION PRIZE!

YOU'LL, UH, ENJOY IT!!

HUH? WHAT?

RUSTLE RUSTLE

JANGLE

IT'S THE KEY TO THE BASE-MENT!!

...

WAIT, WHAT THE HECK?! WE HAVE A BASEMENT?! WHAT BASE-MENT?!

TAKE ME TO A GOOD MEATLOAF PLACE INSTEAD!!

WAAAAAH

...

QUIT YOUR YAPPING!!

WHAAAAM

AAAUGH

WHAT BASE-MENT WAS GRISHA TALKING ABOUT...

AND WILL ANYONE REMEMBER ANYTHING ABOUT EREN AFTER HE GRADUATES?!

(NO. AND YOUR FRIENDS, TEACHERS, AND LOVED ONES WILL ALL FORGET YOU, TOO.)

ATTACK on TITAN
JUNIOR HIGH

SAKI NAKAGAWA

Based on "Attack on Titan" by
HAJIME ISAYAMA

Contents

SCHEDULE FOR TUESDAY, NOVEMBER 3 STUDENT ON DUTY: KRISTA

SIXTY-SIXTH PERIOD: MY CLASSMATE SMELLS SWEET

ガラララ
SHUMMP
YO!
GURK! I MEAN, SORRY FOR BEING LATE.

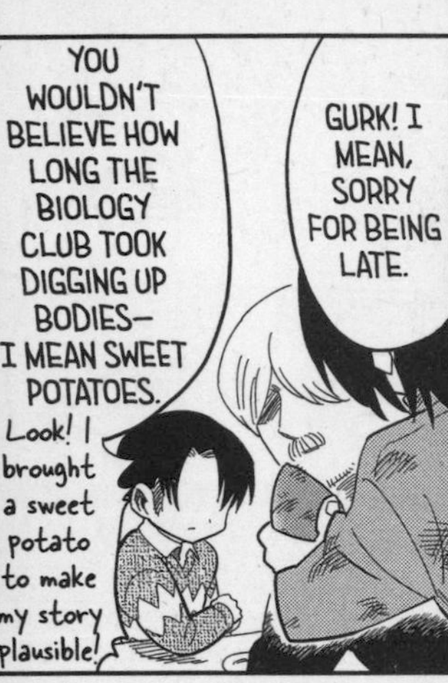
YOU WOULDN'T BELIEVE HOW LONG THE BIOLOGY CLUB TOOK DIGGING UP BODIES— I MEAN SWEET POTATOES.
Look! I brought a sweet potato to make my story plausible!

スンスン
SNIFF SNIFF

HANGE...
HOW LONG HAS IT BEEN SINCE YOU'VE TAKEN A BATH?
ボリボリ
SCRATCH SCRATCH
OH, WHO KEEPS TRACK THESE DAYS?
KACHINK

BWAAAH
I GUESS BETWEEN ELECTRIFYING THE ATTIC AND ACQUIRING ALL THOSE ORGANS, IT'S BEEN...
AH HA HA HAA
...TWO WEEKS, MAYBE?
YOU CAUGHT ME!

BAM
FWOOOOH
WHOA!!
THAT'S ONE COLD BREEZE!!
GRAB
WOOSH
AAAAA!!

GOBLOOSH
ボチャーン
ZPLASH
ザバァ
HEY!!
IT'S MEAN TO DEFENESTRATE YOUR CLASSMATE INTO A KOI POND!!

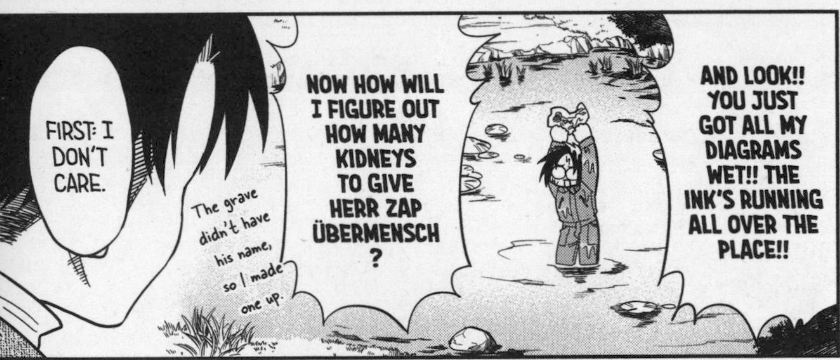
AND LOOK!! YOU JUST GOT ALL MY DIAGRAMS WET!! THE INK'S RUNNING ALL OVER THE PLACE!!
NOW HOW WILL I FIGURE OUT HOW MANY KIDNEYS TO GIVE HERR ZAP ÜBERMENSCH?
The grave didn't have his name, so I made one up.
FIRST: I DON'T CARE.

SECOND: NO ONE WHO HAS NOT BATHED IN TWO WEEKS MAY OCCUPY SPACE ADJACENT TO ME... NOT TO MENTION LIVE NEXT DOOR!
THE FACT THAT I'M BREATHING SOME OF THE PUTRID AIR COMING OFF OF YOU IS AN EVEN BIGGER PROBLEM!
BOO
むっ

NOW YOU'VE DONE IT, LEVI! YOU'RE GOING TO HEAR ME OUT!
YOU SEE, WHEN I WAS A YOUNG...

YOUR FLIGHT HAS BEEN DIVERTED! CONSIDER THIS RESTRICTED AIRSPACE!
KAFF KAFF KAFF KAFF

LEVI... ISN'T IT ONLY POLITE TO HEAR A FRIEND OUT...?!

MAYBE YOU DIDN'T REALIZE IT, BUT I...

I MAY NOT HAVE ...

I MAY NOT HAVE TAKEN A BATH IN TWO MONTHS, BUT...
I HAVEN'T BRUSHED MY TEETH IN ABOUT HALF A YEAR!!
WHADDYA SAY TO THAT?!

GYM EQUIPMENT ROOM
WHAT'S GOING ON HERE?! WHY WOULD YOU TRUSS ME UP LIKE A PIG BEFORE DISSECTION ...?!
WHAT DO YOU INTEND TO DO WITH ME?!

GOOD QUESTION. WELL, TO START WITH...
...WE INTEND TO STRIP OFF YOUR FETID RAGS ...!!
EYAAAH!

THEN I'M GOING TO CLEAN YOU IF IT MEANS SANDING OFF THE TOP LAYER OF SKIN!
EEEEEEEK
WAIT, LEVI...

EVEN SUCH CRUEL AND UNUSUAL METHODS...
...WON'T BE ENOUGH TO CLEAN A BODY THAT DIRTY.

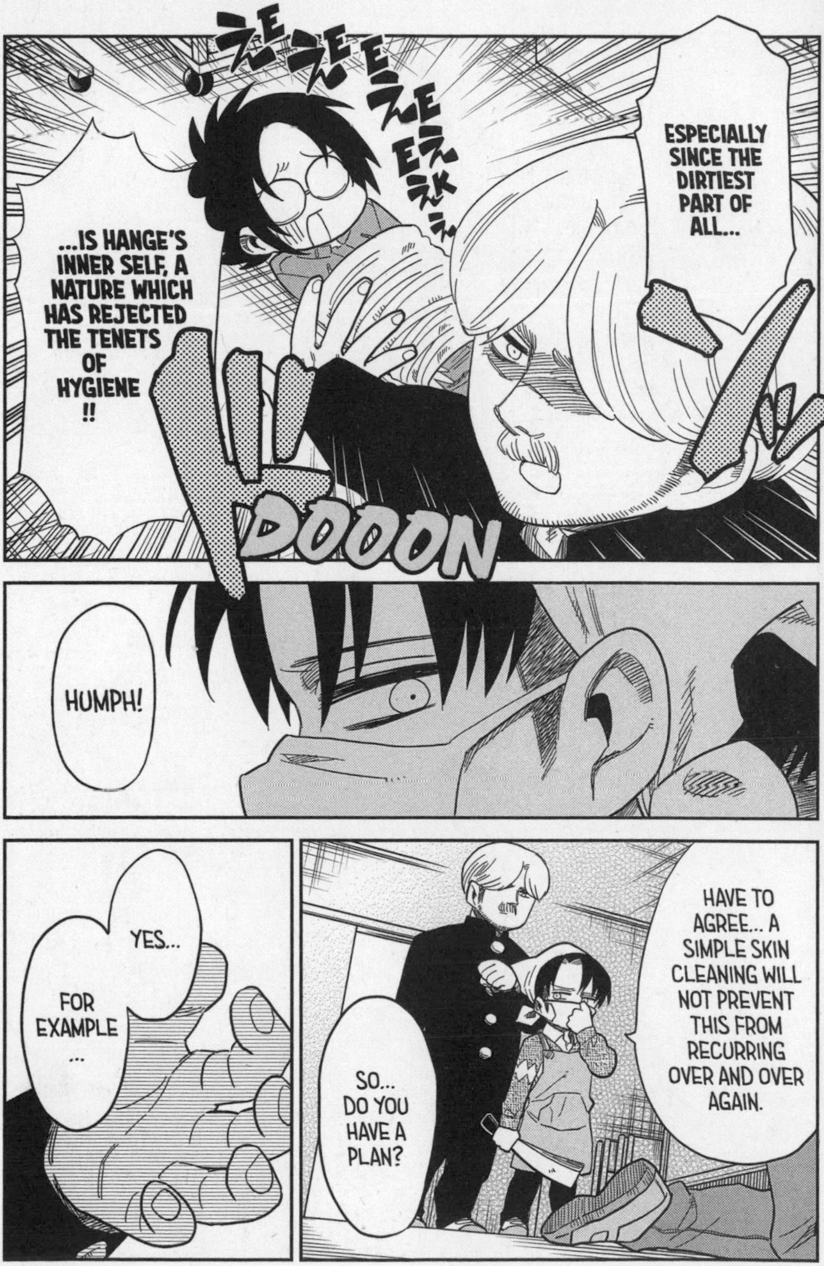

ESPECIALLY SINCE THE DIRTIEST PART OF ALL...

...IS HANGE'S INNER SELF, A NATURE WHICH HAS REJECTED THE TENETS OF HYGIENE !!

DOOON

HUMPH!

HAVE TO AGREE... A SIMPLE SKIN CLEANING WILL NOT PREVENT THIS FROM RECURRING OVER AND OVER AGAIN.
SO... DO YOU HAVE A PLAN?
YES...
FOR EXAMPLE ...

AFTER THE DIRT IS CLEANED COMPLETELY FROM THE SKIN...
...WE TRANSPLANT THE SKIN ITSELF ONTO SOMEONE WITH A BETTER PERSON-ALITY.
JUST WAIT ONE MINUTE THERE!!
ピキーン
SHEEEN

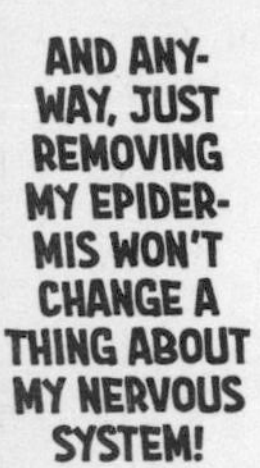
NOW LOOK, IF ANYONE IS GOING TO TRANSPLANT MY SKIN ONTO A DIFFERENT BODY, IT'S NOT GOING TO BE YOU!!
AND ANY-WAY, JUST REMOVING MY EPIDER-MIS WON'T CHANGE A THING ABOUT MY NERVOUS SYSTEM!
ちょっとおおおお
Heey, waait!
...

IS IT NOW?
IF SO, THE FAULT LIES EXCLUSIVELY ON YOUR OWN WEIRDNESS.
ふんっ
HUMPH

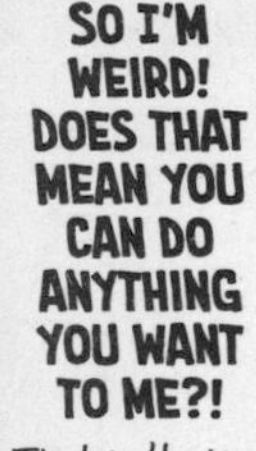
SO I'M WEIRD! DOES THAT MEAN YOU CAN DO ANYTHING YOU WANT TO ME?!
That isn't nice, you know!

THEN...
CHOOSE YOUR OWN PATH.

ゴクッ
GULP

DO WE RETURN YOUR CLEANED SKIN TO YOU?
OR DO WE FIND A MORE FITTING HOST?
YOU DON'T SKIN ME IN THE FIRST PLACE!!

AND WITH THAT, HANGE HAD NO CHOICE BUT TO AGREE TO TAKE REGULAR BATHS.
TWO HOURS LATER...
AHHH...

I SENSE SMOOTH SKIN.
Did you have to use my nice lavender soap, though?
テカ
GLEEEM
WE SHOULD'VE KNOWN HANGE WOULD GET OBSESSED WITH THIS!
BEFORE WE KNEW IT, WE'D RUN OUT OF SOAP AND SHAMPOO BOTH.

DON'T YOU OWN SOAP OF YOUR OWN?
YOU SHOULD DO YOUR BATHTIME ABLUTIONS WITH THAT.
DON'T HAVE ANY.
HUH?
ALSO MY WATER, GAS AND ELECTRICITY HAVE ALL BEEN CUT OFF.
AND BECAUSE OF THAT, I CAN'T USE MY BATH...
ガタッ
SKRRCH

LEVI'S PLACE ...

KACHACK

GLOOOOOOOOM

SHHHHHH

SIXTY-SEVENTH PERIOD: YOU CAN'T BEAT PEER PRESSURE

THERE IS ONE THING IN THIS ENTIRE WORLD...
...THAT IS SO AWFUL THAT I CANNOT MANAGE TO STAND IT.

HEY, LOOK AT THAT!
LET'S ALL THREE OF US TAKE A PURIKURA PICTURE!!

WELL, I...
YES, LET'S DO THAT!
GRAB
ZZZACK!

WHEE! LET'S DO IT! LET'S DO IT!
HOLD ON ONE SECOND!!
...
I... ABSOLUTELY REFUSE TO DO THAT...!
HUUH?
NO! NOT NOW, NOT EVER!!

WH-WHY NOT?
YEAH, WHY YOU GOTTA BE SUCH A KILLJOY ALL THE TIME?
WAIT, YOU DARE ASK WHY?
YOU REALLY DON'T KNOW...?

I'M GONNA EAT YOU!
I'M GONNA EXTERMINATE YOU!
WHAT COULD POSSIBLY BE FUN ABOUT PAYING MONEY FOR PICTURES OF YOUR OWN FACE...!!
NOT TO MENTION WALKING AROUND WITH THEM, TRADING THEM WITH OTHER PEOPLE... IT'S JUST SO... REPULSIVE!
I WILL **NEVER** GET MY PICTURE TAKEN LIKE THAT...!!
GONNG...
I NEVER KNEW ...

GAGONNG
BUT ANNIE, NOBODY WILL FORCE YOU TO WALK AROUND WITH ANY. LET'S JUST TAKE THE PICTURES!
SQUEEZE
THAT MEANS THERE'S EVEN LESS REASON FOR ME TO BE IN THE PICTURE...!!
IF YOU TWO WANT A PIECE OF YOUR SOUL SUCKED OUT, GO RIGHT AHEAD!! I LIKE MY SOUL!!
WHOOSH
BUT... BUT... BUT IF WE DID THAT...
...IT MEANS WE'D HAVE TO PAY 200 YEN EACH...
It's 400 yen for each set!
HAVE YOU NO CON-SCIENCE?!
YOU CAN AFFORD THAT MUCH, CAN'T YOU?!
100 yen = about $1
SO I'M JUST A WALLET TO YOU...?
NO, NOT AT ALL!
HUMPH
OKAY THEN ...
I'LL GIVE YOU A DISCOUNT! YOU PUT UP ONLY 100 YEN!
YOU HAVE NO RIGHT TO SAY "JUST" THERE!!
We'll pay 150 each!
LET'S MAKE THIS CLEAR... I AM NOT HAVING MY PICTURE TAKEN!!
AND IF YOU MAKE ME, OUR FRIENDSHIP WILL BE OVER!!
VISH

HUH?!
OKAY, SO IT'S OVER. NOW LET'S JUST TAKE THE PICTURE...

O...

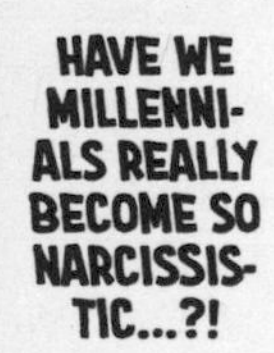
HAVE WE MILLENNI-ALS REALLY BECOME SO NARCISSIS-TIC...?!

WAIT...?! I DON'T GET IT... WHY...?! WHAT THE...
WHY WOULD ANYBODY DECIDE TO BREAK OFF A FRIENDSHIP JUST FOR A PICTURE OF THEIR OWN FACE?!

ANNIE...
I NEED YOU TO NUT UP.

GRAB
THE THREAT TO BREAK OFF A FRIEND-SHIP...

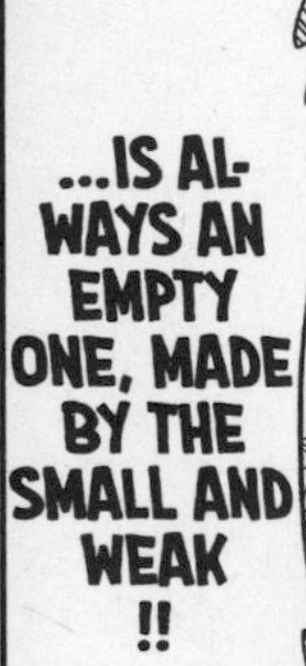
...IS AL-WAYS AN EMPTY ONE, MADE BY THE SMALL AND WEAK!!

SO STOP WITH THE WHINING, AND LET'S GO GET THAT PICTURE TAKEN!!
BUT JUST BE PREPARED FOR ONE THING...
ONCE THE PICTURE IS TAKEN, BOTH YOUR FACE AND BODY WILL BE ALMOST UNREC-OGNIZABLE!!
あははははは AH HA HA HA HA HA HA
I'LL BE AIR-BRUSHED?
...
THEN...
THEN I'LL DIE.
HUH?
I'D RATHER DIE THAN TAKE THOSE PICTURES WITH YOU!!
ぶわあっ BWAAH

W-WAIT...
DASH

HEY! UH, THAT'S ANOTH-ER...
...EMPTY... THREAT. ...RIGHT?
DASH

EVERY-BODY HAS TO DIE SOME-TIME ...
I KNOW THAT.
SO... WHY NOT DIE WITH OUR PICTURES BEING TAKEN?
HAHH HAHH

HEY, ANNIE... !!
JUST LET ME SAY ONE THING... !!

THIS MAKES NO SENSE AT ALL...!!
RIGHT AFTER THAT...

...

YMIR AND KRISTA PINNED DOWN ANNIE AND FORCED HER TO SIT FOR THE PHOTO.

FLASH

SQUEE! HERE COMES THE NEXT ONE!!

FLASH

ANNIE, STOP STRUGGLING OR IT'S CHLOROFORM TIME!!

STRUGGLE

O-OH, NO!

I THINK I FLASHED MY PANTIES!

FLASH

GA HA HA HA HA

STRUGGLE STRUGGLE STRUGGLE STRUGGLE

FLASH FLASH

OH! THERE IT IS! THERE IT IS!

KACHAK

FLASH

HA HA, KRISTA!

YOUR EYES COVER HALF YOUR FACE HERE.

And I like it!

FLASH

TEE HEE HEE! ALL OF YOUR FRECKLES HAVE COMPLETELY DISAPPEARED, YMIR!

OH, AND LOOK HERE!

SNIP SNIP

RIGHT BRAIN, LEFT BRAIN
BONUS MANGA

HANGE'S AMBITION

To be continued on page 316.

SIXTY-EIGHTH PERIOD: FRIENDS ALWAYS SHARE

DINNG
1-3
DONNG
DINNG
LET'S HEAD HOME, BERTOLT.
HM? OKAY.
FIDGET
FIDGET

SHIK
SHIK
SHIK
SHIK
SHIK
W-WAIT UP! REINER, YOU'RE TOO FAST...

GANCH

REINER, WHAT...?!
SHH!
CALM DOWN AND JUST LISTEN...

AH!
JUST TAKE A LOOK AT THIS!
SST

IT'S A PURIKURA PICTURE WITH KIRSTA AND ANNIE!
HUMPH
OH... MY... GUH...

YOU CAN RELAX. I'VE GOT ONE OF THEM FOR YOU, TOO.
SHUFFLE
SHUFFLE
STILL... THERE WEREN'T ANY WITH GOOD PICTURES OF ANNIE.
...
REINER ...

THANK YOU...
REALLY! THANK YOU...!!
HA HA... WHAT ARE FRIENDS FOR?
GRIMP

YOU KNOW, IT FEELS GOOD... MAKING A FRIEND REALLY HAPPY...
OF COURSE I AM! THANKS SO MUCH!
BUT HOW DID YOU GET IT?

WAKE UP!
ANNIE!
YOU MUST HAVE BEEN SO EXCITED TO GET YOUR PICTURE TAKEN THAT THE CAMERA CAUGHT YOU JUST BEFORE YOU WERE READY, HUH?
ANNIE... TO BE CAUGHT WITH YOUR FACE LIKE THAT...

I NOTICED THAT KRISTA HAD THEM...
...SO I GOT DOWN ON MY HANDS AND KNEES AND BEGGED UNTIL SHE GAVE THEM TO ME.
BOW
WOW, GOOD OLD-FASHIONED GROVELING!
I'M IMPRESSED BY YOUR CRINGING MORTIFICATION, REINER!

YEAH...
...SO BE SURE TO TREASURE IT!
SURE WILL!

I MEAN...
...A GUY HANGING ON TO THE PURIKURA PICTURE OF A GIRL HE'S CRUSHING ON FOREVER AND EVER IS... A **LITTLE** CREEPY.
HA HA...!
JUST DON'T THINK ABOUT THAT TOO MUCH, REINER.
I MEAN, I'M JUST REALLY...

FWOOOOOOOOOOH
...REALLY GLAD THAT WE ARE FRIENDS...

FLIPPAFLIPPAFLIPPAFLIPPA

VWIP

MY PICTURE...
MY PICTURE JUST FLEW UP INTO THAT THICK FOREST!
SHUSH SHUSH SHUSH SHUSH SHUSH SHUSH SHUSH SHUSH

ジャリ
SKRICH
...
ガサガサ
SHIFF
SHIFF
ガサ
SHIFFIFFF

ちらっ
ガサ
SHIFF

GRIND
GRIND
GRIND
GRIND
GRIND
GRIND
GRIND
GRIND
GRIND

REINER... HE REALLY LOOKS DEPRESSED.
NO, THAT ISN'T "DEPRESSION," IT'S... WHAT KIND OF FACE IS THAT?!

A-ANYWAY, I HAVE TO FIND HIS PICTURE...FOR HIS SAKE...
BUT...

EYAAAAAH!

R-REINER !!

I-I'M SORRY, BUT I CAN'T!
IT'S LATE, AND THERE'S HOWLING, AND I'M COLD...!

FACE IT, THE PICTURE IS GONE FOREVER !!

HUH?

U-UM... UH...
DID I JUST HEAR...YOU SAY SOMETHING ABOUT GIVING UP ON MY PICTURE...?
THEN... THEN THAT MEANS...

...YOU'RE WILLING TO GIVE ME YOURS ?!
BOOM
WAKE UP!
ANNIE!
BA-
?!

WH...
WHAT ARE YOU SAYING, REINER... ?!
YOU KNOW THAT IS ABSO- LUTELY IMPOSSI- BLE!!
IT BELONGS TO ME!!
WHAM

NO, YOU GOT THAT WRONG !!
I BEGGED THEM OFF OF KRISTA, THEN I ALLOWED YOU TO BORROW ONE...
IT BELONGS TO ME !!
GRIND

GRRRND
IT'S THE PHOTO...! THE PHOTO HAS TURNED HIM INTO A ROIDED-OUT FRIEND-STRANGLER!
IT'S NO GOOD... I CAN'T BREAK FREE... REINER'S GONE MAD...

GUH...
GRINNND

OH... I NEED TO SAY A FINAL PRAYER TO MY GOD...
O PLEASE WATCH OVER ME IN MY FINAL MOMENTS, DAIYA-CHAN...
CRACK

TAP!! TAP!!
HACK!
NGH! FINE!

WHUMP

OKAY, BER-TOLT. HAND IT OVER...
REINER...
YOU'VE CHANGED SOME-HOW...
YOU'RE NOT THE FRIEND I'VE COME TO KNOW!
AS JESUS ONCE SAID... IF YOU LIVE BY YOUR WIENER...
...THEN YOU SHALL PERISH BY YOUR WIENER!

SO YOU'RE SAYING I SHOULDN'T LET FLOPPY WILBUR ORDER ME AROUND?
FINE. I'LL IGNORE THAT PART OF MY BODY FOR NOW.
INSTEAD I'LL USE MY FIST! IT'S TIME FOR...
KLENCH

NAKED ARM WRES-TLING!
BOOM
WELL?
ARE YOU TOO CHICKEN TO PUT IT ALL ON THE LINE, AND LET IT ALL HANG OUT?

GRIMP

NOT AT ALL.

Except the naked part, I ain't doing that..

WAIT... HOW'D YOU GET THAT ARM...?
HEH HEH... SURPRISED? THIS IS MY PRIDE AND JOY.
EVERY DAY FOR THE PAST 287 DAYS, I'VE CUT CHARMS OUT OF EXOTIC METALS TO SELL TO GULLIBLE NEW AGE TYPES ON ETSY.
CHIK CHIK
GRRRN
ONE ARM DIDN'T GROW AT ALL. BUT MY CUTTING ARM GOT ALL BUFFIFIED!

SO YOU'RE A TEENAGE BOY...
...WITH ONE ARM THAT'S GETTING A WORKOUT... AND **THAT'S** YOUR BEST EXCUSE?
SHIF

CLUTCH

KH... I KNOW REINER'S STRONG... PROBABLY STRONGER THAN I IMAGINE...!
BUT I HAVE TO SNAP HIM OUT OF THIS HORMONAL MALAISE...
GRN GRN...
I THOUGHT BERTOLT WAS THE NERDY TYPE... I SURE NEVER THOUGHT HE'D HAVE FULL-BLOWN SWOLEIOSIS!
GRN
GRN
GRN

HYAAAAAAH!
GRUNG
NGAAAAAH!
GRAH
I WILL NOT LOSE THIS!!
I CAN'T... BECAUSE...
KLENCH

...THAT PICTURE...

...IS JUST TOO WUVABLE!!

WAKE UP!

ANNIE!

BOOM

UWOOOOOH!!

AAAAAA!!

FLASH

シュウウウウウウ
SHHHHHHHH

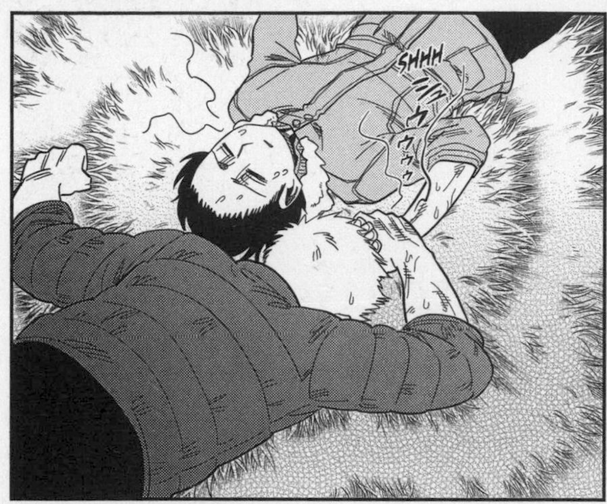
SHHH
シュウウウ

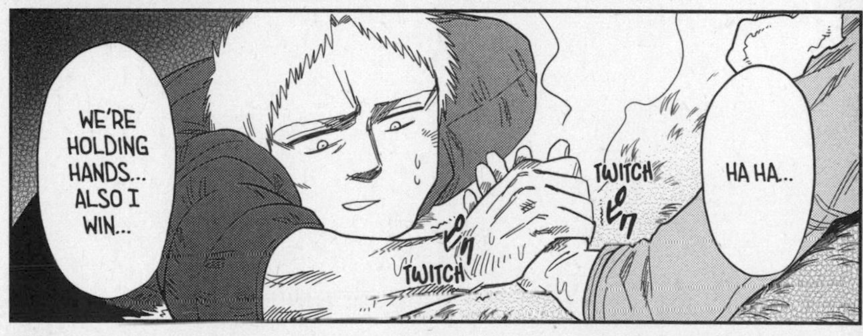
HA HA...
TWITCH
ピク
WE'RE HOLDING HANDS... ALSO I WIN...
ピク
TWITCH

...

REINER...
フッ
HEH

GOOD WARMUP. NOW IT'S TIME FOR THE REAL THING.

HUH...?

WELL, I DON'T REMEMBER YOU SAYING, "BEGIN," OR "START," OR ANYTHING.

SO I JUST FIGURED THIS WAS FOR PRACTICE.

WAIT...

YOU FOUGHT LIKE THAT FOR A PRACTICE MATCH?

THROB THROB

SURE.

I WASN'T EVEN GOING AT HALF STRENGTH.

TWITCH TWITCH

BERT-OLT...
...THAT'S A KARATE-KID-SEQUEL-LEVEL DICK MOVE.
COMPARE ME TO THE BEST MOVIE EVER IF YOU MUST.
AND I HAVE TO SAY THAT YOU'RE NOT BEING FAIR...

REINER, SOMEBODY HAS TO SAY "START!"

I DID! I SAID "BEGIN!" I SAID IT REALLY FAST, BUT...

I DIDN'T HEAR ANYTHING!!

WHATEVER. RIGHT NOW, WE'RE ONE AND ONE. IT'S BEST OF THREE!!

OKAY, IF YOU INSIST, THEN...

START!!

ZWHAM

Will you stop that?! And I meant best three of five!

CHEEP
CHEEP

B-BERTOLT...
TH-THAT MAKES 299 WINS FOR ME...
PANT
WHEEZE
...AND YOU'VE ONLY WON 298 TIMES, SO...
...THE NEXT...
REINER...

YOUR HAND SMELLS LIKE ROTTEN COD...
I DON'T WANT TO HOLD IT ANYMORE. ...HERE.

HUH?
R-REALLY?
YEAH.
B-BERTOLT! YOU'RE...
AW... LOOK, IT'S MORNING ALREADY.
I'M PRETTY SURE WE'VE BEEN ROLLING IN DOG POOP...
I'M GOING TO SKIP SCHOOL AND TAKE A BATH.
...
YEAH!
BERTOLT, YOU'RE...
...SUCH A MATURE GUY!
SNIFF
ぐすっ…
HUH? WHY ARE YOU CRYING, REINER?

THAT WAS
HE NIGHT I
LEARNED...
THANK YOU !!

HERE I WAS GETTING JERKED AROUND BY FLOPPY WILBUR...
...WHILE YOU WERE...
YEAH...
...LET'S JUST END THAT SENTENCE THERE, OKAY?

NOW ON TO MY TRUE QUEST IN LIFE...
1-3

...THAT PHOTOS FOR YOUR SPANK BANK...
...AND WINNING AT ARM WRESTLING...
...AREN'T NEARLY AS IMPORTANT AS FRIENDSHIP.

...TO GET A PICTURE OF HER WHERE SHE'S NOT BLINKING!
OR MAYBE I SHOULD LEARN HOW TO DRAW PICTURES OF LADIES AND GET HIGH OFF MY OWN SUPPLY...
わーい YAAAY
SO, IS ANNIE GONNA SUE THOSE JERKS FOR ALL THAT HORRIBLE STUFF THEY DID? I MEAN, I'M JUST THE NARRATOR, BUT JESUS!

SIXTY-NINTH PERIOD: LET IT SNOW, LET THEM BURN

UM... ALL THE OTHER CLUBS ARE TAKING THE SNOW DAY OFF, YOU KNOW...

WHY DOES THE WALL BEAUTIFICATION CLUB HAVE TO COME HERE?

HOW CAN WE CLEAN THE WALL IN THIS SNOW ANYW...

EVERYONE, I'M GLAD YOU'RE HERE.

WE'RE NOT HERE TODAY TO BEAUTIFY THE WALLS.

WE'RE HERE TO SHOVEL!!
VWAAH
UNF
SHOV-ELING SNOW?!
WHY DO WE HAVE TO DO THIS?!
It's just a pain!
NO MORE OF YOUR TANGENTS ...
Connie, how do you have splinters already?
The shovel is hurting my hands. I hate it?!
When it snows ny religion equires me to ot work nd eat eef tix.
STOP CHATTERING LIKE SMALL DUMB CHILDREN AND LISTEN TO ME...
"WALL BEAUTIFICATION IS STUPID!" "I DON'T KNOW WHAT THAT IS!" "THIS BARELY QUALIFIES AS PARODY!"
CUT
THAT'S WHAT I'M HEARING ABOUT OUR CLUB. NEXT YEAR, OUR ALREADY-TINY CLUB BUDGET MIGHT GET CUT BY ANOTHER TEN PERCENT!
WE'RE SITTING ON A KNIFE EDGE! AND IT'S A SERRATED KNIFE!
AND OUR JUNK IS STUCK ON ONE OF THOSE RIDGES AND THE FIRE DEPART-MENT'S NOT COMING!
FWOOM

GRAB!

AND **THAT** IS WHY WE ARE GOING TO OBTAIN THE GRATITUDE OF THE ENTIRE SCHOOL WITH OUR SHOVELING SKILLS!!

WE'LL FORCE THEM TO NOTICE US, AND THEN THEY'LL HAVE TO GIVE US MONEY!

Like those people in airports dressed as nuns, except they're not nuns!

BAM BAM BAM BAM BAM BAM BAM BAM

FINE, IF IT'LL SHUT YOU UP.
YOU MEAN YOU **WERE** LISTEN-ING?
WE'LL TAKE IT FROM HERE.
NO, WAIT A SECOND.

YOU THREE ARE TEAM A.
THE REST OF YOU ARE TEAM B.

THIS CAN'T BE SIMPLE SHOVELING.
ONLY COMPETITION, THE ENGINE OF CAPITALISM, CAN MOTIVATE YOU JADED MILLENNIALS!
WHAT?!
ええーーっ!?
HUUUH?!
SO WHOEVER SHOVELS A LARGER AREA...

...WILL RECEIVE SNACKS EQUIVALENT TO THE CASH VALUE OF ONE THOUSAND YEN*!!
CARAMEL FOKES
Chagariko
WHAAAAA?!
OOOOH
THEN WE'LL GIVE THIS 100%! WE'LL SPLIT IT THREE WAYS. I GIVE 50, YOU GIVE 50, AND ARMIN GIVES 50!
Y-YEAH!

*About $10

IF WE DON'T WIN I'LL GLAGGLLFLRG!!
BYAH!
GUGLE BLURP DROOPLE!!
HUH?
OH! NICE CLUB SPIRIT, SASHA!

I HEREBY DECLARE THIS SNOW SHOVELING COMPETITION FOR A NEGLIGIBLE AMOUNT OF SNACKS...

BWAAAHH

OPEN!!

UMPH!

WHUMPH
HUP!
I HAVEN'T SEEN A PILE OF SNOW THIS BIG SINCE THAT MOVIE MY DAD LOVES, CARFARCE!
RIGHT... BECAUSE IT'S ABOUT A CAR.
WHUMPH

I THINK WE'VE WON THIS WITH ROOM TO SPARE!
AAAAAAAA AAAAAAAAA
HM?

KERBOOM

OWWWWW
IS THE SNOW OKAY?
YES...

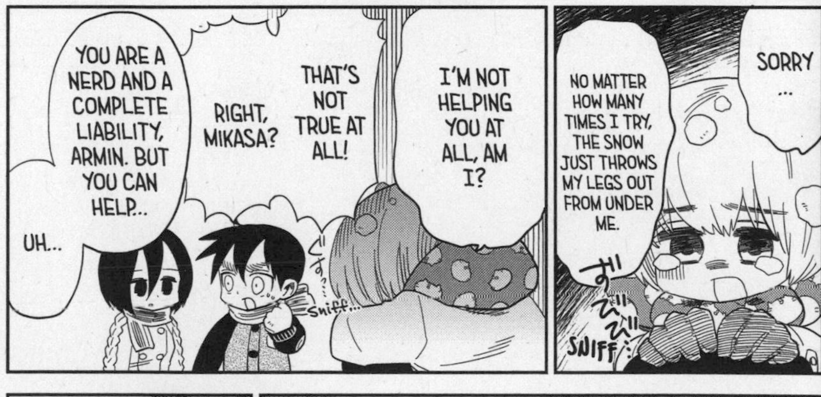
SORRY ...
NO MATTER HOW MANY TIMES I TRY, THE SNOW JUST THROWS MY LEGS OUT FROM UNDER ME.
SNIFF
I'M NOT HELPING YOU AT ALL, AM I?
THAT'S NOT TRUE AT ALL!
RIGHT, MIKASA?
Sniff...
YOU ARE A NERD AND A COMPLETE LIABILITY, ARMIN. BUT YOU CAN HELP...
UH...

JUST STAY HERE AND KEEP WATCH OVER OUR SNOW MOUNTAIN.
STAAARE
Let's do this!

AS JOHN MILTON ONCE SAID, "THEY WHO SIT AND WAIT ARE BIG JERKS AND EVERYONE MAKES FUN OF THEIR DUMB HAIR."
BUT PERHAPS THIS IS FOR THE BEST...

EVEN IF I CAN'T BE OF ANY HELP...
Sorry, everybody...
I guess I spilled the water bucket!
...I CAN AT LEAST BE THE USELESS-BUT-LOVABLE TYPE!
What'll we do with you? You're so clumsy!
アハハー
AH HA HAA
GRIMP

SO UNTIL I CAN BE PLUCKY COMIC RELIEF, I'LL JUST SIT HERE QUIETLY...
SHIK

YO.
I'M ONLY GONNA ASK ONCE. GET OUTTA THE WAY.

HUH?

WAAAGH!!

THAT'S ARMIN'S VOICE...?!
TUMP
TUMP
WHAT COULD HAVE HAPPENED TO HIM?!

AAA!!
ALL THE SNOW WE SHOVELED ...!!
I'M SORRY... I...
...REALLY AM NO HELP AT ALL, AM I?

BUT WHAT COULD HAVE HAP-PENED HERE?!
WHO DID THIS TO YOU?!
JEAN ...
...AND CONNIE...

HUH?!
THEY DID THIS ?!

THOSE WHINY LITTLE SNOW-FLAKES...
I'M GONNA MELT THEM DOWN WITH MY HOT FISTS!!
DASH
W-WAIT!
IT'S JUST A PILE OF SNOW!

I NORMALLY HOLD EREN BACK, BUT YOU'RE RIGHT, THIS IS IMPORTANT!
THEY MUST BE ANNIHILATED!
THAT'S NOT WHAT I —!!
DAAASH

I MEAN, I'LL COME TOO...
TRIP
ZLIP
ZLUUSH
ZUWHAM
UMPH

SHIK
SHIK
SHIK

OPERATION EREN SUCKS AND I HATE HIM IS A SUCCESS!! NOW WE'RE ASSURED OF A COMPLETE VICTORY, RIGHT?!
YEAH...
SHIK
HEY! AREN'T YOU EXCITED, JEAN?!
AH! I GET IT. YOU'RE HOLDING IN A BIG HONKING DOODY, AREN'T YOU?
NO, I'M NOT, YOU IDIOT!!

I WAS JUST THINKING... MAYBE I, JEAN, DIDN'T NEED TO STOOP SO LOW...
I JUST WOULDN'T WANT ANY BAD FEELINGS BETWEEN ME AND MY PRECIOUS MIKAS... I MEAN, CLASSMATES.
AH, BOOGER TIME...
OH, AND ALSO ...
I ALSO DON'T LIKE TAKING ORDERS FROM THE POTATO GLUTTON—
UMPH!
VWAAM

SHIK
...HOW POOR ARMIN FEELS?!
DO YOU UNDERSTAND NOW...
WHA?!
HUH?!
HEY!! I DON'T WANT ANYBODY TO GET THE WRONG IDEA! WE JUST SMOOSHED YOUR SNOW PILE!
WE DIDN'T DO A THING TO ARMIN!
SHIK
NO MORE LAME EXCUSES!! IT'S CIVIL WAR TIME!
FWOOM
HYAAH !!
SKRRRCH

HUH?
ZWOOSH
GRRRRUN
ぐぎぎぎぎ
WAIT, HE'S FIGHTING CONNIE?
SO THAT MEANS...
MY SKIN BRUISES AT THE LIGHTEST CARESS...
DAMMIT! I'M NOT REALLY AFRAID OF EREN'S NAMBY-PAMBY PUNCHES, BUT...
JEAN!
APOLOGIZE TO ARMIN OR I WILL BE FORCED TO SNAP YOUR BALLS OFF WITH MY ELBOW.
HUUUUUH ...?!
ZWATCH
OR, IF YOU APOLOGIZE TO HIM, YOUR BALLS REMAIN.
WHICH WILL YOU CHOOSE?

JEA...
PANT
PANT
PANT
PANT
BLUUUSH

......?
IS HE AFRAID ...?
UH... SO, LET'S GO TO ARMIN, AND...
NO!!

I'M NOT GONNA APOLOGIZE! EVER...!
NO! NO APOLOGIES FROM ME!!
BWAAAH!!

WHAT ?!

I MEAN...
IS SHE SERIOUS?!

IF I DON'T APOLOGIZE...

IS SHE REALLY GONNA KEEP... TOUCHING ME?

SLAAAAP
JEAN!!
Whoa! Dat's gotta hoit!
CONNIE, THIS IS...
...THE END FOR YOU TOO!!
WHAM
CRAAAK
CRAK
POK
AAAAA!!

I...
I GIVE UP!!
ワァァァァァ!!
YAAAAAAY
DING
DING
DING
DING
DING
THE WINNERS AND CHAMPIONS!!

EREN, THIS ISN'T ABOUT WINNING, IT'S ABOUT ARMIN...
AND WHO WAS RINGING THAT BELL...?
OH, YEAH. YOU'RE RIGHT.
My tender face...

OKAY, YOU GUYS. YOU'RE GOING TO GO APOLOGIZE TO ARMIN NOW.

DAMMIT...
IT'S NOT OUR FAULT. WE WERE JUST FOLLOWING ORDERS.
THAT'S RIGHT...! WE HAD NO WAY OF KNOWING THAT ARMIN WOULD SLIP, FALL, BUMP HIS HEAD, AND GET STUCK IN A PILE OF SNOW...
...AFTER WE PUSHED HIM INTO A PILE OF SNOW.

IT ISN'T ARMIN'S FAULT EITHER!
HE'S AN INNOCENT LITTLE WEEPY CHERUB!
WHEN YOU SAY ORDERS...
YOU MEAN THOSE WERE **HER** ORDERS?

SURE WAS! THAT WOMAN!
SHE'S OBSESSED! SHE'LL BREAK ANY RULE AND ANYONE TO GET HER HANDS ON THOSE SNACKS...
HEH HEH HEH HEH HEH
BU HEH HEH HEH
JUST REMEMBERING IT GIVES ME THE SHIVERS. THE EVIL IN HER EYES... HER DEMONIC CACKLE...
...THE VISCOUS DROOL POURING OUT OF HER MOUTH AND DOWN HER JACKET.

THEN, EREN...
...WE WILL NEED THEM TO LEAD US TO HER LAIR.
HUH?!
IF SHE IS THE RINGLEADER, THEN **ALL THREE** OF THEM SHOULD GO APOLOGIZE TO ARMIN.
GOOD IDEA!
AND WE CAN HAVE THEM REBUILD OUR...
THERE'S NO NEED FOR THAT!!
VROOM

VROOOOM
VROOM
BECAUSE I'M NOT APOLOGIZING TO ANYONE!
WHAT THE?!
ZWAAAASH
WHERE DID YOU GET AN INDUSTRIAL SNOW PLOW ...?!
THUD
DAMMIT ...
AAAGL GRGL...
ARMIN !!
FWOOOOOH
...
E...REN...?

SEVENTIETH PERIOD: THE SNOW-SHOVELING FANCIERS CLU

FOR A SECOND, I THOUGHT... THAT I HEARD EREN'S VOICE... CALLING...
BUT...

NO MATTER HOW FAR I GO, I CAN'T FIND THEM...
I SUPPOSE IT WAS JUST MY IMAGINATION...
WAVER
ふらっ
AHH... I ALWAYS ASSUMED...
...I WOULD OUTLIVE MY GRANDFATHER...
Now I'll never inherit his vintage Robotech action figures...
SNIFF
ずびっ

FWOOOH
WOBBLE
AH...

AAAAAAAAA!!
TUMBLE
TUMBLE
TUMBLE
TUMBLE

THWAK
OW!
WHUMF

AAACHOO!
AHCHOO!

ZWIP

HUH...?
SASHA...?

JEAN...AND CONNIE...?!
EREN AND MIKASA TOO...?

WHAT COULD BE GOING ON...?!
HEE HEE
HEH HEE HEE... NOW THE SMALL AMOUNT OF SNACKS IS MINE! ALL MINE...!!
MY PLAN WAS PERFECT! PERFECT!!
YES, THE GOD OF A SMALL AMOUNT OF SNACKS IS SMILING ON ME NOW!!
HEE HEE
GU H

SO THE ONE WHO SABOTAGED OUR SNOW PILE, DECAPITATED EVERYONE, AND THEN PLANTED THEIR HEADS IN GIANT SNOWBALLS... WAS SASHA?!
ALL JUST TO GET HER HANDS ON A SMALL AMOUNT OF SNACKS?!

AND NOW ...
I'VE GOTTA GO.
GRN GRN
BUT WHAT CAN I DO...?!
I CAN BARELY MOVE IN THIS SNOW...!!
PLUS, I DON'T EVEN KNOW WHERE THEIR BODIES ARE...
I'M COLD ...
EREN ...
I DON'T... KNOW IF I CAN...
H-HEY, MIKASA! ARE YOU ALL RIGHT?!
YOU HAVE TO HOLD ON! JUST A LITTLE LONGER!
IF YOU DO...
THEN ARMIN WILL COME SAVE US!!
WE'LL BE JUST FINE!! I KNOW WE WILL!!
WAIT...
DID THOSE HEADS JUST TALK...?

THAT MEANS THERE'S STILL A CHANCE...!
...I CAN STILL SAVE THEM!
ぎゅっ
GRIMP

I LEFT MY SPELLBOOK AT HOME...
...BUT IF THEIR HEADS ARE STILL ALIVE, THEN I CAN CRAFT NEW BODIES FOR THEM SOMEHOW!

...MOST OF ALL, I'M TOUCHED...

I NEVER REALIZED THOSE TWO...
...THOUGHT SO HIGHLY OF ME!!

WHAT THEY JUST SAID IS THE BEST MOTIVATION THEY COULD'VE GIVEN ME...

THEY KNOW I'M THE ONLY ONE WHO CAN SAVE THEIR LIVES...

I'M THE ONLY ONE IN THE WORLD WHO CAN SAVE THEM...

ARMIN...

SLUMP

...AND ATTACH THEIR HEADS TO NEW BODIES.

SNIFF SNIFF

SASHA, YOU BIG MEANIE!!
ROLL
ROLL
ROLL
WHAM
POP
ROLL
YOU'VE ACTU- ALLY COME FOR US!!
A...
ARMIN!

BWUMPH
ZWOOCH
SHKK
HAHH
ハァ
HAHH
ハァ

Y-YOU GUYS!
CRAWL
CRAWL
CRAWL
よちよち
I'LL GET YOU OUT OF THAT SNOW...
THANKS!

...
AAA...
GRIMP

YOU'RE THE MEANIE, SNACK-BLOCKER!!
AAA!!
DOKAAAM

もぞもぞ SQUIRM
I CAN'T BELIEVE YOU'D GO THIS FAR...
SASHA...
SQUIRM もぞ もぞ SQUIRM

FRIENDS DON'T SURGI-CALLY REMOVE FRIENDS' BODY PARTS!!
YEAH, ARMIN!! ...WAIT, WHAT?
ZWHAM

Y-YOU THINK YOU'RE JUST SO SMART... YOU...

LITTLE FUTON-WEARING NERD!
A B-BRIDGE MOVE...?!
VWAAAM

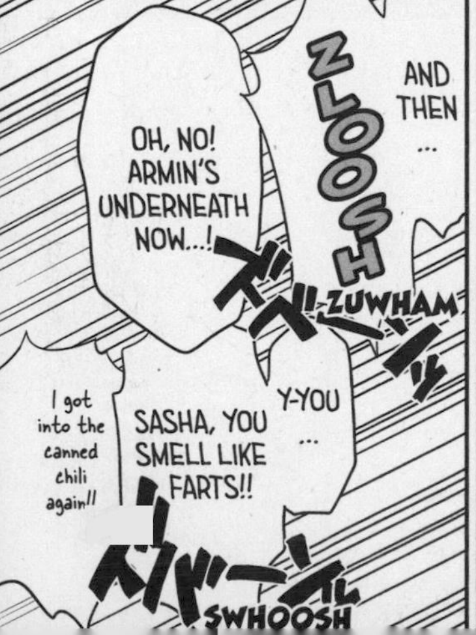
AND THEN ...
ZLOOSH
OH, NO! ARMIN'S UNDERNEATH NOW...!
ZUWHAM
Y-YOU ...
SASHA, YOU SMELL LIKE FARTS!!
I got into the canned chili again!!
SWHOOSH

DUH-DUUM
ZLOOOSH

HAHH
HAHH
HAHH
HAHH
SASHA...

GIVE YOURSELF UP, NECROMANCER!
BAAAAM

THROW YOURSELF ON THE MERCY OF THE MAGIC COURT...!
GASP

UFF!!
ZLOOOSH
DODGE

TH- THAT'S THE FIRST TIME...
...THAT ARMIN'S ATTACK HAS MISSED!!

HA HEE HEE... IT LOOKS LIKE THE GOD OF A SMALL AMOUNT OF SNACKS IS FRIENDS WITH THE GOD OF DODGING!!
SHIK
ARMIN!

I JUST NOTICED ...
...THAT YOU CAN'T EVEN STAND UP ON SNOW WITHOUT FALLING OVER!!
!!
OH, NO... SHE'S SEEN RIGHT THROUGH HIM!
IN THE THIRD HOUR OF THEIR LIFE-OR-DEATH STRUGGLE, SHE FINALLY...
...FOUND ARMIN'S WEAK POINT!!
I'VE RUTHLESSLY TURNED YOUR FRIENDS INTO SNOWBALLS...
GRAB
NOW... YOU'RE GOING TO BECOME A SNOW-BALL, TOO!!
ARMIN!!
ROLL ROLL ROLL ROLL

BOOM

NOO...!! I CAN'T FEEL MY BODY AT ALL!!

THE TUBER WITCH HAS CURSED ME, TOO, RIGHT WHEN I WAS ABOUT TO SAVE EVERYONE...

FYUUUUUUUH
OH NO... I'M SO COLD, I'VE BEGUN TO SEE HALLUCI-NATIONS!
VYUUUM
BRAIN FREEZE MUST BE SO MUCH WORSE WHEN YOU'RE ONLY A BRAIN!
SASHA, YOU DASTARDLY...
ACHE
TH... THAT WAS COLD!
KOFF
ROLL
AND NOT JUST ANY HALLUCINATION...
BUT A HALLUCINATION OF MR. HANNES!
UUUUH
YOU KIDS PICKED A WEIRD TIME TO PLAY OUTSIDE.
AREN'T YOU, UH, COLD?
WOW. I DIDN'T KNOW HALLUCI-NATIONS TALKED...
I'M NO HALLUCINATION. I'M HANNES!

YOU AREN'T A HALLUCINATION?
THEN MR. HANNES, WHAT ARE YOU DOING IN A PLACE LIKE THIS?

I'M HERE BECAUSE I'M YOUR FACULTY ADVISOR! DID YOU FORGET?!
...JUST BECAUSE I'VE BEEN HANGING OUT IN THE TOOL SHED WITH A BOTTLE OF DEWER'S...
BESIDES, YOU SHOULDN'T EVEN BE DOING CLUB ACTIVITIES ON A DAY LIKE THIS!!

YOU'VE BEEN FREEZING LOOKING FOR US ALL THIS TIME?
ARE YOU CRAZY? OF COURSE I HAVEN'T!!
FWOOOH

I KNOW BETTER THAN THAT! I SNUCK THE KEROSENE HEATER OUT HERE FROM THE FACULTY OFFICE!
PUFF
PUFF
WHY DON'T YOU WARM YOURSELF UP A BIT?

A...
...STOVE...
ヒュ FWOOOOOH
AND...
...SASHA'S SNOW-PLOW...?
FWOOOH ビュウゥ
AH!
MR. HANNES, I CAN'T DO MUCH AS JUST A HEAD, BUT...
...COULD YOU PUSH ME AS HARD AS YOU CAN AT THE STOVE?!
HUH?! WHAT ARE YOU TALKING ABOUT?!
HAS THE COLD ADDLED YOUR BRAINS?!
IF I DO THAT, IT'LL BREAK THE STOVE...
IT'LL BE ALL RIGHT! HURRY!
YOU HAVE TO DO IT QUICK...
IF YOU DON'T, I'LL TELL THE OTHER TEACHERS THAT YOUR ENTIRE CLUB WAS DECAPITAT-ED...
...AND ALSO THAT YOU STOLE THE STOVE!!
NOOO

I HAVE NO IDEA WHAT YOU'RE SAYING, BUT FINE!!
I'M GONNA TELL YOUR GRANDFATHER ON YOU!!
GANCH
VWOOM
THANK YOU, MR. HANNES!!
ROOOOOOOOOLLLL
HYAH!
BAM

UH HEH HEH HEH... NOW, IT LOOKS LIKE THE ONLY ONE WHO HASN'T EATEN THE SNOW YET IS MIKASA!
I'M GOING TO FILL YOUR BELLY TO THE BRIM WITH SNOW, SO YOU **CAN'T** EAT A SMALL AMOUNT OF SNACKS!
HO HO HO! MIKASA THE FIGHTER HAS BECOME SUCH A WEAKLING...

N-NO!!
MIKASA'S ARMS AND LEGS ARE PINNED!! THERE'S NOTHING TO BE AFRAID OF!!
SHAKE SHAKE
NOW EAT THIS SNOW, AND REGRET EVERY MOMENT...
...WHEN YOU LOOKED AT ME WITH YOUR "I THINK SASHA'S AN IDIOT BUT I'M TOO GOOD TO SAY IT OUT LOUD LIKE EVERYONE ELSE" FACE!!
ZWIP
VWAM

VYOOOOOM
BOFOOOM
HUUUUUUH?!
IT JUST BLEW UP...!!
WOW !!
IT'S A MIRACLE...
...A ST. XAVI'S DAY MIRACLE.
MY SNOWPLOW ...!! THAT WAS A RENTAL!!
DRIP
AH... WARM...

THE SNOW...
...IS MELTING!
BLOOSH
ボコォッ
BLOOSH
ボコォッ
YEAH!
ACK!!

ボォォォォォォォォ
BWOOOOOOGH

I...
BWOOOGH
I DID IT...
He really did it!

I HOPE EVERY-ONE'S OKAY.
TO THINK SASHA WOULD STOOP SO...

Hold on a minute. Where'd these limbs come from?

YOU GUYS!! YOUR LIMBS ARE BACK!
VWAAH
ARMIN! I ASSUME YOU DID SOMETHING TO SAVE US !!
HUG
THANK YOU.
LOOK. SORRY ABOUT WHAT I DID BEFORE.
WH-WHAT HE SAID.
AH, SASHA...
SNIFF SNIFF SNIFF SNIFF SNIFF SNIFF SNIFF
WAAAAH!
WAAH! I-I'M SO SORRY!
I KNOW I WAS REALLY STUPID...
I KNOW THAT NOW YOU'LL ONLY GIVE ME CANDIED YAMS AND A PEPPERMINT PATTY...

HOW ABOUT I FEED YOU MY FISTS INSTEAD?
HUH? BUT I...
YEAH!! YOU FED US ICE, WE FEED YOU PUNCHES!
WAAAAAAAAH
EVERYONE, DON'T YOU THINK SHE'S SUFFERED ENOUGH?

SASHA JUST GOES A LITTLE CRAZY, AND ACQUIRES MAGICAL POWERS APPARENTLY, WHEN SHE'S HUNGRY.
SO INSTEAD, DO YOU THINK YOU CAN JOIN US IN ALL SHOVELING SNOW TOGETHER?
YES!
I CAN!
SMILE

RIGHT! WELL THAT TIES UP ALL THE LOOSE ENDS!

WELL...I GUESS IF ARMIN SAYS SO, WE'LL GO EASY ON HER.

SASHA ...

...ONE MORE SCHEME AND I SWEAR, I'LL CANDY YOUR YAMS.

HUH?

I DON'T GET IT!

SHUT UP, CONNIE, YOU STUPID MONKEY.

BUT LOOK! IT'S BEEN SO WARM SINCE THE EXPLOSION THAT THE SNOW IS MELTING ON ITS OWN.
OH! IT'S TRUE!
とろ…
DRIP...

GWAHOOOM

THAT MEANS THAT WE DON'T HAVE TO SHOVEL AT ALL!! TWO CHEERS FOR LAZINESS!
HIP, HIP!! I'M TIRED!
YAAAAAY

WHA?!

シャアアアアア
ZHOOOM
OH, MAN. I LOST TRACK OF TIME CHOOSING BETWEEN THE SOUR LINGONBERRY KITKAT OR THE SALTED BEEF KITKAT!
MY FINAL ANSWER WAS BOTH, OF COURSE! HA HA HA!

I WONDER IF THOSE LAB RAT REJECTS STAYED MOTIVATED.
DID THEY SHOVEL AT ALL...?
OOOH!!
さぱっ
SPOTLESS
THERE'S NOT EVEN A SNOW-FLAKE LEFT OUT HERE!!

THAT'S AMAZING!! HOW COULD THEY HAVE DONE IT ...?!
TUMP
TUMP
I'LL HAVE TO GIVE THE LOSING TEAM SOMETHING, TOO...

THE WHOLE SCHOOL'S ON FIRE ?!
BWOOGH
YAAGGH!
My precious skin!!
GOOOOOOOOOOOOONG
WOW! IT'S SO WARM!
THE NEXT DAY ...
I SEE... SO THERE WAS NO MALICE AFORE-THOUGHT.
AND I'M GLAD TO SEE YOU TURNED YOUR-SELVES IN.
AND SO...
...YOUR CLUB BUDGET HAS BEEN CUT BY 90%!
CASE CLOSED !!
YES, SIR !!
SLAM
IN THE END, RICO ATE ALL THE SNACKS IN FRUS-TRATION.

LAST CHAPTER, WHAT WITH ONE THING AND ANOTHER, YADDA YADDA YADDA, THE SCHOOL BURNED DOWN.
SO EVERYONE GOT ONE DAY OFF.

I'M BORED.

COME TO THINK OF IT, RECENTLY ...
...I GET THE FEELING WE HAVEN'T BEEN ABLE TO EXTERMINATE ANY TITANS AT ALL. MAYBE IT'S JUST MY IMAGINATION ...
NO, I DON'T THINK YOU HAVE AN IMAGINA-TION.

SEVENTY-FIRST PERIOD: A DAY OFF IS THE TIME TO TRY A CHANGE AND MATURE LIKE NOBODY'S BUSINESS

SO IT'S TRUE...? WE'VE MADE NO PROGRESS ON OUR PLAN? I WAS AFRAID OF THAT.
I MEAN, SOON WE'LL MOVE UP AND BECOME SECOND-YEAR STUDENTS.
WHAT'S THE WORRY THERE?

I MEAN, WHEN WE'RE IN THE SECOND YEAR, WE'LL HAVE TO TEACH THE FIRST-YEARS HOW TO EXTERMINATE TITANS, RIGHT?
THEY'LL LOOK UP AT US WITH THEIR SHINING, YOUTHFUL EYES, AND THEY'LL SAY...
"WISE OLD EREN, TEACH US HOW TO EXTERMINATE TITANS JUST LIKE YOU!"

IMAGINE HOW CRESTFALLEN THEY'LL BE WHEN THEY REALIZE THAT WE HAVEN'T DONE ANY EXTERMINATING AT ALL!
YOU TRY LOOKING INTO A FRESHMAN'S EYES AND TELLING THEM WE HAVEN'T MURDERED ANYONE!
E

WHO COULD RESPECT AN UPPER-CLASS-MAN LIKE THAT?!

THEY'LL MAKE FUN OF US!!

BAM

EREN, I CAN IMAGINE HOW YOU FEEL...

...BUT WE'RE A SECRET CLUB. WE CAN'T JUST GO OUT AND EXTERMINATE TITANS WILLY-NILLY.

GRRRRR

THEN WHY ARE WE IN THE SURVEY CLUB IN THE FIRST PLACE?!
HMM...
EREN, ARMIN...

I'M GOING OUT TO GET INGREDIENTS FOR DINNER, SO YOU TWO WATCH THE HOUSE.
UH... WHY?
WHAT'S IT GONNA DO?
KACHAK
パタン

...
MIKASA LEFT KINDA ABRUPT-LY.
?
YEAH...
HEY, ARMIN...

WANT TO INVITE MR. LEVI OVER?
BWAH?! MY ORANGE!

EVEN IF YOU COUNT ALL THE UPPER-CLASSMEN, HE'S THE ONLY ONE WHO HAS REALLY FOUGHT FACE-TO-FACE WITH TITANS.
BESIDES, SINCE IT'S A DAY OFF... THERE'S NOTHING FOR HIM TO CLEAN, ANYWAY!
IT'S THE PERFECT TIME TO ASK HIM ABOUT BUTCHERING OUR ENEMIES!

Y-YOU MEAN CALL HIM OVER NOW...?!
BUT WE DON'T KNOW WHEN MIKASA WILL GET BACK...
OH! HELLO?
YOU'RE ALREADY CALLING HIM?!
Are you listening to me?!

THIRTY MINUTES LATER...
DING DONG
ピンポーン
COME IN.
ZWAAAAN
スパァン
THIS FILTHY HOUSE MAKES ME WANNA PUKE!!
NOOOO!
おわーっ
THAT TELEVISION IS COVERED IN DUST!
PANIC
あわ
VACUUM THAT FUTON!
PANIC
あわ
CLEAN OUT THE CREVICES! THOSE TRICKY CREVICES... I HATE CREVICES!
PANIC
あわ
NOW...

...WHAT DID YOU WANT TO TALK ABOUT?
UM...
I FORGET...

Oh, yeah!
I WANT YOU TO TEACH ME HOW TO DEFEAT TITANS!!
WE'VE HAD LIKE 1,500 PAGES OF THIS MANGA AND NOBODY'S GOTTEN EXTERMINATED!!

PLEASE!!
I DON'T THINK THERE'S ANYONE ELSE I CAN ASK!

HO?

ARE YOU REALLY THAT SERIOUS ABOUT THIS?

YES!!

D-DO YOU MEAN YOU'LL TEACH ME?!

YES... BUT!
FIRST I NEED TO PROBE YOU.
PROBE ME?!
SHIK

YES, I NEED...
...TO PROBE YOUR POWER OF SELF-CONTROL.

"POWER OF SELF-CONTROL"...?!
GULP

THUNK
WHAT KIND OF PROBE IS HE TALKING ABOUT...?!

CURRY...
...UDON...
DOON

MR. LEVI, YOU WANT ME...
...TO PUT THIS SOUP UP MY BUTT?!
OH MY GOD...
YOU ARE SUCH A REPUGNANT LITTLE COCK-ROACH...

NO!! EAT IT!!
AND DO IT WITHOUT SPRAYING A SINGLE DROP OF THE SOUP!

THIS IS THE PROBE YOU WERE TALKING ABOUT?
YES, THIS IS THE TEST I HAVE SELECTED FOR YOU.
DIDN'T I TELL YOU BEFORE?

EATING CURRY UDON WITHOUT SPRAYING A DROP OF SOUP...

...REQUIRES THE SAME LEVEL OF STRENGTH OF WILL AND CONCENTRATION THAT IT TAKES TO BRING DOWN A 15-METER TITAN...

I NEVER KNEW...!!

CONCENTRATE ON EATING? I SUCK DOWN MY SUGAR POLYPS SO FAST IN THE MORNING I CAN'T EVEN GET THROUGH A FULL EPI-SODE OF ROAD ROVERS!
Where'd you get these noodles from, by the way?
GROSS.

CAN YOU DO THIS, EREN?

I ATE CURRY UDON 3,572 TIMES AS A CHILD, BUT...

SLURP ずぞぞ…
SLURP

EVERY LAST TIME, I SPLASHED THAT SPICY GOODNESS ALL OVER MY OSHKOSHES...

WELL... IF IT MEANS I CAN TAKE DOWN TITANS...

ぶる TREMBLE

ぶる TREMBLE

EREN, YOUR HAND!!

MY ARM ISN'T SHAKING OUT OF FEAR...

HUH?

I'M JUST THINKING ABOUT HOW EATING THESE EARTHY NOODLES IS THE SAME AS SLAYING A TITAN...!!

VWAAH

I'M TREM-BLING...

...AT THE JOY OF A CHALLENGE!!

SLURP
ちゅるっ
Plip
ぴ

plitch

NOW GROVEL BEFORE ME!!
AAAAAAAAA!!

FORGIVE ME!! PLEASE LET ME HAVE ANOTHER CHANCE! I'M SORRY! I'M REALLY SORRY!
I KNOW I CAN EAT CURRY RICE WITH-OUT SPILL-ING!!
UWAAAA

PLIP

I'M LETTING YOU OFF EASY THIS TIME.
Yes sir...
CHUP
CHUP

UM... ABOUT THE TITANS...
THE PROBE HAS COME BACK NEGATIVE.
SO I HAVE NOTHING AT ALL TO TEACH YOU.

Y-YEAH, I GUESS THAT'S TRUE...
I HAVE NOTHING TO TEACH YOU, BUT...

...HE MIGHT.
?!
THEN CALL THIS HIM!

DINNG DONNG
ピンポーン

KOCHOK

HELLO, EVERYONE!

I HOPE YOU'RE ALL HEALTHY IN BODY AND SPIRIT (AND AVOIDING CAFFEINE)!

MR. SMITH ...!!

I SEE. YOU WANT TO LEARN HOW TO DEFEAT A TITAN...

Spill food and choke on my fist!

I WAS JUST THINKING THAT MAYBE IT WAS TIME WE MADE PROGRESS IN THAT AREA, THIS BEING THE LAST VOLUME AND ALL...

MR. SMITH... YOU MEAN...!

SHIK
BUT BEFORE I CAN DO THAT, EREN...
...I'M AFRAID **I** SHALL HAVE TO PROBE YOU!
WHAT?! AGAIN?!

THIS NEXT PROBE ...
...WILL TEST YOUR STRENGTH AND BALANCE!
VWAM

A CREAMPUFF ?!
A C...
PUUUUUUUUFF
CREAMY CREAM CREAMPUFF

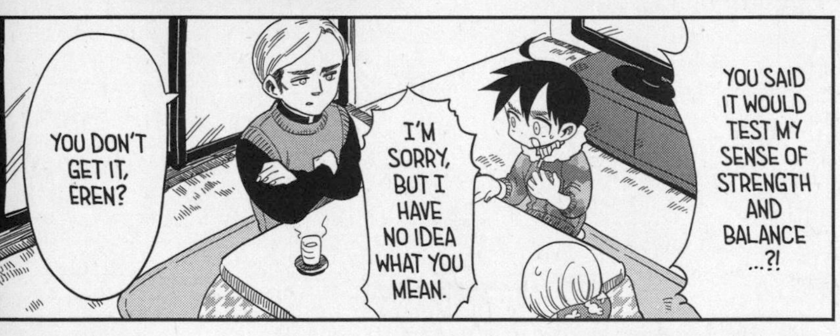
YOU DON'T GET IT, EREN?
I'M SORRY, BUT I HAVE NO IDEA WHAT YOU MEAN.
YOU SAID IT WOULD TEST MY SENSE OF STRENGTH AND BALANCE ...?!

IF YOU WERE TO EAT IT WITHOUT SOME KIND OF PLAN, WHAT DO YOU THINK WOULD HAPPEN?
AH!

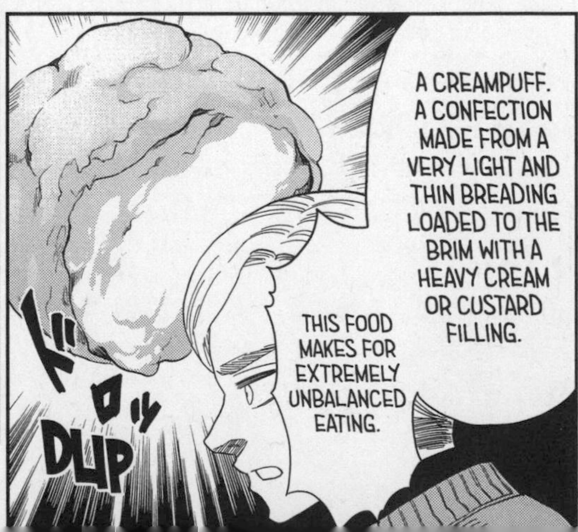
A CREAMPUFF. A CONFECTION MADE FROM A VERY LIGHT AND THIN BREADING LOADED TO THE BRIM WITH A HEAVY CREAM OR CUSTARD FILLING.
THIS FOOD MAKES FOR EXTREMELY UNBALANCED EATING.
DLLP

IT EXPLODES AND YOU GET CREAM ALL OVER YOUR FACE!
EXACTL— WHAT?! NO!
BLETCH
I WOULD GET THE RUNS WORSE THAN GRANDMA AT THE HOT'N'SPICY DEEP-FRIED CHICKEN'N' OREO FACTORY...!!

OH YEAH! WHENEVER I EAT ONE OF THESE, THE CREAM ALWAYS COMES DRIPPING OUT BEFORE I'M DONE!
BUT I ALWAYS FIGURED IT WAS JUST A CONSPIRACY BY THE NAPKIN INDUSTRY.
HEH... I THOUGHT SO TOO, AT FIRST.

BUT YOU HAVE TO RETHINK YOUR AP-PROACH.
IF YOU WANT TO DEFEAT THE TITANS...
...YOU NEED TO BECOME THE KIND OF MAN WHO EATS A CREAM PUFF WITHOUT SPILLING A DROP OF THAT SWEET, MILKY ESSENCE!

REALLY?! THAT'S WHO I HAVE TO BECOME ?!

SO YOU'RE SAYING I HAVEN'T TAKEN DOWN A TITAN SO FAR...
...BECAUSE I WASN'T GOOD ENOUGH AT SWALLOWING CREAM?!

EREN... WE'VE ALL SEEN THE DOJINSHI, BUT CAN YOU DO IT FOR REAL?!
I SURE CAN!
THIS IS A CINCH, COMPARED TO LAST TIME! AFTER ALL...
...THIS CREAM PUFF ALREADY HAS THE CREAM INSIDE THE PUFF!!
VWAM

M-MY GOD, HE'S RIGHT...!!

I AM GOING TO EAT THIS PUFF WHOLE...

...AND THEN, I'M GOING TO DEVOUR THE TITANS...!!

ぱひ
SHUP
GRIP
BLITCH
...
SHUUUUUUP
WELP, YOU FAIL.

EREN...
ONE MORE TIME!! AND THIS TIME, GIVE ME A CREAM PUFF WITH TOUGHER SKIN!!
OH, AND COULD YOU MAKE IT WHIPPED CREAM INSTEAD OF CUSTARD? AND THE KIND WITH A CHOCOLATE COOKIE CRUST?
WHAM

THERE ARE NO DO-OVERS WHEN FIGHTING TITANS, EREN... TRUST ME, I HAVE TWO INTACT ARMS.
RIP
NOW DO YOU UNDER-STAND?

Y...
YEAH, I GET IT...!!
SNIFF
EREN...
BLETCH

HE REALLY WANTS TO KILL ALL TITANS...
...SO WHY IS IT THAT HE CAN'T PASS THE TESTS...?
CHOMP
CHOMP

THEN AGAIN... LOOK AT THE CIVILIZED WAY THAT MR. SMITH EATS HIS CREAM PUFF...
AND MR. LEVI IS EATING HIS UDON WITH A FORK?!

AND THEN THERE'S ERIN...
WAAAAAH
HIS FACE IS JUST A MESS OF CURRY, CREAM, AND SPIT...!!

LOOK AT THAT...
CHOMP

MUNCH
もぐ
もぐ
MUNCH
HORLK

GULP
WAAH
SNIFF

MR. SMITH! MR. LEVI! IT ISN'T RIGHT TO TURN EREN INTO A SLOBBERING WRECK!

SPLURTZ

BAM

I DEMAND YOU STOP PROBING HIS MOUTH! PROBE SOMETHING ELSE!!

A-ARMIN!
HO...?
THUNK
WELL, I SUPPOSE IT'S TRUE THAT HIS EATING HABITS MAKE A PIG TROUGH LOOK LIKE AN ICU.
TO TELL THE TRUTH, WATCHING HIM FILLS ME WITH COMPLEX AND AWKWARD FEELINGS.
VERY WELL.
Guilty...
KREEK

WE SHALL CALL HIM!
AN-OTH-ER HIM?!
AND MAKE SURE HE BRINGS THAT.
THAT SHALL BE HIS FINAL PROBING.

KCHACK...

FOR CRISSAKES, WHAT'S THE BIG RUSH HERE?

SO, UH, WHERE'S MIKASA?

Glance Glance

きょろきょろ

...UH. SHE'S OUT.
HUH...?! YOU MEAN IT'S JUST THIS SAUSAGE-FEST?!
You have no idea, Jean...

SO MR. LEVI, IS THIS THE NEXT **HIM?**
Gah! Mr. Smith is here?!
YES...

WAIT, ARE YOU SAYING HE ACTUALLY KNOWS A WAY TO TAKE DOWN A TITAN?!
HUH?!

WHAT'RE YOU TALKING ABOUT?!

YOU CREEP!! WHEN DID YOU LEARN?! HOW'D YOU GET AHEAD OF ME LIKE THAT?!

JEAN, COME THIS WAY A MOMENT.

WHISPER

Yeah... Yeah...

HUH? ARE YOU SERIOUS? YES... YES...
OHHH... OH, YEAH! YEAH, SURE.
Is Erwin saying the word "whisper"?
YEAH... OKAY. YEAH, I GET IT.
WHISPER
WHISPER
WHISPER
WHISPER
WHISPER
WHISPER

UH, YES. IT'S TRUE. I HAVE IN HAND A WAY TO DEFEAT TITANS.

HEH HEH

I-I KNEW IT!

MR. SMITH! MR. LEVI! WHY WOULD YOU TEACH A STUCK-UP HORSE-FACE LIKE THAT...?!

WHY? BECAUSE WE PROBE HIM... AND HE PASSED
JEAN, SHOW HIM.
SNAP
HUUH ?!
WHAT? OH, SORRY! I'M SUPPOSED TO PULL IT OUT NOW?
LET'S SEE...
Y-YES, I AM ONE WHO PASSED THE TEST !!
POTATO CHIPS
RICE OMELET FLAVOR
I USED THIS TO TEST MY "COOPERATIVE POTENTIAL"!!
P-POTATO CHIPS ?!
WAAAAAAAM

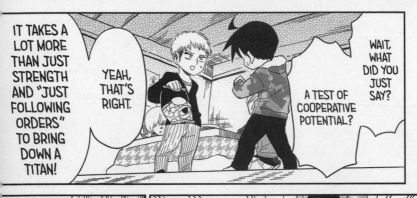

WAIT, WHAT DID YOU JUST SAY?
A TEST OF COOPERATIVE POTENTIAL?
YEAH, THAT'S RIGHT.
IT TAKES A LOT MORE THAN JUST STRENGTH AND "JUST FOLLOWING ORDERS" TO BRING DOWN A TITAN!

YOU'VE GOTTA COOPERATE WITH YOUR FELLOW TITAN HATERS!
YESSIREE, COOPERATION IS A MUST!
MR. SMITH ...!!
MR. LEVI ...!!
SO WHAT KIND OF TEST IS THIS GOING TO BE?

WHISPER WHISPER WHISPER
Okay... Sure...

YOU HAVE TO OPEN THIS BAG...
..SO IT'S EASY FOR EVERYONE TO EAT THE EGGY, TOMATOEY CHIPS INSIDE!!

JUST OPEN IT?
YOU MEAN THAT'S ALL I GOTTA DO?!
HEY! WERE YOU ACTUALLY LISTENING
IT WASN'T "JUST OPEN IT"!
I KNOW.
IN A WAY THAT'S EASY FOR EVERYONE TO EAT?
WELL, THERE'S ONLY ONE WAY TO OPEN A BAG OF CHIPS FOR THAT PURPOSE!!
POTATO CHIPS
HO?
AND WHAT WAY IS THAT?
THE ANSWER IS THE "PARTY OPEN"!!
EVEN I CAN DO THAT...
THIS TIME, I'M SURE TO PASS!!
PIP
POTATO CHIPS
Rice Omelet Flavor
OHHHH!
OHHHH!
OHHHH!

BWAAA
RIP
AASH

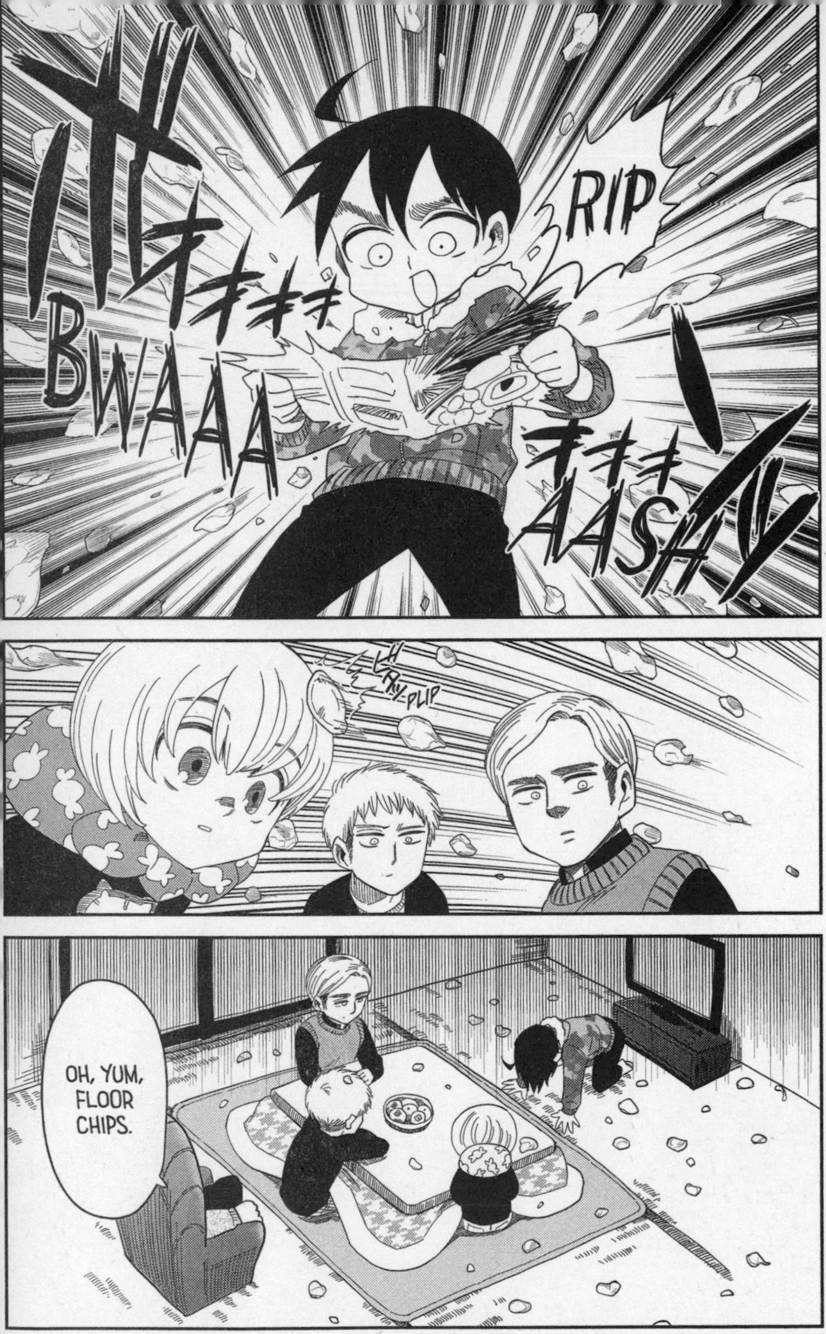

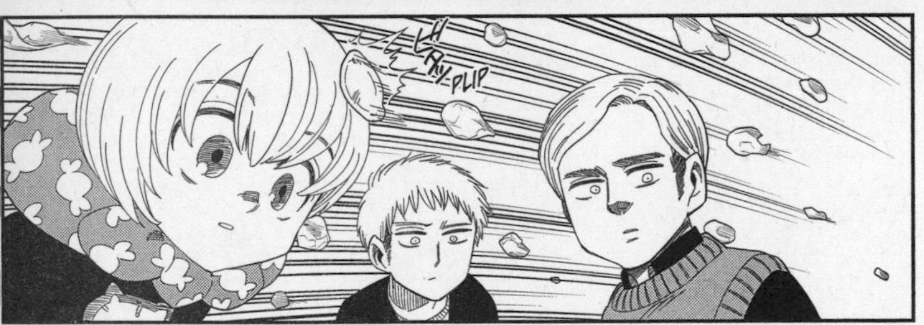
PLIP

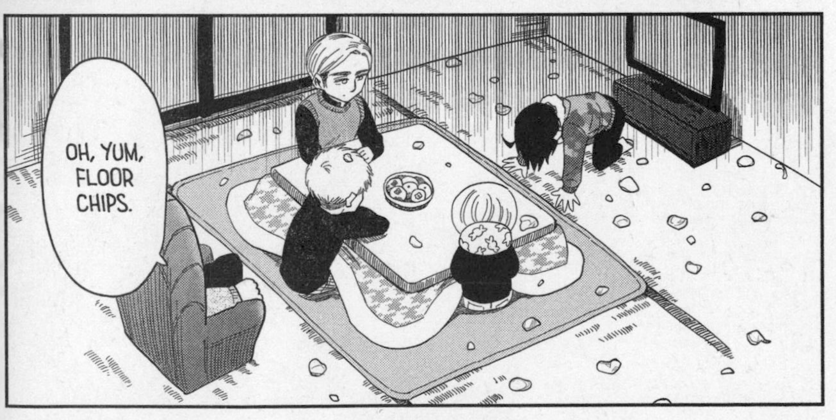
OH, YUM, FLOOR CHIPS.

UH... I'LL GET THE DUST-BUSTER.
HI'A
SKRRT
GLAD YOU'RE ON TOP OF IT, LEVI.
WAAAAAAAH
EREN!
A-ARE YOU ALL RIGHT?!
DUST BOX

ALL HE DID WAS OPEN A BAG OF CHIPS! HOW CAN HE POSSIBLY NOT BE ALL RIGHT?
JEAN!
I... I CAN'T...

I CAN'T TAKE DOWN THE TITANS, AND THIS IS WHY...
I'M A COMPLETE FAILURE! A LOSER! A WASHOUT! A NE'ER-DO-WELL!!
A FLOP, A FIASCO, A JOHNNY-COME-NEVER! EREN WAS A MISTAKE! A FLASH IN THE PANERA BREAD BATHROOM! A FIZZLED-OUT, FLOUNDERING BUMMER!
ALL THE THINGS PEOPLE SAY ABOUT ME ON THE INTERNET ARE TRUE!!!

HEH HEH
Eren, SOME fans like you, kinda!
WAAH!
びぇー

MR. SMITH, EVEN I THINK LAUGHING AT THAT IS PRETTY MEAN.
HEH HEH HEH HEH HEH HEH
M-MR. SMITH...?

IS IT SO FUNNY THAT I'M SUCH A FAILURE?!
AH HA HA HA HA HA HA HA
WAAAAAAAA

HEH!
WAAAAAAAH

KON
KONK
OW!
THERE IS NO WAY THAT THOSE "PROBES" WOULD TELL YOU IF YOU COULD DEFEAT A TITAN OR NOT.
ARE YOU STUPID?
HUH?!

THEN... WHY WOULD YOU DO ALL THAT STUFF TO ME?!
You're cleaning those up already?
WHY TORTURE ME WITH CURRY UDON, CREAMPUFFS AND POTATO CHIPS...?

UH, HOW DO I PUT THIS?
...WE WERE BORED.
GONNNNG

I CRIED.
WAAAAAAH
IT WAS A RICH MIXTURE OF ANGER AND HUMILIATION. IN THE TOP TEN MOST PAINFUL OF MY 2,452 SCHOOL-RELATED CRIES.

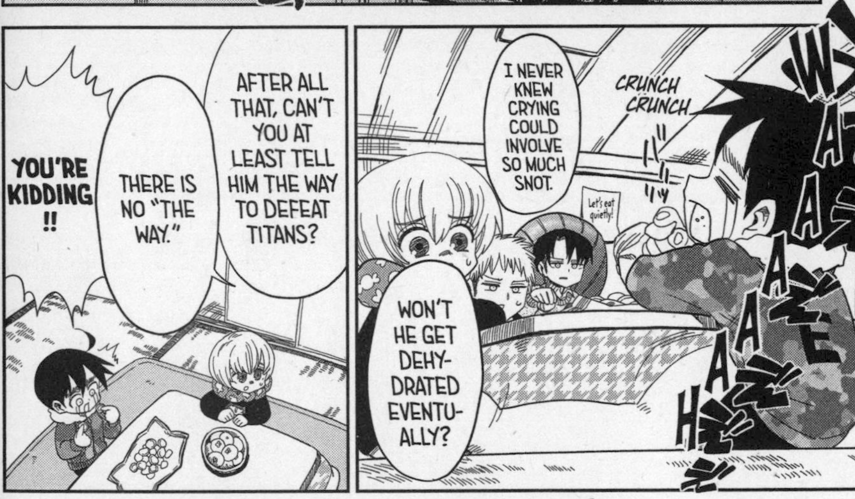
WAAAAAH
CRUNCH CRUNCH
I NEVER KNEW CRYING COULD INVOLVE SO MUCH SNOT.
Let's eat quietly!
WON'T HE GET DEHYDRATED EVENTUALLY?
AFTER ALL THAT, CAN'T YOU AT LEAST TELL HIM THE WAY TO DEFEAT TITANS?
THERE IS NO "THE WAY."
YOU'RE KIDDING !!

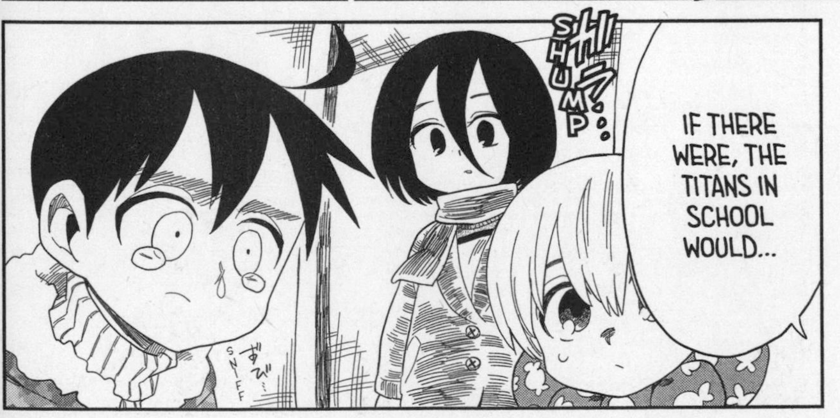
IF THERE WERE, THE TITANS IN SCHOOL WOULD...
SHUMP
SNIFF

HELLO, MIKASA! COFFEE IS FROM THE DEVIL.
ALSO WHY IS MR. SMITH AND THIS PERSON HERE...?
IT'S JUST POLLEN. YEAH, THAT'S IT. TREES ARE TO BLAME.
I-I'M NOT WEEPING LIKE A MISERABLE BABY!
WHOO MAAADE EREEEN CRYYY ??!!1!

SNORT
THAT AGAIN ...?
EREN SAID HE WANTED US TO TEACH HIM THE WAY TO DEFEAT TITANS.

Coming up on the Convenient-ly-Timed Evening News...
AND THERE'S NO WAY THAT ANYBODY COULD DEFEAT TITANS SO EASILY...
EREN, YOU HAVE SO MANY BIGGER PROB-LEMS...
WHAT DO YOU MEAN, "THAT AGAIN"?! IT'S MY BIGGEST PROBLEM!!

At about 4 PM this evening, the Shiganshina Shopping District was attacked by a Titan!

BREAKING

SHOPPING DISTRICT AT MIDDAY

ATTACK OF TITAN

FACING IT WAS...

However a mysterious girl, her face covered by a winter scarf, knocked the Titan out cold using nothing but a loaf of French bread!

Immediately afterwards, the girl in the scarf left the area, so her identity is still unknown...

UH, I'LL START COOKING DINNER...

EREN... UM...
TITANS ARE ARE DANGEROUS, Y'KNOW? MAYBE STAY AWAY FROM THEM.
THERE HAS TO BE SOME WAY...!!
MAYBE IF I WATCH YOU CUT VEGGIES I'LL LEARN THE SECRET!

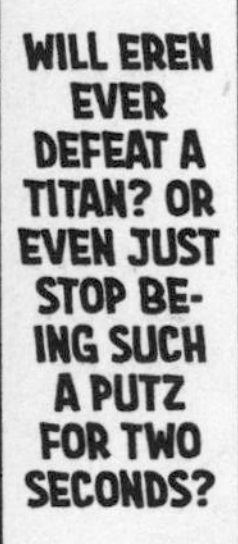

WILL EREN EVER DEFEAT A TITAN? OR EVEN JUST STOP BE-ING SUCH A PUTZ FOR TWO SECONDS?

You know, yesterday...

TEE HEE HEE
うふふ

Aww...!
えー

AH HA HA
あはは

THOSE TWO ALWAYS SEEM LIKE THE HAPPY COUPLE!
IT'S TRUE... IT COULD MAKE A GUY JEALOUS.
HOOTING HOLLERING
ひゅーひゅー

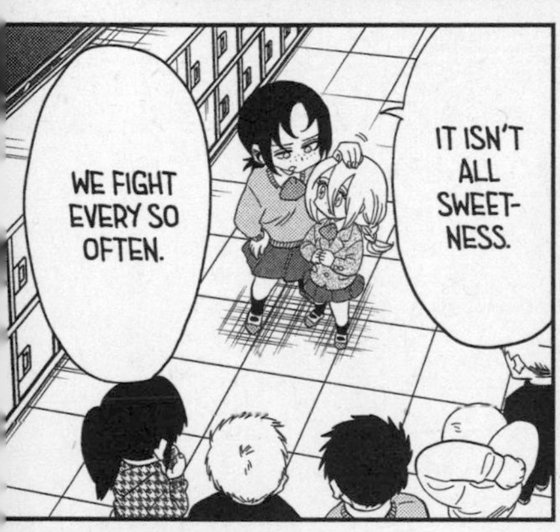

IT ISN'T ALL SWEET-NESS.
WE FIGHT EVERY SO OFTEN.

BUT IN THE END, WE ALWAYS MAKE UP AND GO BACK TO CUTESY HUGGING!!
RIGHT, YMIR?!
FWEE! MWAH MWAH! HOOOO! LOVEY-DOVEY!
HUG

YOU ARE SO RIGHT, KRISTA!
RUB RUB
WHAT WILL I DO WITH YOU, YMIR?

RUB RUB RUB RUB RUB RUB RUB RUB RUB RUB RUB RUB
OH, HONESTLY! YOU'RE OVER-DO-ING IT, YMIR!!
GONNNK
...OWWW!
OH...!
I-I'M SORRY, YMIR!!
HA HA...
I'M FINE, YOU DUMMY!
REALLY ?!
WHA ?!
...IS YOUR VERY LIFE!!
ALL I REQUIRE FOR A LITTLE BUMP LIKE THIS...
SPLOSH

SEVENTY-SECOND PERIOD: FRIENDSHIP SHINES...AND SOMETIMES IT DOESN'T

1-3
YMIR AND KRISTA ARE FIGHTING?

I WAS THERE THIS MORNING WHEN IT ALL STARTED.
YMIR'S VOICE GOT ALL DEEP AND GROWLY.

I'M SORRY, YMIR!
I NEVER MEANT TO ACTUALLY HURT YOU!
CHATTER
CHATTER
YOU HAVE DRAWN BLOOD AND NOW YOU ARE MINE!!

TUMP
PLEASE FORGIVE ME!
AAA!!
UNHAND ME!!
WHASH

I HAVE COME TO A DECISION...
YOU AND I ARE FINISHED!!
WHAT?! NO! WE'RE, LIKE, THE ONLY ACTUAL COUPLE!!

I WILL FIND ANOTHER CUTE, SHORT, BLONDE-HAIRED GIRL TO HANG AROUND!!
GOODBYE FOREVER, KRISTA!!

NO, WAIT, YMIR... WITHOUT YOU...
WHO WILL I LOOK AT AND THEN FEEL BETTER ABOUT MYSELF?!
HMM...
SLURRRRP
AND THAT'S WHAT HAPPENED.
OH, RIGHT, I JUST REMEMBERED. YOU'RE ALL IDIOTS AND I DON'T CARE.
HUH? COME ON, THIS IS BIG...
NOPE. IDIOTS. DON'T CARE.
ANNIE!

RUB
ARE YOU BUSY TODAY AFTER SCHOOL?
DO YOU WANT TO WALK HOME TOGETH-ER?
NUZZLE ME WITH YOUR FACE AGAIN AND I WILL REMOVE IT.

SOUNDS GREAT.
SEE YOU AFTER SCHOOL, THEN.
DID YOU HEAR WHAT I JUST SAID?

WHAT WAS THAT ABOUT...?
OH...
CUTE, SHORT, BLONDE-HAIRED...
HUH?
TUMP
YOU'RE SAYING THAT SHE WANTS TO GO HOME WITH ME AS A SUBSTITUTE FOR KRISTA?!

KRISTA WAS SO ANNOYING! HOW MANY MAKEUP TUTORI-ALS CAN ONE GIRL WATCH?
DING DONG
ANNIE, WHERE ARE YOU HEADED?
DIRECTLY HOME, TO STARE CYNICALLY AT TV.
YOU MUST BE HUNGRY. SHALL WE STOP FOR A CREPE?
ANYONE EVER TELL YOU YOU'RE AN AWFUL LISTENER?
CREPE

I'LL HAVE THE TUNA SALAD.
YES, MA'AM!
...

SAME.
It sounds gross, but choosing another one would take effort.

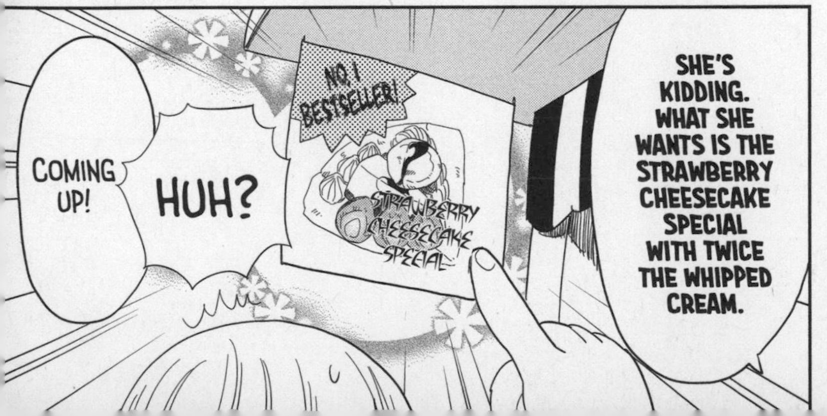

SHE'S KIDDING. WHAT SHE WANTS IS THE STRAWBERRY CHEESECAKE SPECIAL WITH TWICE THE WHIPPED CREAM.
NO. 1 BESTSELLER!
STRAWBERRY CHEESECAKE SPECIAL
HUH?
COMING UP!

WHAT IS HER DAMAGE ?
KR...
ANNIE... ?
THIS IS HEAVY!

COULD I HAVE A TASTE.
...I DON'T CARE.
HUH?

DON'T BE STINGY. IT'S JUST ONE BITE.
WHAT?
SHE'S ...
IF YOU EAT THAT ENTIRE PILE OF SUGAR ON YOUR OWN, YOU'LL GROW DISGUSTINGLY FAT!
UH, REALLY, HAVE AS MUCH AS YOU WANT.
...TALKING TO SOMEONE WHO ISN'T ME...
WELL, IF YOU INSIST, I SUPPOSE ...

...I CAN EXCHANGE IT FOR A BITE OF MINE.
OPEN WIDE!
GWIM
...

VWUP
I DON'T WANT YOUR GROSS CREPE.

WHAT IS WRONG WITH YOU, KRISTA ?!
GRIMP
?!

THIS IS WHERE YOU SAY, "AAAH!"

WHAT DID YOU JUST SAY TO ME, YOU UN-BALANCED COW?!

GRRRRNNNNNNNN

"UNBAL-ANCED"?! WHAT DO YOU MEAN BY THAT...?
YOU LOVE THIS!! YOU DO IT EVERY DAY...!!

MY NAME IS ANNIE! NOT KRISTA!
YOU BARELY ACKNOWL-EDGED MY EX-ISTENCE UNTIL THIS MORNING!
GRRRNN..

H-HOW COULD I HAVE DONE SUCH A THING...?!
WU
I SLIPPED INTO OLD HABITS...
BUT I CAN NEVER GO BACK TO HER! WE ARE THROUGH, FOR ALL TIME!
HAAAAA

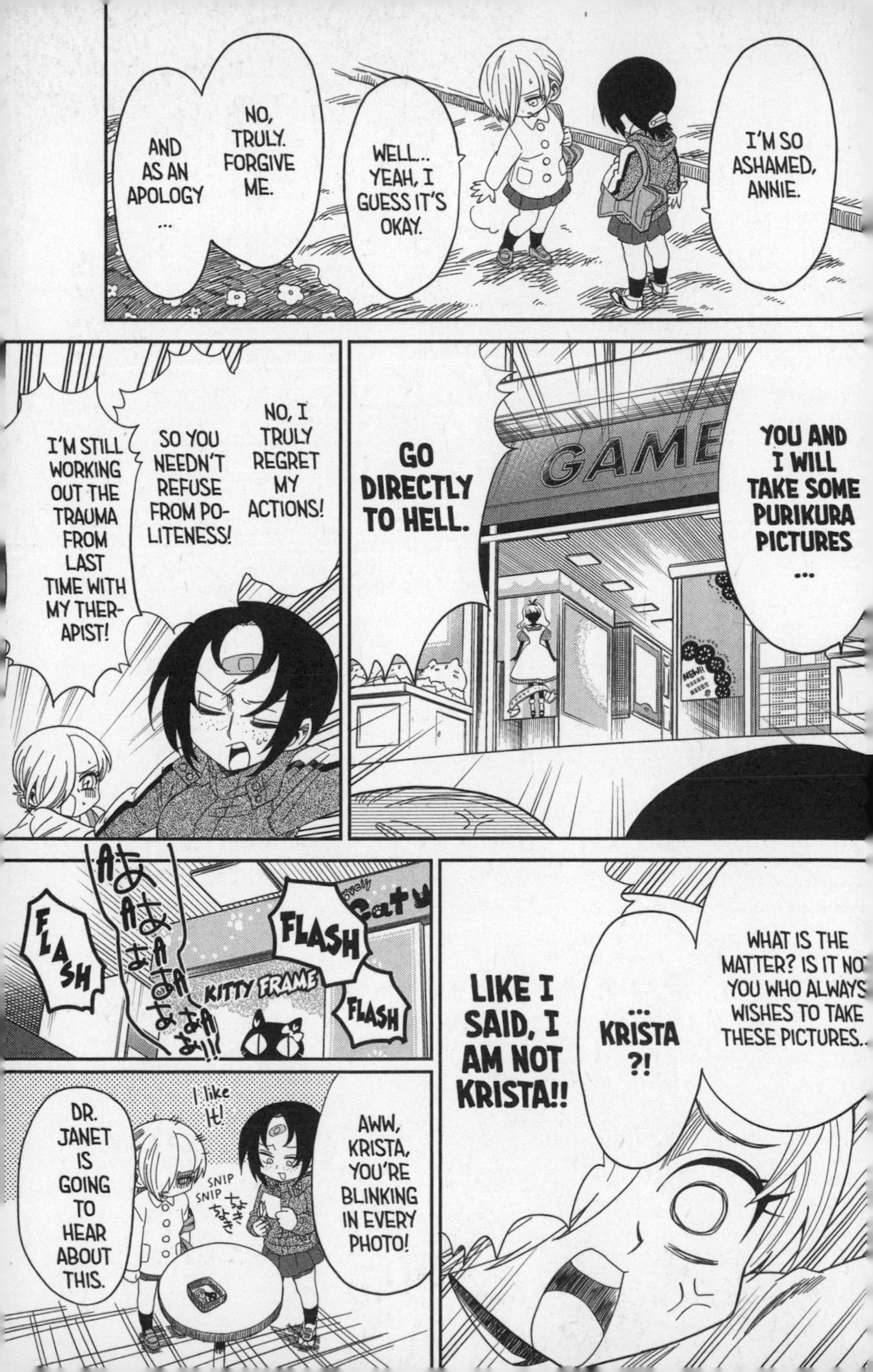

I'M SO ASHAMED, ANNIE.

WELL... YEAH, I GUESS IT'S OKAY.

NO, TRULY. FORGIVE ME.

AND AS AN APOLOGY ...

YOU AND I WILL TAKE SOME PURIKURA PICTURES ...

GO DIRECTLY TO HELL.

NO, I TRULY REGRET MY ACTIONS!

SO YOU NEEDN'T REFUSE FROM PO-LITENESS!

I'M STILL WORKING OUT THE TRAUMA FROM LAST TIME WITH MY THER-APIST!

WHAT IS THE MATTER? IS IT NOT YOU WHO ALWAYS WISHES TO TAKE THESE PICTURES...

... KRISTA ?!

LIKE I SAID, I AM NOT KRISTA!!

FLASH

FLASH

FLASH

KITTY FRAME

Cat

Aあ Aあ Aあ あA あ!!

AWW, KRISTA, YOU'RE BLINKING IN EVERY PHOTO!

I like it!

SNIP SNIP ちょきちょき

DR. JANET IS GOING TO HEAR ABOUT THIS.

WHAT WAS THAT?
WHOOSH
UWAA
AH, YES! I FORGOT AGAIN THAT YOU WEREN'T KRISTA!!
SHE WOULD DIE BEFORE SHE BLINKED IN A PHOTO!
HOW MUCH FORCE DOES IT TAKE TO CRUSH A HUMAN SKULL, I WONDER?
... FORGIVE ME FOR DRAGGING YOU THROUGH THIS...
LOOK, YMIR, IF YOU WANT HER TO FORGIVE YOU...
...MAYBE YOU COULD ASK INSTEAD OF TORTURING ME?
...
I'M SORRY, WHATEVER YOUR NAME IS...
..I AM AFRAID SUCH IS NOT POSSIBLE.
SHE'S GONE ENTIRELY MAD! HEAD-BUTTING PEOPLE LIKE A BULL IN A SHOP FULL OF HEADS! SOME SORT OF HEAD SHOP!
HOW COULD I EVER FORGIVE...
YMIR...!!
BESIDES ...
SST

I DISAGREE.
RUB ぐり RUB ぐり RUB ぐり RUB
THIS ISN'T SO BAD.
RUB ぐり RUB ぐり RUB ぐり RUB

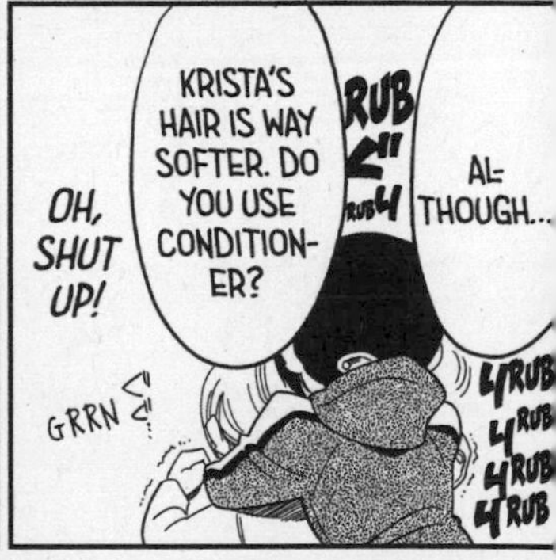
AL-THOUGH...
RUB ぐり RUB
KRISTA'S HAIR IS WAY SOFTER. DO YOU USE CONDITION-ER?
OH, SHUT UP!
GRRN
RUB RUB RUB RUB

ZakkaYa
AH!
THIS LOOKS RIGHT UP YOUR ALLEY, KRISTA... ER.

HERE! I BET THIS IS YOUR STYLE, KR- ANNIE.
NOT EVEN CLOSE!
Is that Bigfoot?

I SEE... I THOUGHT FOR SURE THAT...
...THESE JUST SCREAMED "KRISTA."
WELL, NOT BEING KRISTA, I CAN'T REALLY SAY.
nd your head's heavy!

KRISTA, WHAT ARE THESE?
I AM NOT KRISTA.

THIS IS NOT KRISTA?
YOU'RE LOSING YOUR MARBLES.

THEN, IS **THAT** KRISTA?
YOU NEED A LOBOT-OMY.

KRISTA
STILL NOT KRISTA HERE.

NOT KRISTA HERE?
...

THEN KRISTA WHERE?!

HAHH HAHH

THAT'S IT, SHE'S FINALLY GONE.

KRISTAAA-AAAAAA!!
ER, YMIR... IT ALL RIGHT. WE GO NOW TO PLACE WHERE KRISTA.
OR MAYBE TO A HOSPITAL.

I-I CAN NOT GO ON! THE... WITH-DRAWAL ...
MY BODY CAN'T...
URRRRRRG
WHAT AM I SUPPOSED TO DO NOW?!

H-HERE, TAKE THIS, KRISTA...
HURRY AND TAKE IT...
WHAT ?!

I CAN'T GO ON... UNLESS WE HAVE... MATCHING KEYRINGS!!
KAFF KAFF
HUH?!

IS THIS SOME KIND OF ELABORATE JOKE? ARE YOU ACTUALLY SACHA BARON COHEN OR SOMETHING?
PANT PANT
IT'S 2018! I DON'T KNOW WHO THAT IS!
H-HURRY!!

KRISTA WOULD PUT HER KEYS ON THIS AND TELL ME WOW SO CUTE WOW YMIR SO CUTE?
THAT'S WHAT KRISTA DO?!
I HAVE NO CLUE!
OH, FOR PITY'S SAKE. OKAY, I'LL USE IT.
...HUH?
PANT PANT
KACHIK KACHIK
CAN'T SEEM TO... OOPS, IT BROKE.
TWITCH TWITCH
KACHIK KACHIK

HUUUUUUUUUUSH
SLUMP

HUH? WAIT! ARE YOU DEAD?!
DON'T DIE IN THE GIFT SHOP!
I don't have an alibi this time!
SHAKE
SHAKE

UH... CALL AN AMBULANCE!!
PEEEPOHH
PEEEPOHH
SHINGEKI HOSPITAL
SHINGEKI HOSPITAL
ZakkaYa

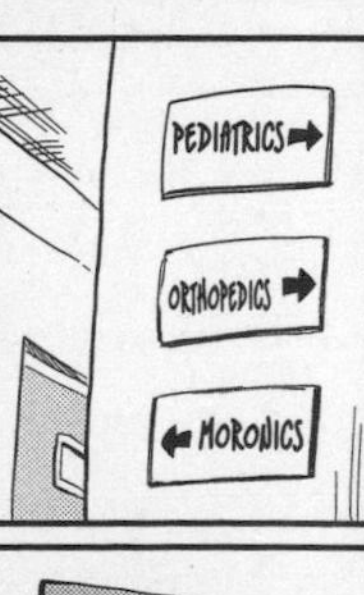
PEDIATRICS
ORTHOPEDICS
MORONICS

217
YMIR

BLINK

I MEAN...
CAN IT BE... THAT I HAVE DIED?

...THERE IS SOMEONE WHO LOOKS LIKE AN ANGEL RIGHT BEFORE MY EYES...

YMIR...?!

ARE YOU ALL RIGHT?

YOU COULD SAY I'M ETERNALLY ALL RIGHT...
SINCE I'M DEAD...
SIGH
?
YOU AREN'T DEAD.

HUH?
UM, LISTEN ...
I CAME TO THE HOSPITAL IN AN AMBULANCE JUST LIKE YOU.
SHUMP
OH, SO SHE'S AWAKE NOW?
HITCH!

I WAS WALKING HOME WITH HER.
It was a huge pain.
I REALIZED THAT SHE REMINDED ME A LITTLE OF YOU, YMIR... I MEAN, SHE'S GOT A DEEP VOICE, SHE'S SUPER MEAN, AND SHE SMELLS LIKE CLEAN LEATHER.
SO I THOUGHT THAT LIFE COULD BE FUN AGAIN WITH HER, LIKE IT WAS WHEN I WAS WITH YOU, YMIR...
BUT SHE'S NOT FUNNY MEAN, SHE'S ACTUALLY MEAN!
YMIR...
I WANT TO STAY WITH YOU!
KRIS...
...TA...
GRRN
IT'S ALL MY FAULT!! I'M SO SORRY THAT I OVERRE-ACTED!
WITHOUT YOU, I'M A GIB-BERING MESS!
HUG

I'M SORRY, TOO!
I'LL BE MORE CAREFUL NEXT TIME WE PLAY THE HEADBUTT GAME.
I TOO ...
...WILL MAKE SURE I DO NOT OVERDO THE RUB-RUBS.

GREAT!
RUB RUB RUB
AH HA HA HA HA HA
TIME FOR US TO GO HOME, I GUESS.
YEAH...
AND SO...

YMIR AND KRISTA PLAYED OUT THEIR MAKE-UP SCENE AND FINALLY WENT HOME AS FRIENDS.
AH HA HA HA HA HA HA HA
I FEEL LIKE LIKE I'VE BEEN DUMPED, SOME-HOW...
AND... THE LATEST ANNIE PURIKURA PHOTO MADE ITS WAY INTO BERTOLT'S SWEATY FISTS.
I'VE GOT THIS REALLY AMAZING PICTURE OF ANNIE. WELL?
I'LL BUY IT!!
Hm?
FLIP FLIP

SPECIAL EDITION: A NICE MORNING, FEELS DREAMY

BUT WE'RE GOING TO HAVE TO AWAKEN HIM...
OH, RIGHT...
HEY, ARMIN!
WAKEY WAAGH!
VWATCH

RRRRUUUMMMBLE

RRRRRRRRUUUUUUUMMMMBBLE

...
FLIP
ZZZZ

EREN...
HA HA... USUALLY HE'S THE TYPE WHO WOULDN'T HURT A FLY!
BUT WAKING HIM UP IS JUST THE WORST...
SLEEPY ARMIN IS LIKE A SCARY PAINTING BY THAT CREEPY GUY... VINCENT VAN PRICE.

CAN'T WE...
...JUST LET HIM BE? WOULDN'T THAT BE ALL RIGHT?

BUT SCHOOL...

IT'S JUST ONE DAY! WHAT'S THE HARM?

LOOK AT HOW CUTE HE IS DOZING AWAY...

すやすや

LIKE A BABY PHOTO BY THAT PHOTO LADY, ANNIE GETTYS.

I COULDN'T BRING MYSELF TO WAKE HIM EVEN IF I TRIED!

YES...

I KNOW...

JUST LOOKING AT HIM IS MAKING ME SLEEPY AS WELL.

YEAH...

YAWN ふぁ...

THEN WHY DON'T WE ALL...

...JUST GET A LITTLE MORE SHUTEYE OURSELVES...

TAK

YAWN ふわー

EREN, THAT WOULD BE ONE OF YOUR BAD IDEAS.

NOW GET OUT OF THE WAY.

CHATTER

CHATTER

Who's sleeping there?

Armin...

CHATTER

CHATTER

WHY ARE YOU GUYS ALWAYS TREATING SCHOOL LIKE IT'S YOUR HOUSE?
I'D HAVE GOTTEN ARRESTED BY NOW! THIS IS MAIN CHARACTER PRIVELEGE!
KEEP IT DOWN, JEAN...
AND WHAT'S WITH THE ATTITUDE?

DA-DAHN
WE'VE BEEN TRYING TO WAKE HIM UP LIKE THIS...
...EVER SINCE HE WENT TO SLEEP AFTER SCHOOL ON FRIDAY!!
HOW LONG HAS HE BEEN SLEEPING?!
It's Monday morning!!
ARMIN IS A HIBERNATING LIFEFORM.
ZZZZ すや
ZZZZ すや

THERE'S A CERTAIN CANDY SHOP BETWEEN ATTACK JR. HIGH AND DISTRICT 2 JR. HIGH.
IT WAS A HANGOUT FOR ALL THE KIDS FROM THE "BAD SIDE OF TOWN"*, INCLUDING LEVI AND HIS FRIENDS.
Reevez Coco
CANDIES TOYS
SNACK ATTACK
*NO WHOLE FOODS
I'LL TAKE THIS ONE, AND THAT THERE.
CHOCO
POTATO CHIPS
SQUID
OKAY, TODAY'S THE DAY... TODAY I TAKE ON...
GRAB
TASTY!
BIG CHOCO
THE SUPER BIG CHOCO!
YAAAY

D R A A A A G
すずるるるるる
HUH ...?
B-BOSS !!
WAIT! MY SUPER BIG CHOCO ...
WHEN WILL YOU FINALLY GROW OUT OF SNACK ATTACK TIME?!
OUR MEETING PLACE TODAY IS...
SHUUSH SHUUSH
*SIGN: SHINZERIA. EDITOR'S NOTE: THIS IS A PARODY OF A JAPANESE ITALIAN RESTAURANT CHAIN WHERE I ONCE HAD A GLASS OF WHITE WINE THAT COST ABOUT 70 CENTS. IT WAS 6 AM AND, AT THE TIME, I REGRETTED EVERYTHING, BUT TODAY, LOOKING BACK, I MERELY MOURN FOR MY YOUTH. AH, WHERE DID THOSE DAYS GO...
シンゼリア
MMMBBBLLLEE
RRRRRRUUU
A FAMILY RESTAU-RANT!
SPECIAL EDITION: A FULL-OUT DASH UP THE STEPS TO ADULTHOOD

N-NO... ANYTHING BUT THAT, BOSS...! DON'T MAKE US GO TO SHINZERIA...!!
NOOOOOOO
IT SMELLS WEIRD... AND THEY PUT KIWI ON PIZZA... AND...

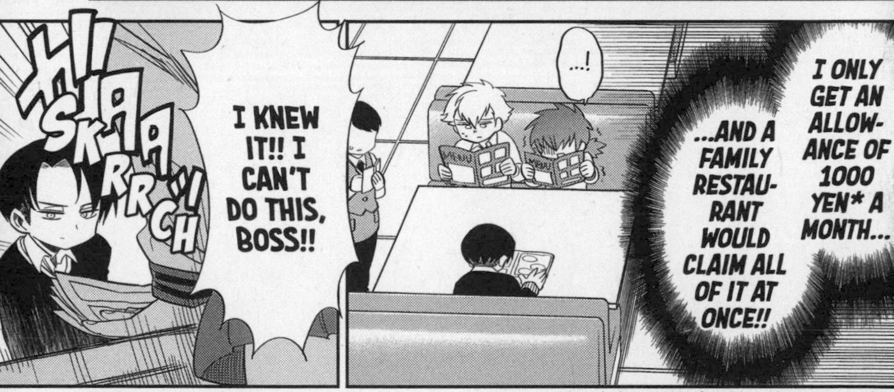

I ONLY GET AN ALLOWANCE OF 1000 YEN* A MONTH...
...AND A FAMILY RESTAURANT WOULD CLAIM ALL OF IT AT ONCE!!
...!
I KNEW IT!! I CAN'T DO THIS, BOSS!!
SKRRRCH

*Like ten bucks. Haven't you figured this out by now? Come on already

LOOK AT THIS! THIS CAN-DRINK THING IS AN ENTIRE 190 YEN!*

THAT GUY MIKE SELLS OLD CANS OF JOLT COLA OUT OF HIS VAN FOR LIKE 60 YEN...!!

ISABEL...

VWAM

RINK BAR 19

ALA CART
250 YEN

*About $1.90. I'm so tired of doing math for you people

DRINK BAR

IT'S NOT "CAN DRINK" ...

...IT'S "ALL YOU CAN DRINK."

?!

FLOOM

"ALL YOU CAN DRINK"...?! W-WHAT MADNESS IS THIS...?!

MEANING YOU COULD KEEP DRINKING FOREVER?! DO YOU EVER HAVE TO PEE AGAIN?! IT CAN'T BE...

n Umaibo costs about 10 yen, which is about 10 cents. Seriously, if you still need these notes, there's something wrong with you.

B-BUT, LEVI!
I CAN'T! I HAVE CHIL-DREN TO THINK ABOUT!
SKRRRT
MY LITTLE UMAIBO BA-BIES! LIKE ONE GIANT CHEETO EXCEPT IT TASTES LIKE OLD SHRIMP!
I CORNERED THE NEIGH-BORHOOD MARKET ON HOSE THINGS FOR 2,000 YEN, BUT HERE THAT WON'T BUY ME SQUAT!
TWO THOUSAND YEN
YEAH, WHAT HE JUST SAID!

I CAN'T EVEN AFFORD AN ORDER OF THE RASP-BERRY YAMS!
THANK YOU FOR WAITING! HERE IS YOUR ORDER!!
VAAAAAAM!!
L-LEVI! YOU ORDERED ALL THIS...?!
WHY WOULD YOU DO SOMETHING LIKE THAT?!
FURLAN...
HOW MUCH DO YOU THINK ALL THIS COSTS...?
HUH...?
I'm sorry I snapped at you on the last page. It's just, it's so easy. Just move the decimal two points. Like, 1196 yen is about $11.96. See? So. Easy
1196 YEN, TAX INCLUDED.
TH-THAT'S CHEAP!!
Salad 299 yen
Did you get $2.99?
Pepperencino Spaghetti 299 yen
If so, you're right!
Doria 299 yen
Wait, these are all the same.
Chicken 299 yen
Then why do I have to write notes for them a–
WOOOOOOW

FIVE HOURS LATER...
MORE ASPARAGUS JUICE PLEASE!
ANOTHER PEPPERENCINO! EXTRA SPAGHETTI!! CHOP CHOP!!
KACHUNK
KACHUNK
KACHUNK
KACHUNK
KACHUNK
WOW, I'M SO FULL! I DON'T THINK I COULD EVER GET THIS FULL ON SNACKS...
AND THE OWNER OF SNACK ATTACK WOULD HAVE KICKED US OUT HOURS AGO!
SKRITCH
COME TO THINK OF IT, BOSS, WHAT ARE YOU DOING HERE?
ARE YOU STUDYING?
NO, MORE IMPORTANT THAN THAT.
SKRITCH
THE CLEANING SCHEDULE FOR SCHOOL THIS WEEK.
SHIFF SHIFF
WAX
OHH!
I SHOULDA KNOWN!
YOU'RE THE EPITOME OF A CLEANING DEMON!
IS THAT THE REASON YOU CAME HERE TODAY?
YES...
WOOOW

REALLY...
NOW THAT I LOOK, THERE ARE PEOPLE PLAYING YUGIOH, WRITING NETFLIX PITCHES, WATCHING ADULT FILM PARODIES...
...DOING ALL SORTS OF THINGS THAT DON'T INVOLVE SPENDING MONEY!
THIS IS AMAZING!
I NEVER KNEW FAMILY RESTAURANTS WERE SO MAGICAL...!!
BOTH ISABEL AND FURLAN...
...FINALLY REALIZED WHAT THEY'D BEEN MISSING.
BUT JUST THEN...
シンゼリア
GRUUUUNCH
WH-WHAT WAS THAT THAT RUMBLING...
C-COULD IT BE...?
KAPAPAM
YAAARGH!
A TITAN STOMPED INTO THE RESTAURANT!!

HOOOOOOSH
...
AAAAAAA!!
EEEEK!
N-NO, WAIT! PAY UP BEFORE YOU FLEE!
YOU CHEAP-SKATES!
H-HOW CAN THIS BE?!
A TITAN JUST TRASHED THE RESTAURANT, AND ALL THE CUSTOMERS RAN OUT ON THEIR BILLS!!?
MR. HERGÉ IS GONNA FIRE ME FOR SURE!
WWAAAAAH
UR... URRN...
AND WHEN I'D JUST GOTTEN THE WAITERS TO STOP HUCKING EGG YOLKS AT MY CAR...
SNIFF
SNIFF
SHIK
SHIK
HM?
...WAIT! WHAT... IS THIS?!
HEY, SOME-BODY LEFT BEHIND SOME GREAT CARBONARA!!
WHEEEEE!
THERE ARE CUSTOMERS EATING THE LEFTOVERS!!
AND SOMEONE LEFT A STEAK!!
SCRITCH
SCRITCH

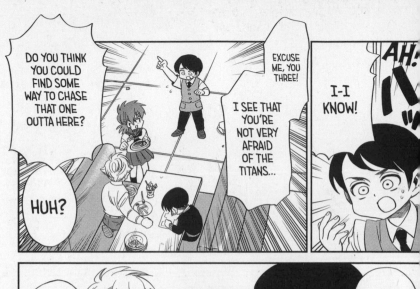

DO YOU THINK YOU COULD FIND SOME WAY TO CHASE THAT ONE OUTTA HERE?

HUH?

EXCUSE ME, YOU THREE!

I SEE THAT YOU'RE NOT VERY AFRAID OF THE TITANS...

AH!

I-I KNOW!

UH, NO. WE'RE EATING.
PLEASE, I DON'T WANT TO BE EGGBOY AGAIN!
IF YOU MANAGE IT, I CAN FIND SOME WAY TO THANK YOU!!

RIGHT! THIS TIME, I'LL MIX THEM ALL IN ONE CUP!

KACLICK

SSS

I'LL GIVE YOU MY VERY WARMEST SMILE!!

I DON'T NEED A SMILE!!

P-PLEASE, I'M ON MY KNEES HERE!!

GRAB

I DON'T SEE WHY WE HAVE TO DO ANYTHING FOR YOU.

YOU'RE AN EMPLOYEE HERE, RIGHT? WHY DON'T **YOU** DO IT?

...

PUNCH

BLOOOSH

IT'S...
IT'S ALL OVER!!
SLUMP
WITH THE RESTAURANT THIS DESTROYED, I'M FIRED FOR SURE...
I'M GOING TO HAVE TO START ALL OVER AT AN APPLEBEE'S OR... GOD FORBID... RUBY TUESDAY!!
SHIK

NO... DRINK BAR... YOU WERE MY ONE LOVE...
HOW CAN I DRINK ALL I CAN DRINK NOW, HUH?! HOW CAN I...

THIS PASTA HAS SODA ON IT?
HEY! I CAN'T EAT THIS! I HATE MR. PIBB!

LEVI...?
... FILTHY...

GET OUT!!
SWAAM

YOU MEAN...
...THEY COULD'VE DONE THAT ALL ALONG?!
SPING

I THINK I'VE HAD ENOUGH OF THIS!
シンゼリア
シンゼリア

I'M NEVER COMING TO THIS RESTAU-RANT AGAIN!!
HEY, YOU THREE, WAIT A SECOND!

YOU **DID** EVENTUALLY CHASE OFF THE TITAN, SO THANK YOU!
AND HERE'S A LITTLE THANK-YOU GIFT.
HUH?!

A LITTLE 10% OFF CHEESE LUMPS WON'T MAKE US CHANGE OUR MINDS!
SNACK ATTACK IS BOTH CHEAPER AND SAFER...
THESE ARE SUPPOSED TO BE ONLY FOR VETERANS' DOGS' BIRTHDAYS, BUT...

*So, we're back here again, huh? It's $10. Well, 1,000 yen is about $10, and there are five of these, so that's… no, you know what? I'm not doing this anymore. Buy a calculator.

WHOOOOOAAAA!

HERE. FIVE 1,000-YEN GIFT CARDS.*

¥1,000

AND SO THEIR NEW LIVES BE-GAN AS "THOSE WEIRDOS." YOU KNOW, THE ONES WHO KEEP ORDERING FOR FIVE HOURS.

CHA-CHING

DINNG
DONNG
DINNG
KUKLO!
I WAS WONDERING. WHAT YOU WILL DO AFTER YOU LEAVE SCHOOL?
?
WHAT I DO...?
YOU KNOW! MOST KIDS WILL EITHER GO TO COLLEGE OR TRY TO GET A JOB.
YOU HAVE TO DECIDE YOUR LIFE PATH BEFORE YOU ACTUALLY LEAVE SCHOOL.
HMM...
I NEVER THINK ABOUT THAT...
OF COURSE, THERE ARE OTHER PATHS TO CONSIDER.
FOR EXAMPLE...
MUNCH
MUNCH
...MAYBE YOU AND I COULD...
YOU TWO!!
SHIK
YEAH, YOU, TARZAN AND VAIN JANE! THIS IS A SCHOOL, NOT A MONKEY PICNIC GROUND!
ZWACK

SPECIAL EDITION: OUR LIFE PLAN, AND BEYOND!!

ME NOT SEE WHY THIS HAPPEN...
ぷく
SWeee
eeeLL

HUH? DO YOU TRULY NOT UNDERSTAND, KUKLO?
WHAT?!
ぷぷ
TEE HEE!

YOU MEAN CALDINA UNDERSTAND ALL THIS?
I SUPPOSE SO. ANYONE ASIDE FROM YOU WOULD UNDER-STAND.
WHAT'S HAPPENED IS THAT YOU...
HEY, RODENT!!

I HEAR YOU MADE MY SISTER CRY...
THAT'S A DEATH SENTENCE!!
XAVI...!

THAT MEAN YOU UNDER-STAND?
THEN WHY SHARLE CRY?!

GRRRN
YOU MEAN YOU DON'T KNOW?!
THE REASON IS...

FLAAAAAAAAASH
YOU OPENED THE ONE PANDORA'S BOX OF SHARLE'S THAT SHOULD NEVER BE OPENED!
YOU BROUGHT THE SUBJECT OF BUST SIZE INTO THE CONVERSATION!!
IS THAT WHAT HAPPEN ?!
NO, IT WASN'T !!
ZWACK

IT NOT ?
WELL, IT MAY HAVE BEEN A LITTLE BIT, BUT...
...THE REAL REASON HAD NOTHING TO DO WITH IT!!

YOU SHOWED AN INTEREST IN A GIRL...
...AND THAT'S WHAT SHE FINDS SO OFFENSIVE!!

THAT ...!!
THAT MEAN ...!!
GULP

THE NEXT DAY...
DINNG
DONNG
DINNG

SHARLE...I SORRY FOR WHAT HAPPEN BEFORE...
OH, KUKLO ...!

NO, I SHOULD APOLOGIZE FOR SLAPPING YOU LIKE A CIRCA-2000 HAREM ANIME CHARACTER!!
NO, THIS MANGA SO FACE HEAL FAST, SEE?

SO, UM...
AFTER THAT, I CAME TO REALIZE...
...THAT I MUST CHANGE MYSELF FOR YOUR SAKE, KUKLO...

SHARLE...
AND I HAVE. I HAVE CHANGED!
RUSTLE

KUKLO, LOOK...
THIS IS THE NEW ME...
FWUMPH

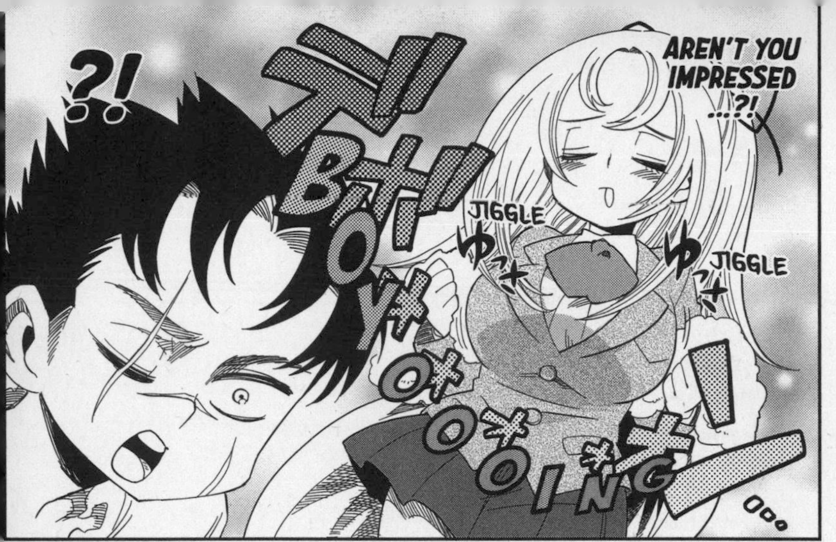
AREN'T YOU IMPRESSED ...?!
JIGGLE
JIGGLE
BOYOING!
?!

I'VE DONE ALL I CAN TO BE-COME...
UM... KUKLO ...?!
POKE
POKE

STOP POKING ME WITH THAT BRANCH, OR I'LL... !!
ZWAP
TASH

KUKLO, YOU JERK !!
ZWACK

DO YOU REALLY LOVE HUGE GAZON-GAS THAT MUCH?!
NO, SHARLE!! I NOT KNOW WHO THIS GAZONGA!!
YOU'RE A LIAR !!
WAAAAAAAAAH

I WANT MAKE UP WITH SHARLE!!
AH!

CALDINA TEACH ME WHAT IT ALL ABOUT!
THAT SHARLE REALLY MAD BECAUSE I SHOW INTEREST IN WOMAN...
BUT THAT JUST SHARLE'S MISTAKE!!
KUKLO...
I PROVE IT, I...

I NOT INTEREST IN GIRL AT ALL...!!
SEE?! I KIDNAP MAN...
...FOR KISSY TIME!

KUKLO, YOU JERK!!
ZWACK
I WANT TO BE TO-GETHER WITH KUKLO FOREVER AND EVER!!
IN JUNIOR HIGH, HIGH SCHOOL, AND EVEN BEYOND THAT!! FROM NOW ON!!
THAT'S WHY I GET SAD WHEN I SEE YOU GETTING CLOSE TO ANYONE ELSE, KUKLO!!

WHAT ...
...I DO TO...
...DE-SERVE... ?!
WHAT WRONG WITH THAT?!
ZWAK ZWAK ZWAK ZWAK ZWAK ZWAK

I WILL WITH YOU FOREVER!
IN THE HIGH SCHOOL AND ANY OTHER. ALWAYS IN SAME PLACE!

AT THE TIME, SHARLE'S FACE GOT ALL PUFFY AND HER MAKEUP WAS COMPLETELY RUINED...

...BUT KUKLO DIDN'T EVEN SEEM TO NOTICE.

TO BE CONCLUDED!

ATTACK on TITAN JUNIOR HIGH

CONTINUED FROM PAGE 180.

COME QUICK ...!
HUH? YOU MEAN ARMIN?!
YES! KIDNAPPED BY HANGE...
...AND FORCED INTO BECOMING A CHEESEBURGER STREETWALKER!
WE HAVE TO GO SAVE HIM!!
DASH
WAIT A SECOND, EREN!! IT'S TOO DANGEROUS FOR YOU TO JUST GO BARGING IN!
YOU'RE UP AGAINST MAD HANGE, AND YOU NEVER KNOW WHAT A MAD HANGE IS CAPABLE OF...!
YOU NEED A PLAN BEFORE YOU GO...
A PLAN? BUT WHAT KIND OF PLAN...?
EREN!
WE HAVE A PLAN!
JUST COME WITH US!!
OHH! IT'S YOU GUYS!
OKAY, THEN...

COME GET THEM WHILE THEY'RE HOT!
HOW ABOUT A DELICIOUS, SATISFYING CHEESEBURGER?!
WHEET
WHOO
YOU'RE STILL NOT ALLURING ENOUGH!!
DO YOU REALLY THINK ANYONE WOULD BUY A CHEESEBURGER ON THAT PITCH?!
VWASSH
OWW
REMEMBER, RIGHT NOW, YOU'RE 100 TIMES CUTER THAN THE ANIME VERSION OF YOU!!
WHAT DOES THAT MEAN?!
SO THERE YOU ARE!!
WHAM
WH-WHO ARE YOU?!
SHF...
SORRY WE'RE SO LATE, ARMIN.
THE BAD HANGE WON'T HURT YOU ANYMORE!
WE'RE NOT GOING TO STAND BY AND LET ARMIN GET SHAMED ALONE!!
EVERYONE IS BUNNIES!!
VWAAM

I HAVE NO IDEA WHY YOU GUYS ARE ALL DRESSED LIKE ME, BUT...
CAPTURE THE MAD HANGE!!
...THANK YOU, SO MUCH, EVERYBODY!!
I'M SO GLAD YOU'RE OKAY!
IT'S ALL BECAUSE YOU GUYS SHOWED SUCH BRAVERY!
REALLY! THANK YOU, YOU GUYS!
HA HA! THAT'S WHAT FRIENDS ARE FOR!
AH! OVER THERE!
OH, THE POLICE?
EXCUSE ME, BUT THIS PERSON...
OH, HIM?
LOOK AT THAT GETUP! YOU'RE A MORAL MENACE! BOYS IN SKIRTS CAUSE BANK FRAUD!
KACHANK
IT'S A HARD WORLD...
A VERY, VERY HARD WORLD...
PEEPOHH
PEEPOHH
POLICE

THE END

ATTACK on TITAN
JUNIOR HIGH

By
SAKI NAKAGAWA

Based on "Attack on Titan" by
HAJIME ISAYAMA

Contents

SCHEDULE FOR TUESDAY, NOVEMBER 3 STUDENT ON DUTY: EREN

DANG.
ANOTHER DAY THAT I COULDN'T ERADICATE THE TITANS...

MAYBE IF I POKE EVERYTHING A CLUE TO DEFEATING THEM WILL POP UP!
LIKE IN THOSE PROFESSOR WEIGHTON GAMES...
RAH
RAH
Guh...
LEVI!
DON'T FORGET OUR DEAL! IF I STRIKE YOU OUT, YOU BUY ME LUNCH FOR A WEEK!!
BOOM
GAAAAH

BRING IT ON, FOUR-EYES.
HERE I GO!!
KTCH...
HNNNNNNGGGGGH
WHIP

SEVENTY-THIRD PERIOD: DAD ON A WEEKDAY

FWIP
CLAAAAANG
HE HIT MY SUPER-SLOW PITCH!!

OAAAAAAR

C'MON, I'M RUBBING AS HARD AS I CAN...!!

GIVE ME A HINT, ACE ATTORNEY FIXIT RIGHT!

GAAAAAAH

THWAAAAAACK

NNNGH

EREN ?!

OOOWWWWWWWWW!!
EREN, ARE YOU ALL RIGHT!?
ROLL
ROLL
ROLL
I'MBM DFDEFI-NINTA-LOLY NOT ALOLOL RIGHT!!
GUH... MY CHEST HURTS...
IT MUST BE ALL MY RIPPED ABS AND STUFF, BECAUSE...
HM?
GRAB
IT WASN'T MY RIPPED ABS...
IT'S... !!
THAT'S RIGHT!! I HAVE THIS!!

AFTER SCHOOL
I'M HOME!!

OH, WEL-COME H...
STOMP STOMP STOMP STOMP

HI, MR. AND MRS. YEAGER!
OH, HELLO, EVERYONE. LOOK AT HOW CUTE YOU ALL ARE.
INTENSE

YOU HAVE THIS MANY FRIENDS, EREN? DON'T THEY KNOW WHAT A CHUCKLEHEAD YOU ARE?
DAD!!

TAKE US TO THE BASEMENT !!
!
SLAM

I REMEMBERED WHAT YOU TOLD ME!!

THIS KEY... IS GOING TO BE THE CLUE TO UNLOCKING THE MYSTERY OF THE TITANS!

EREN...!!

DID I SAY A THING LIKE THAT?
YOU DID, ACTUALLY!
I don't remember that page...
SEVERAL MONTHS AGO...
WHEN KEITH VISITED THE YEAGERS' FOR A PARENT-TEACHER MEETING...
WHAT THE HECK IS THIS KEY?!

I DON'T CARE ABOUT THIS!! CAN'T YOU REMEMBER SOMETHING ABOUT THE STUDENT WHO TRIED TO DEFEAT THE TITANS?!
BWAAAAAH
GAH, QUIT YOUR BAWLING!
EREN, CALM DOWN.
THAT KEY WILL LET YOU GO INTO THE BASEMENT...
Attack on Titan

WHERE THE CLUE TO UNLOCKING THE MYSTERY OF THE TITANS IS HIDDEN!
WHAT ?!

CAN YOU TAKE ME TO THE BASEMENT RIGHT NOW?!

NO.

WHY NOT?!

BECAUSE WE HAVE TO DRAG THIS MANGA OUT...

ER, I MEAN...

KCHAK

I'M HOME!!

TIME FOR DINNER!!

BA-DUMP

YAAAAY

AND THEN, AFTER FINISHING DINNER, I...
KCHAK

...FELL STRAIGHT ASLEEP...!!
AND I FORGOT ALL ABOUT THIS KEY UNTIL TODAY...!!

SEE? THE FLASHBACK SAID SO! AND BY CHANCE, I REMEMBERED IT TODAY.
THAT CAN ONLY MEAN THAT THE TIME HAS COME FOR THIS MANGA TO FINALLY, MERCIFULLY END!

YOU'LL TAKE US, WON'T YOU... DAD?!
IF- IF IT MEANS THE END OF THIS MANGA...
WOW! SO IT REALLY EXISTS!
JOOOY
SEE?! JUST LIKE I TOLD YOU!
FOLLOW ME, KIDS.

I CAN'T BELIEVE YOU GUYS HAVE A BASEMENT.
THAT'S PRETTY UN-USUAL HERE IN...GERMA-NO-JAPAN-AMERIC...ER, WHEREVER THIS STORY TAKES PLACE!

SO THE MOMENT HAS FINALLY ARRIVED...
DAD...?

EREN... TO TELL YOU THE TRUTH, I'VE ALSO BEEN INVESTIGATING THE TITANS ON MY OWN...
WHAT?!
THE BASEMENT CONTAINS THE MANY FRUITS OF THAT RESEARCH.
I MADE IT TO PRESERVE THEM AND TO PROTECT THEM FROM THE WORLD...

BUT I WILL GIVE IT ALL TO YOU, EREN...!!
DON'T MESS IT UP, CHUCK-LEHEAD.

THANKS ...!!
I'LL MAKE YOU PROUD, DAD!!

IT'S DOWN HERE.

WOAH!
THERE'S A DOOR DOWN THERE!!

CHILL

WHAT IS THIS ...?
L-LET'S GO...
WHAT IS THIS UNEASY FEELING...?

WHAT IS CAUSING THIS ANXIETY PRODDING MY CHEST...?
THERE'RE ONLY FILES ABOUT THE TITANS HERE...
CLAK
CLAK
CLAK
GASP

STOP
EREN, THE KEY.

AND WAIT HERE FOR A MOMENT.
HUH?
I HAVEN'T BEEN IN HERE IN A WHILE. I JUST WANT TO DOUBLE CHECK WHAT'S IN HERE.
THEN LET ME GO WITH YOU...
JUST WAIT HERE!

SLAAAAM

WHAT'S GOING ON?
HE SAID SOMETHING ABOUT CHECKING WHAT'S INSIDE...?
YOUR DAD'S SO DRA-MATIC.
KCHAK
CLICK
HE LOCKED IT...?
D-DAD...?
EREN?

UH... I CAN'T SHOW YOU THE BASE-MENT AFTER ALL...
WHAT ?!

BUT THIS MANGA WILL GO ON FOR-EVER!
RATTLE
RATTLE
RATTLE
RATTLE
IS THERE SOMETHING IN THERE SO EMBARRASSING THAT YOU CAN'T SHOW ANYONE?!
...

HOW DID YOU KNOW...?
BLUSH
FOR REAL?!
!?

NO, YOU CAN'T DO THIS TO US, DAD...
WHAT IS THIS EMBARRASSING THING, ANYWAY? I PROMISE NOT TO LOOK AT IT...
...

NO. THIS WHOLE ROOM IS EMBARRASSING...
JUST WHAT'S GOING ON IN THERE?!

I'M SORRY... BUT COULD YOU WAIT A FEW MONTHS?
I'LL RE-DECORATE IN HERE, AND THEN...
I CAN'T WAIT THAT LONG, DAD!

THEN WOULD IT BE POSSIBLE FOR YOU TO JUST RETRIEVE THE DOCUMENTS ABOUT THE TITANS?!
OH, RIGHT!

OH, RIGHT...
HOLD ON A SECOND...
UM...

I CAN'T DO THAT, EITHER...
?!
BUT WHY?!

I'VE SCRIBBLED... EMBARRASSING... THINGS ALL OVER THEM...
WHAT THE HECK, DAD?!

THEN YOU LEAVE US NO CHOICE...
DAD, EMBARRASS YOURSELF... FOR US!!
WHAT?!

EREN... ARE YOU TELLING ME TO OPEN THIS DOOR AND FACE HUMILIA-TION...?
THERE'S NO OTHER OPTION, IS THERE?!
YOU'RE RIGHT... AND IT WAS ME WHO BUILT SUCH AN EMBARRASSING ROOM AND PUT TOGETHER THESE DOCUMENTS...
ALL RIGHT...

カチャ... KCHAK...
SLAM
NO, I JUST CAN'T!!
DAAAAAAD!!

THEN WHAT ABOUT THIS, EREN?
I MAY BE ABLE TO GET MYSELF TO OPEN THIS DOOR IF EVERY-ONE ELSE IS EMBARRASSED, TOO!!
HUH?

WHAT'RE YOU SAYING ...?
BUT DON'T YOU SEE, EREN?!
DON'T YOU THINK IT'S UNFAIR THAT I ALONE SHOULD FEEL EMBAR-RASSED?!
WE'LL BE ON EQUAL FOOTING IF YOU ALL FEEL THE SAME THING!!
BUT ISN'T IT ALL YOUR OWN FAULT?!

SO WHAT SPECIFICALLY DO YOU WANT US TO DO?
LET'S SEE... I CAN ONLY HEAR YOUR VOICES, SO LET'S HEAR SOME STORIES.
I KNOW YOU'RE KIDS, BUT I WANT SOME REAL SHIT!
EREN, WHY DON'T YOU START?
WHAT ?!

BUT IT'S TOO SUDDEN... I CAN'T COME UP WITH AN EMBARRASSING STORY JUST LIKE THAT...
Hmmm
IT CAN'T BE THAT HARD, EREN... YOU ACCIDENTALLY WORE YOUR MOTHER'S UNDERWEAR TO SCHOOL TODAY.
HOW ABOUT THE TIME YOU DRANK ALL THAT YOOHOO AND PEED YOURSELF ON YOUR FIRST DAY OF GRADE SCHOOL...?
Happy first day of school
SEEP
HEY! JEAN DIDN'T KNOW THAT YET!
CHORTLE
PFFFT PFFFT
FOR-REAL?!
OR THAT TIME WHEN THE DOG NEXT DOOR BARKED AT YOU AND YOU RAN CRYING AND WET YOUR PANTS...
Bow wow
SEEP
THAT DOG WAS A MENACE! IT SHOULD'VE BEEN PUT DOWN!
GIGGLE
GIGGLE
PFFFFT
OR HOW YOU USED TO PEE IN THE POOL IN THIRD GRADE...
PEEEEE
BWAHA
...
STOOP!!
AHAHAHAHA

OKAY, EREN. NOW TELL ONE MORE...
YOU STILL WANT ANOTHER ONE?!
BWAHAHAHAHAHA
だはははは
BUT I KNOW ALL OF THOSE ALREADY...
IF YOU DON'T SHARE, YOU'LL NEVER MAX OUT MY "EMBARRASSMENT METER"!!
PIIING
ピコーン
SHAME
PIIING
ピコーン
WHAT MESSED-UP GAME MECHANIC IS THAT?!

SO, UH... DO YOU HAVE SOMETHING MORE EMBARRASSING THAN THOSE STORIES?
C'MON, HURRY UP AND TELL US!
I DON'T HAVE ANY, YOU JERK!!
UM...
OH, THAT'S RIGHT.
THE OTHER DAY...

...AFTER I WATCHED A SCARY MOVIE, I WANTED TO GO TO THE BATHROOM LATE AT NIGHT...
SHUDDER
TINKLE
SHUDDER
BUT I WAS SO SCARED THAT I PEED MYSELF A LITTLE ON THE WAY...
AHAHAHAHAHAHA
WHY'RE THEY ALL ABOUT PEE?!
YOU'RE SUCH A LOSER-RRR!!
WHEEZE
EEZE
STOP LAUGHING!!
EREN...

YOU SEEM TO PEE YOURSELF A LOT...
MAYBE YOU SHOULD GO SEE A UROLOGIST...
HMMMM
SHUT UP!!
MY HEART IS IN A LOT WORSE SHAPE RIGHT NOW THAN MY BLADDER!!

MMM, DUNN ABOUT THAT STORY.
I DIDN'T GET A GOOD LAUGH OUT OF IT, SO YOU DON'T GET THAT MANY POINTS...
PIIING PIIING
SHAME
WHY ARE YOU ALWAYS TRYING TO FIND REASONS TO LAUGH AT ME?!
CHORTLE...
WHO WANTS TO GO NEXT?
JEAN!! YOU'RE NEXT!
HUH?!

I BET YOU HAVE A TO OF EMBARRASSING STORIES!!
I DO NOT!!
WE NEED SOME, JEAN.
YOU SAY THAT, BUT I'M NOT LIKE YOU MORONS. I'VE LED A QUIET AND DIGNIFIED LIFE, BOUND FOR THE ELITE...
...I'VE LIVED KNOWING THAT MY LIFE WOULD BE SCRUTINIZED BY HISTORIANS ONE DAY...
WHA?
What are screwtoon eyes...?

WAIT, I SAW YOU IN TOWN THE OTHER DAY!

WHAT?

I WAS SHOPPING WITH MY MOM...

SHOUT

SHOUT

WHAT'S ALL THAT RUCKUS...?

SETTLE DOWN!! I TOLD YOU I'M MAKING CHICKEN STEW TONIGHT!!

BUT I WANT AN OMELETTE WITH RICE!!

ACK, ENOUGH!!

OH!!

YOU SAID JUST A MINUTE AGO YOU DIDN'T CARE WHAT'S FOR DINNER!!

SPANK

SPANK

JEAN...!!

AAAAAAUGH

Oh my.

STOP IT, KIDS!!
YOU SHOULDN'T MAKE FUN OF THE MISTAKES OF OTHERS LIKE...
CHORTLE

YOU SHOULDN' LAUGH AT PEOPLE...
PFFFFT
CHOKE
ゴホッ
ゴホッ
CHOKE
PFFT
ぷひ
あ AHA
は HA
は HA
は HA
は HA
は HA
は HA
TWITCH
ぴく
ぴく
TWITCH
AW, SHOOT!!
I'M GOING TO TELL THE WHOLE SCHOOL ABOUT WHAT'S IN THAT ROOM!!

ARMIN IS NEXT
UMMM,
I...

...
...

YOU DON'T HAVE TO DO THIS, ARMIN!
WE ALL KNOW YOU'RE A DEL-ICATE SPRING BLOSSOM. JUST IGNORE MY DAD.
Eren!
N-NO, IT'S FINE!!

WELL, I DON'T MIND TELLING.

BUT I'M WORRIED THAT YOU MIGHT NOT THINK IT'S THAT EMBARRASSING...

FIDGET FIDGET もじもじ

MAYBE YOU'VE ALL HAD THE SAME EXPERIENCE AND IT WON'T BE THAT FUNNY...

FIDGET FIDGET もじもじ

SOMETHING THAT WE'VE ALL EXPERIENCED...?

I THINK SO...

WITH A DICTIONARY...

HM?

AN EMBARRASSING THING WE DO WITH A DICTIONARY...?

WHAT'S THAT?

I CAN'T THINK OF ANYTHING.

WHAT?!

BARK BARK BARK BARK BARK BARK

YOU'VE NEVER DONE IT?!

LOOKING UP DIRTY WORDS IN THE DICTIONARY?!

MEOW MEOW MEOW MEOW MEOW MEOW

LOOKING UP DIRTY WORDS...

IN THE DICTIONARY?!

WHAAAAAT?!

Huh...

!?

BLUUUUSH
BWUH, I'M SO EMBARRASSED!!
A-ARMIN!
I-I'VE NEVER DONE THAT...
BUT I THINK IT'S NO BIG DEAL
GUUUH
R-RIGHT, ME TOO.
DON'T WORRY, ARMIN.
I THINK EVERYONE WHO'S GONE THROUGH PUBERTY HAS HAD SIMILAR EXPERIENCES.
HA HA HA HA HA HA HA HA HA
BUT WOW, YOU JUST SAID IT IN FRONT OF EVERYONE!!
WOW, HOW EMBARRASSING, ARMIN!!
CLAP CLAP
AND WHOSE FAULT IS THAT?!
SLAAAM
GUH
BWUUUUH

AND SO EVERYONE TOLD THEIR STORIES...

LISTEN TO THIS!

I USUALLY GET BELOW 10 POINTS ON TESTS...

SO MY PARENTS TOOK ME TO THE DOCTOR, BUT THEY GOT MY BRAIN SCAN CONFUSED WITH ONE OF A ROTTING SALMON!

SHAME

ピ DIT ピ DIT ッ

LAUGHTER

THIS ONE TIME, SOMEONE STOMPED AROUND IN THE CLASSROOM AND MADE THIS BIG NOISE...

AND FOR SOME REASON, EVERYONE DECIDED THAT IT WAS ME FARTING!!

...

AHHH

Are you sure you didn't fart?

SHAME

ピ DIT ピ DIT ピ DIT ッ

あははは AHAHAHAHA

EREN'S DAD'S EMBARRASSMENT METER CLIMBED UP STEADILY.

AND THEN...

SO WE'RE DOWN TO THE LAST ONE...

...

...

WHAT'S WRONG, KIDS?

ISN'T IT MIKASA'S TURN?
COME, TELL ME YOUR STORY!

...
IT'S NO GOOD, DAD...
WHAT?!

AS A STRONG FEMALE CHARACTER™, MIKASA HAS NO EMBARRASSING STORIES!
SHE'S ALWAYS JUST BEEN ASSERTIVE, SWEET, BADASS, LOYAL, AND COOL!
IT CAN'T BE...
THERE COULDN'T POSSIBLY BE SUCH A PERSON!

HAVE YOU EVER PEED YOUR-SELF?
NEVER.

HAVE YOU PARENTS EVER CHEWED YOU OUT?!
NEVER.

HOW ABOUT FARTS?
I AM INCAPABLE OF FARTING.

IS SHE EVEN HUMAN?!
GULP

NO...!!
BUT THAT MEANS...
I CAN NEVER LEAVE THIS ROOM...!!
SHOCK
NO, YOU TOTALLY CAN!!
At any time!!
...
WILL EREN'S DAD EVER COME OUT?!
GOD, I DUNNO.

TO SOLVE THE MYSTERY OF THE TITANS, THE GROUP HEADED TO EREN'S BASEMENT...
HRRRMMMMM
BUT EREN'S FATHER TURNED ON THEM, WHICH, I MEAN, THEY PROBABLY SHOULD'VE SEEN THAT COMING.
TAP TAP TAP

I FIGURED IT OUT!
I KNOW HOW TO OPEN THIS DOOR!!
REALLY ?!
WHY DIDN'T I REALIZE IT SOON-ER? IT'S SO SIMPLE!!
YES!

ALL YOU HAVE TO DO IS GIVE UP AND COME OUT, DAD!!
BAM
K-BAM
HEY EREN, STOP! OW OW!
DON'T MIN-IMIZE YOUR DAD'S ADULT CON-CERNS!
K-BAM
K-BAM
EREN, WAIT.

SEVENTY-FOURTH PERIOD: THE CONFESSIONS OF THE PERFECT PERSON

I JUST REMEM-BERED...
AN EMBAR-RASSING STORY ABOUT MYSELF...
WHAT ?!
EVEN MIKASA HAD ONE AFTER ALL!
WHAT A RELIEF! SHE'S HUMAN AND NOT SOME KIND OF ROBOT!
GO ON AND ELL US, IKASA!!
JUST THE OTHER DAY...
AS I WAS HEADING HOME FROM THE GROCERY STORE...
MM HMM
ふん
ふん
THERE WAS A FIRE IN AN APART-MENT COMPLEX I WAS PASSING...
MY SON IS STILL IN THERE!!
NANA !!
KITTY!!
DASH
HEY, STOP!!
ROOOOAAAR
?!
THERE'S NOTHING WE CAN DO!!
HROOOOAAAAR
AAAAAAAH
EVERY-ONE, GET BACK!!
BOOM!!

I WAS THERE, SO I HELPED EVERYONE THAT WAS LEFT BEHIND...
THEY'RE ALL SAFE!!
RAAAAAAA
HOLD ON, MIKASA!!
AAAAH
DAMN, WHA A DISASTER...
HUH?!
PLEASE WAIT!!
I TRIED TO GET ON MY WAY BECAUSE I HAD TO PREPARE DINNER, BUT...
I'M GETTING THERE...
IT GETS EMBARRASSING AFTER THAT?!
WHAT'S S EMBARRASSING ABOUT THIS STORY?!
YANK
HEY, EVERYONE!!
I'M SORRY, BUT I'M IN A HURRY...
PLEASE LET US REPAY YOU SOMEHOW!!
MISS, WON'T YOU TELL ME YOUR NAME?!
WHAT?! MODEST AND A HERO?!

RAAAAAH
WE'VE GOT NO CHOICE ...
THROW HER INTO THE AIR!!
HURRAY
HURRAY
HURRAY
HURRAY
SO THAT'S WHAT HAPPENED...

OH, I'M SO EMBAR-RASSED ...!!
BLUSH
WAIT, WHY IN THE NAME OF PETE?

IT'S NOT LIKE I DID ANYTHING THAT GREAT.
I DIDN'T DESERVE TO BE AIR-BORNE.
BLUSH
Wow
NO NO, YOU DID DO SOMETHING GREAT!!
BUT WAIT, THAT'S WHAT EMBAR-RASSES YOU, MIKASA?!
WHAT DO YOU THINK, MR. YEAGER?
...

WOMP

SHAME

WOW, MIKASA. FOR YOU TO FIND THAT EMBARRASSING, YOU HAVE TO BE A WONDERFUL...

...COMPLETELY BORING PERSON.

DROP

THE METER WENT DOWN!!

M-MY STORY WASN'T ANY GOOD?!

WELL NO, IF I HAD TO CALL IT GOOD OR BAD, IT'S DEFINITELY A GOOD STORY...

BUT THAT'S NOT WHAT I'M LOOKING FOR...

I WANT TO HEAR ABOUT PEOPLE WORSE THAN ME SO I CAN FEEL BETTER ABOUT MYSELF!!
SHOCK
DAD, YOU'RE THE WORST!!

CLAMOR
I-I HAVE MORE.
YOU CAN KEEP GOING, MIKASA?!
PLEASE TELL ME SOMETHING ACTUALLY EMBARRASSING THIS TIME!
THERE WERE NATIONAL EXAMINATIONS THE OTHER DAY...
AND I GOT PERFECT SCORES ON EVERY SUBJECT...
?!

MY NAME WAS PRINTED IN 37 NATIONAL NEWSPAPERS...
Most difficult tests in history
PERFECT SCORES IN EVERY SUBJECT
From a public school in the middle of nowhere
THE SCHOOL MADE THIS HUGE BANNER.
TOP RANK IN NATIONAL EXAMS
FIRST TIME IN SCHOOL HISTORY
THE WHOLE TOWN WAS TALKING ABOUT IT.
AND THEN STRANGERS STARTED GREETING ME ON THE STREET AND WRITING WEIRD LETTERS TO ME.
LIKE, "OOH, DID YOU GET TO BE SO SMART BECAUSE YOU EAT SO MUCH KALE?"
WAIT... IS SHE UMBLE BRAGGING?!

THIS ONE ISN'T JUST EMBARRASS ING...
IT WILL FORCE ME TO BARE MY SOUL AND TELL YOU SOME-THING...
...THAT I HAVEN'T BEEN ABLE TO TELL ANYONE UNTIL NOW...!!

YOU'D TELL MIKASA A STORY LIKE THAT FOR ME...?!
I MUST HAVE BEEN IN THE FIFTH GRADE...
MOOOVED
BWA HAHA
AND...
I WAS DEEPLY MOVED BY THE NOVEL INFINITE JEST.

SO I SET OUT TO WRITE MY OWN MEAN-DERING EPIC FULL OF MAG-ICAL-REALIST METAPHORS, PAGE-LONG FOOTNOTES, AND TENNIS.
WRITE
WRITE
WRITE
WRITE
WRITE
?!

I SENT IT IN TO A NEW WRITER'S CONTEST IN A MAG-AZINE...
TOSS

AND IN THE NEXT VOLUME, WHEN THEY ANNOUNCED THE WINNERS...
MIKASA, WAIT.

THAT NEW WRITER'S CONTEST ...
DID YOU WIN FIRST PLACE?

...
NO.

WHAAT?!
DID YOU REALLY THINK THAT MY FIRST, TURGID ATTEMPT AT IMITATING DAVID FOSTER WALLACE WOULD WIN?

WELL, IF IT WERE ANYONE ELSE...
MY NOVEL DIDN'T WIN FIRST PLACE.

IT WON THE EDITORS' CHOICE AWARD.
WOMP

THEY TOLD ME THAT I HAD ENOUGH VOTES FROM THE JUDGES TO WIN FIRST PLACE...
So you did win an award?!
BUT THEY COULDN'T GIVE IT TO ME BECAUSE OF MY AGE...

OH, I GET IT!

DID NOT WINNING HURT YOU...?
NO, I DIDN'T CARE ABOUT THAT.
HUH?

!
I BOUGHT THAT VOLUME BECAUSE THEY'D BEEN SERIALIZING **GRAVITY'S RAINBOW.**
AHAHA
BUT ONCE I GOT IT HOME AND OPENED IT, I SAW SOMETHING TERRIBLE... THEY CANCELLED PYNCHONFEST...
AND...
NOTICE ABOUT THIS NOVEL

THE MAGAZINE RAN MY NOVEL INSTEAD!
SPECIAL FEATURE
EDITORS' CHOICE FOR NEW WRITER'S AWARD
"SCARF"
by Mikasa Ackerman
WHAAAA?!
AMAZING !!
Head of Selection Committee

IT WAS SUCH A SHOCK THAT I WOULDN'T GET TO FINISH READING...
...AND THAT MY NOVEL WOULD BE PUBLISHED INSTEAD...

OH, IT'S SO EMBARRASSING...
PLEASE, GUYS... DON'T TELL ANYONE!!
FLUSH
UM, SURE, BUT...
YOU'VE GOT SOME WEIRD STANDARDS.

...
...
DAD?!
BAM
BAM
NGH?
OH, SORRY.
RATTLE
I WAS ASLEEP...
WAKE UP ALREADY!!

BUT I CAN GUESS.
IT WAS ANOTHER ONE OF MIKASA'S SELF-DEPRECATING HUMBLE-BRAGS, HUH?
Come on.
I MEAN, YEAH, BUT YOU SHOULD'VE BEEN LISTENING!
IT WON'T HELP, EREN.
MY METER'S PRACTICALLY RUNNING ON FUMES RIGHT NOW...
SHAME
BEEP
BEEP
WHY?! YOU SHOULD BE EMBARRASSED ABOUT SLEEPING!!

KIDS... PLEASE G HOME FO TODAY...
I DON'T THINK THERE'S ANY WAY THAT I CAN OPEN THIS DOOR...
WHAT ?!
YOU MEAN WE EMBARRASSED OURSELVES FOR NOTHING?!

I'M SORRY GUYS, IT'S ALL MY FAULT...
NO, IT'S NOT YOUR FAULT, MIKASA! IT'S ALL BECAUSE OF THAT MIDDLE-AGED FREAK IN THERE!
THAT'S RIGHT.
BAM
PLEASE, DAD, OPEN UP!!
ISN'T IT MORE EMBARRASSING TO TURN EVERYONE AWAY LIKE THIS?!
E-EREN ...
BAM
BAM

THAT MIGHT BE TRUE, BUT I CAN'T BEAR TO HAVE YOU SEE THIS ROOM...!!
BECAUSE... BECAUSE...
HONEY !!
EREN!
KIDS!!

WOULDN'T YOU LIKE TO HAVE SOME DINNER BEFORE YOU GO?!

MOM!

CARLA...!!

HEY MOM, CAN'T YOU HELP US CHANGE HIS MIND?
DAD WON'T COME OUT OF THE BASEMENT!
OH?

SWEETIE, WHAT ARE YOU DOING?
EVERYONE IS WAITING FOR YOU.
YEAH... WELL...

IF YOU DON'T COME OUT OF THERE, I'M GOING TO CALL THE LOCKSMITH TO OPEN THIS DOOR!!

N-NO, DON'T DO THAT!!

I CAN'T HAVE ANYONE SEE THIS ROOM...!!

HUH?!

WHAT IS THIS ALL ABOUT?! THIS HOME BELONGS TO THE WHOLE FAMILY, BUT YOU BUILT A ROOM THAT YOU CAN'T SHOW ANYONE ELSE...?

YOU KNOW "MAN CAVES" ARE FOR PATHETIC, INSECURE, OVER-GROWN BABIES!!

IT'S NOT THAT...

THEN WHAT?!

OPEN THIS DOOR, RIGHT NOW!!

OR I'LL KNOCK IT DOWN, COME IN WITH THIS SPOON, AND START GOUGING!!

P-PLEASE, CARLA, WE CAN WORK THIS OUT LATER!

CAN'T YOU SEE THAT I'M SUF-FERING, TOO?!

YOUR FAMILY IS OUT HERE, GRISHA!

THE DINNER I MADE WILL GET COLD BECAUSE OF YOU!!

IF YOU DON'T OPEN UP BEFORE I COUNT TO TEN...

I'M FILING FOR DIVORCE !!

BOOOM

SHOCK

WHAAAAM

ANY-THING BUT THAAAT!

PANT PANT
GASP

A-AMAZING... SHE GOT HIM TO OPEN THE DOOR!!
WHAT WAS ALL OUR HARD WORK FOR?!

NOW LET ME IN THERE.
C-CARLA, WAIT!
I'M STILL NOT READY...
LUNGE
WILL YOU STOP IT?!
WHAT ARE YOU HIDING?

H-
HONEY ...
THIS...

WHAT IS IT?!
DASH

TH...
THIS IS...

C-CARLA.
I CAN EX-PLAIN ...
HONEY, YOU ALWAYS HAVE BEEN...
...A REALLY STRANGE MAN...
I NEVER KNEW...

...THAT YOU GOT OUR WEDDING PORTRAIT FRAMED!!

OH, HOW EMBARRASSING...!!

EEEEK

I HAD IT MADE IN SECRET... BUT I WAS TOO EMBARRASSED TO TELL YOU...
LET ALONE SHOW SOMEONE ELSE...
FIDGET
FIDGET
FIDGET
I SEE. WE CAN'T SHOW THE NEIGHBORS.
SPECIALLY OT IF YOU FRAMED THAT OTHER PHOTO, TOO.

SO THIS WAS WHAT YOU WERE ALL THIS TIME?
OF COURSE...
IT'S A MEMORY OF A VERY IMPORTANT DAY.
I'm sorry for saying I'd divorce you..
I'm sorry, too.
LOVEY
DOVEY

G- GUYS...
NO NEED TO LOOK SO DOWN!!
Although I know how you feel!

THAT'S RIGHT, YOU GUYS! LET'S GRAB TH FILES ON THE TITANS AND GE OUT OF HERE!!
SEE HOW STRONG EREN IS...?
IT'S 100 TIMES HARDER ON ME...
...TO SEE MY PARENTS ACTING SO GROSS!
E- EREN ...

SHOOT! THIS IS AL BECAUSE OF THOSE TITANS.....

THEY'LL NEVER GET AWAY WITH THIS!!

AHA HA はは

ふ HA ふ HA ふ HA

BUUUURN

AND SO EREN AND THE GANG STEELED THEIR RESOLVE TO DEFEAT THE TITANS...

...AND ALSO ENTERED A REBEL-LIOUS PHASE.

EREN, WHY ARE YOU DRESSED LIKE THAT?!

SHUT UP, MOMMY—

I MEAN, OLD LADY!

ATTACK on TITAN
JUNIOR HIGH

LET'S GET TO THE CHAMPIONSHIP

THUMP

THUMP

THUMP

THUMP

THUMP

SEVENTY-FIFTH PERIOD: WANNA BE A SEMPAI

WELL?!

NOTHING OVER HERE!!

SEARCH IN PROGR— OH!

ITEMS FOUND !!

A HAND-KERCHIEF OF A TITAN RUGBY TEAM MEMBER!!

I FOUND... LARGE UNDER-WEAR!!

FLAP

Survey Club
WOAH !!
AMAZING!! YOU STOLE THE INTIMATE BELONGINGS OF THAT FIERCE TITAN RUGBY CLUB?!
HMPH
WE KNEW YOU'VE ALWAYS WANTED THEM, HANGE.
I SURE DID, BUT THEY WERE SO HARD TO GET MY HANDS ON.
THEY TACKLE YOU IF THEY CATCH YOU! WITH NO HELMETS!
YOU GUYS ARE AMAZ-ING!!
HEH HEH HEH
WE WERE JUST DOING OUR JOBS FOR THE SURVEY CLUB!!
WE'LL BE THIRD-YEARS SOON... WE WANT TO ACT ACCORD-INGLY...
EMPAI !!
WE BROUGHT SOME-THING, TOO!
OH, WHAT IS IT?
RESEARCH FILES ON THE TITANS FROM MY HOUSE!!
TADAAAA
WOAAAAH!!

CROWD CROWD
THIS IS AMAAAZ-ING!!
CROWD
LOOK AT ALL THAT...!
NOT BAD AT ALL...
HEY, WAIT...!

ALL OF THIS WAS SITTING AT YOUR HOUSE, EREN?
WOOOOOO
うひょ
IT'S WHAT MY DAD'S BEEN UP TO INSTEAD OF RAISING ME!
SHIRYO

ALSO... ALTHOUGH WE HAVEN'T READ ALL OF IT YET...
What?
WE LISTED THE THINGS THAT WE THOUGHT WERE IMPORTANT IN WHAT WE'VE READ SO FAR.
File
AH.
WAIT A...

THIS IS SOMETHING ELSE, EREN... SO MANY FILES...
NO, MY DAD WAS THE ONE WHO DID ALL THE RESEARCH ...
I DIDN'T REALLY DO ANY-THING!
OH, YEAH.
I MEAN, YOU OULDN'T HAVE ONE ALL THIS.
YOU BROUGHT MORE QUANTITY, YES.
BUT WHAT'S IMPORTANT IS QUALITY!
AFTER ALL, WE BROUGHT THINGS FROM THE RUGBY CLUB...
FIRST YEARS, THIS IS WONDER-FUL!!
INCREDIBLE... THESE DISCOVERIES WILL GO DOWN IN THE HISTORY OF THE SURVEY CLUB... NO, OF HUMANITY ITSELF!!
YOU DID WELL, FIRST YEARS!
THANKS, DAD! I MEAN, UH, MR. SMITH!
YAAAAY!

REALLY? EREN, I'M SURPRISED! YOU CAN READ?!
OH, WE'LL GO THROUGH THE REST OF THE FILES, SIR!
HOW DO YOU KNOW THEY'RE ALL SO MARVEL-OUS?!
YOU'VE ONLY READ A SMALL PART OF THOSE FILES, RIGHT?!
He's right!
HOLD ON A SEC-OND!!
H-

I'M SURE OUR SEMPAI ARE ALL BUSY WITH OTHER SURVEY ACTIVITY!!
SPARKLE
SPARKLE
WE HAVE TO SUPPORT YOU BY TAKING CARE OF THE BUSY WORK!!
STAB
STAB
HNNG

FIRST-YEARS ...!!
YOU'RE THE PRIDE OF THE SURVEY CLUB!!
Super amazing!
I learned to read from a book with a frog on it!

ARE WE...
...GOING TO BE ENTIRELY FORGOT-TEN?

OUR KOUHAI BEAT US TO A BIG SCOOP...
あははははは
AHA HA HA HA HA
...
NEITHER OUR SEMPAI NOR OUR TEACHERS ARE PAYING ANY ATTEN-TION TO US...

WHEN WE BECOME THIRD-YEARS...
...HOW WILL WE CONTRIB-UTE TO THE SURVEY CLUB?

SECOND-YEARS, OVER HERE!
Y-
YES, SIR!

WE'RE GOING ON A SURVEY EXPEDITION TO THE TITAN FOREST!!
HIKTCH
N-NOW?!
I'M GOING TO GIVE YOU YOUR ASSIGNMENTS!

THE THIRD YEARS ARE TO PREPARE AND HEAD OUT ON THE EXPEDITION!
YESSIR!

THE SECOND-YEARS WILL JOIN THE FIRST YEARS TO STUDY THE FILES!
OH!
UH, Y-YESSIR!
WE'RE NOT GOING ON THE SURVEY?!
DOES IT MEAN... THAT THEY DON'T TRUST US...?!
S-SIR?
HEY.

I DON'T NEED THESE TWO.

I'LL TAKE THE SECOND-YEARS INSTEAD.

M—
MR. LEVI?!

WHAT? WHY, LEVI?
You don't like me?
No, I don't.
THEY'LL BE THIRD-YEARS SOON.

I THINK IT'S TIME WE GAVE THEM THE EXPERIENCE COMMENSURATE WITH THAT.
AND I THINK THEY HAVE THE ABILITY TO HANDLE IT...

AT LEAST, THEY'RE RECKLESS ENOUGH TO STEAL RUGBY EQUIPMENT.
...PROBABLY.

I SEE... YOU WANT TO USE THIS OPPORTUNITY TO TEST THEIR METTLE.
SOUNDS GOOD! GO GET 'EM, GUYS!

ARE YOU UP TO IT, SECOND-YEARS?
S... SIR,
YES SIR!!
WE'RE NOT HOPELESS...!

TITAN FOREST
WE'RE GETTING STRONGER...!
KTCH...!

EVERYONE, MIND YOUR SURROUND-INGS AND ADVANCE!
YESSIR!
THERE'S NO MISTAKING THAT!

THOMP
AFTER ALL...
THOMP
THOMP
THOMP

...MR. LEVI SAYS SO!
うAHA はHA はHA はHA はHA はHA は
ARE YOU GUYS, UH... NORMAL?

MR. LEVI THINKS WE CAN HANDLE ANYTHING!
Hey.
HE'S THE FIRST AUTHORITY FIGURE TO VALIDATE ME SINCE MISTER ROGERS!
Ok, so let's—
HEH... YOU'RE SOFT.
THAT'S ENOUGH TO SATISFY YOU?
HUH?
NOT ME! I WON'T REST ON MY LAURELS, OR MY TITAN UNDERPANTS!
BAM
I'M GOING TO SCORE BIG IN THIS EXPEDITION AND TAKE MR. LEVI'S OFFICIAL POSITION IN THE NEXT THIRD-YEAR CLASS!!
WHAAT ?!
MR. LEVI'S OFFICIAL POSITION...
HOT SHIT
KING OF THE SUCK-UPS
UNDERLINGS
SMALL FRY
EVERYONE ELSE
YOU MEAN "HOT SHIT" ?!
BUT I WANT TO BE HOT SHIT, TOO!!
ME, TOO!
ME, TOO!
HEY
HUH? YOU GUYS AREN'T WORTHY OF THE NAME!!

I'M THE ONLY—
HNGG
SMAAACK

WANT ME TO LEAVE YOU HERE?
S-SORRY, SIR.

OH, WHAT ARE WE AFTER IN THIS EXPEDITION, ANYWAY?
OUR GOAL IS TO USE THESE FILES...
...TO FIND SPECIFIC TITANS.

GO LOOKING FOR TITANS?!
THESE ONES.
WHAT KIND OF TITANS...
Let's see
HUH?
THESE ARE...
BOOM...

TADAAAAAAA

HERE THEY ARE !!

WE CAN'T GO BACK UNTIL WE CONFIRM THAT THEY'RE THE SAME TITANS DESCRIBED IN THESE FILES.
SAME AS WHAT...?

THE TITANS THAT HAVE BEEN AT THIS SCHOOL FOR OVER 30 YEARS.
THIRTY
じゅう
WHAT?!
さし

HOW MANY TIMES HAVE THEY FLUNKED HISTORY?!
HNNNG
AND HOW DO WE TELL?! ALL TITANS LOOK THE SAME TO ME!
WE NAME THEM BASED ON THEIR TERRIFYING TRAITS.
FLIP...

DADAAAA
THE BAMBOO HELI-COPTER TITAN!!
TEDEEE
THE CUP AND BALL TITAN!!
THERE'S THE SPINNING TOP TITAN!!
TADAAA
DATAAAA
RATTLE RATTLE RATTLE
THE GOOD-AT-GUESSING-THE-TOY-IN-THE-CRACKER-SNACK TITAN!!
GASP
THE MUD BALL TITAN!!
DEEDEEEE

THAT'S NOT TER-RIFYING AT ALL!!
TADAAAA
THEY ALL LIKE TO PLAY REALLY OLD GAMES!!

BUT IT MAKES SENSE, IF THESE TITANS REALLY HAVE BEEN HERE FOR OVER 30 YEARS.

OH, RIGHT.

AND ALL OF THEM ARE WORLD-CLASS EXPERTS AT THEIR FAVORITE GAMES.

HUH?

IN OTHER WORDS, OUR MISSION WILL BE COMPLETE ONLY AFTER WE VERIFY THEIR MASTERY OF THEIR GAMES.

SQUEEZE SQUEEZE

DO YOU UNDERSTAND WHAT THAT MEANS?

TWIRL TWIRL

VERIFY THEIR MASTERY...
THAT MEANS WE HAVE TO FACE OFF AGAINST THEM AT THESE LAME GRANDMA GAMES!

I'M NOT SURE IF I'M DOING THE RIGHT THING, PITTING YOU AGAINST THESE MON-STERS...

BEAT THEM.
I THINK YOU'RE READY FOR THAT.
YES, SIR!
HEY! HOW ABOUT THE ONE THAT WINS AGAINST THESE TITANS THE MOST GETS TO BE THE NEXT HOT SHIT?!
OH, THAT'S A GOOD IDEA!
I'M IN!
DASH!!
HEY WAIT, YOU CAN'T JUST CHANGE THE HOT SHIT RULES!
WOAH!
Y- YOU'RE ...
HEH...
THE CUP AND BALL CHAMP!!

THIS LOOKS LIKE...
KTCH
...A JOB FOR ME.
HUH?!
HEY, YOU CAN'T TAKE ALL THE GLORY...
HEH... WHAT A NASTY THING TO SAY.
RUSTLE RUSTLE
ごそごそ
BOOM
I ONLY MEANT THAT THIS IS A JOB FOR SOMEONE WITH THE PROPER SKILL.
I HAVE A QUADRUPLE ROSÉ BELT IN CUP AND BALL.
Oluo

OLUO...! I NEVER KNEW THAT...!
WHAAAT?!
なにー!!?
SHOOT! HE'S GOT THE LEAD IN THE HOT SHIT RACE NOW!

ARE YOU SURE ABOUT THIS, LEVI?
YES.
THEY HAVE WHAT IT TAKES.

I KNOW, BECAUSE I'VE WATCHED THEM ALL THIS TIME.
FSH
FSH
FSH
FSH
FSH
FSH
FSH

HEY... DON'T TELL ME THAT'S ALL YOU'VE GOT.

TAKE THIS...

TWIRL-ING FANCY BALLS!!

WATATATATATATATATATATA

HE'S... REALLY AMAZ-ING!

LOOK! THE TITAN'S OVER-WHELMED, TOO...

WOAH

SMAAACK

RUMBLE
RUMBLE
WILL THE SECOND YEARS SURVIVE THEIR TITAN ENCOUN-TER...?
OR WILL LEVI KILL THEM FIRST?
OHHHHHHHHHH
RUMBLE
RUMBLE
THAT WAS JUST... A PRACTICE ROUND... RIGHT...?
OLUO ...
GASP I-I'M SORRY, SIR!!
KTCH

MY LUNCH
D-DAMN TITANS...
WHAT DID WE DO TO DESERVE THIS...?!
I BIT MY TONGUE!!
I HAD NO IDEA THAT JUNIOR HIGH WOULD BE LIKE THIS...
WAAAAAH
うわあああん
DAMN IT, I WANT MY MAN-WICH!
HEY.
KTCH
KEEP IT DOWN.
CRYING WON'T BRING YOUR LUNCH BACK.

W-WHO DO YOU THINK YOU ARE?
AND ALSO, WHO ACTUALLY ARE YOU?
LOOK, BE-TWEEN YOU AND THE TITANS, I'VE BIT MY TONGUE AGAIN!
WHO CARES?
HUH?!
KTCH
LEAP
SMAAACK

TH-
THANK YOU!!

UM... SO... WHO ARE YOU...?

LISTEN TO ME.

CRYING WON'T CHANGE ANYTHING.

IT'LL JUST MAKE YOU HUNGRIER.

IF YOU TRULY WANT YOUR MAN-WICH...

...BECOME STRONGER.

SEVENTY-SIXTH PERIOD: WORKING TOGETHER

"WE WANT TO BE AS STRONG AS YOU, STRANG-ER..."
"HOW... HOW DO WE BECOME STRONGER?"
CHILL...

"WE WANT TO BEAT THE TITANS WITH OUR OWN HANDS!!"
SHAKE SHAKE
PANT
PANT PANT

SO HOW ABOUT IT, SECOND-YEARS...?
HOW STRONG DID YOU GET...?

CHOKE...
WHEEZE
WHEEZE
WHEEZE
BLEED BLEED

WHEEZE
BOOM
ALL OF US...
GOT THRASHED ...!
WHEEZE
WHEEZE
PANT

SORRY..
PANT
WE'RE REALLY GOOD AT CATAN...
MAYBE IF WE PLAYED THAT WITH THEM...?
PANT

...
What's the point of that?
OUT OF MY WAY.
HUH? WAIT! MR. LEVI!
ARE YOU TAKING ON THE TITANS?!
KTCH
PLEASE DON'T!!
FACING FOUR TITANS BY YOURSELF...? IT'S—

BOOM
KABOOM
SHOOM
BAANG

HE DIDN'T BREAK A SWEAT.

WE'RE SO SORRY, MR. LEVI!!

YOU GAVE US AN OPPORTUNITY TO PROVE OUR WORTH, AND WE FAILED...
PLEASE GIVE US ONE MORE CHANCE!!
HUH?

THAT ONE!!

PLEASE LET US FACE THE MUD BALL EXPERT!!

BOOM

I USED TO MAKE MUD BALLS WHEN I WAS IN PRESCHOOL!
ME, TOO!
ME ME MEE
I... DIDN'T! BOYS ARE GROSS!
I DIDN'T, EITHER, BUT MY CONFI-DENCE WILL OVERCOME MY LACK OF SKILL AND EXPERIENCE!

PLEASE APPOINT WHOEVER BEATS THAT TITAN AS THE NEXT SURVEY CLUB HOT SHIT!
PLEASE !!

NO.

YOU CAN'T BEAT THAT ONE.

H-HOW CAN WE KNOW UNTIL WE TRY?!
YES, WE LOST TO THE OTHERS, BUT...
I'VE SEEN ENOUGH.

THAT TITAN IS THE STRONGEST OF THE FIVE.
!!

THEN YOU MEAN...
WE STILL AREN'T STRONG ENOUGH...?

THAT'S RIGHT.
TO BE HONEST, I WAS DISAPPOINTED IN YOUR ABILITIES.
N-NO...!!

STILL...
SNIFFLE...
I'LL BE GONE FROM THIS PLACE SOON.
BUT YOU'LL STILL BE HERE.

SO GET BACK SAFELY.

AND GROW STRONGER FOR THE FUTURE.

MR. LEVI!!

DASH

WE LET MR. LEVI DOWN...
SOB...
WHEN HE WAS THE ONE WHO SAW THE MOST IN US...!
ALL ALONG, I WAS RIGHT TO HATE MYSELF...!
HOW DO WE GET STRONGER...?!
HOW... CAN WE BE LIKE MR. LEVI...?
THUD
WHEEZE...
WAIT, MR. LEVI?!
WHAT HAPPENED? I WAS TOO BUSY PITYING MYSELF TO LOOK!
WASN'T ANYONE WATCHING? GOD, WE'RE PATHETIC!
THE TITAN DIDN'T DO ANY-THING.
HUH?!
LOOK AT LEVI'S FEET.

HE WORE H
FRESHLY-
CLEANED
WHITE
SNEAKERS
TODAY!
SUPERFLY!!
...PSYCHO-
LOGICALLY,
HE MAY
NEVER BE
THE SAME
AGAIN!!
BUT NOW
THEY'VE
GOT MUD
ALL OVER
THEM...
WHAAAT?!
I NEVER KNEW MR. LEVI HAD SUCH A WEAK-NESS...!
HIS HYGIENE HAS A HUGE EFFECT ON HIS HP...
AT THIS RATE ...
WE HAVE TO HELP HIM!!
RIGHT !!
DASH
STOP !!

IF YOU COME ANY CLOSER ...
STAGGER...
...I'LL SMACK YOU A HUNDRED TIMES EACH...!
BUT...
MR. LEVI...!
GLARE
SHOOM
SHOOM
SHOOM
SHOOM SHOOM
SHOOM
SHOOM
WHACK
WHACK
FLICK
WHACK
WHACK
FLICK
SOME OF THEM ARE GETTING THROUGH ...!
USUALLY, E'D HANDLE THAT ATTACK EASILY...!

WHACK
WHACK
UGH!
DASH
I-I HAVE TO GO--
I TOLD YOU TO STAY THERE!!
B-BUT--
JUST STAY BACK.
YOU WON'T BE SAFE...
STANDING THERE...
HOW DO YOU BECOME STRONG?

I DON'T KNOW.
WHAT!!
WE JOINED THE SURVEY CLUB, TOO. PLEASE TEACH US!
HUH?
FWIP
ROAAAR
IT'S A HUGE BALL!!

SMACK
EEEEK!!
TWINKLE
HEY.
OH, SORRY--
WE TRIED TO RUN AWAY AGAIN--

THAT'S RIGHT...
MR. LEVI!...

...
ARE YOU ALL RIGHT?

IS INCREDIBLY STRONG WHEN HE FIGHTS TO PROTECT US.
COME ON.

FALL

FLING

STEP
NOW IT'S OUR TURN...
...TO PROTECT MR. LEVI!!
WHAT?!
THWACK
HNNG
ARE YOU ALL RIGHT?!
HEH... WHAT A DUMB QUESTION... DID YOU THINK AN ATTACK LIKE THIS WOULD BOTHER—
HE'S FINE!
HEY...
DRIP
DRIP
UNGE
L-LOOK OUT!!
SHOVE

SLIDE
WOAH!
JUST IN TIME!!
THUD

YOU ALMOST GOT MR. LEVI DIRTY AGAIN!
SORRY, SORRY.
I'M, UH, MOVED ...
GUYS! I FINISHED THE MUD BALLS!!
TADAAAA
WE CAN USE THESE AS WEAPONS, RIGHT?!
OH, GREA—
THEY'RE A TOTAL MESS!!

WHAT?! I PUT A LOT OF WORK INTO THESE!
YEAH, ABOUT AS MUCH AS YOUR HALLOWEEN COSTUME LAST YEAR!
Yeah, a "ghost," real original!
HEY.

CAN'T YOU JUST DO AS I SAY?
Ahaha...

MR. LEVI...

WE'RE SORRY TO WORRY YOU ALL THE TIME.

HUH?

BUT WE'RE OKAY NOW.

WE AREN'T STRONG NOW...

...BUT I THINK WE KNOW NOW HOW TO BECOME STRONG.

CATCH

HEY, IT'S YOUR WHAPPIN' FAN...!

LISTEN TO ME... BY YOURSELVES EACH OF YO IS LIKE A LLAMA IN AN ICE DANCINC CONTEST.

BUT THE FOUR OF YOU TOGETHER AREN'T AS BAD.

Why did I get a rag...?

SO FIGHT TOGETHER.

WE WON!!

HEH...

ALL RIGHT. ALL OF YOU.
HEAD BACK AND TAKE A BATH.
YES, SIR!
AND SO THE FOUR OF THEM DISCOVERED THAT, WHEN THEY WORK TOGETHER...
...THEY'RE NOT QUITE AS USELESS AND PATHETIC. SOMETIMES.
WE'RE BACK!

THE FOUR OF YOU BEAT A TITAN...
WOAH
うおお
...THAT NOT EVEN MR. LEVI COULD BEAT?!

THAT'S RIGHT
AND YOU GOT THESE SMACKING FANS FROM HIM?!
THAT'S RIGHT.
AWE-SOME!!
THAT'S AMAZ-ING!!
WELL, TODAY'S BATTLE WAS REALLY TOUGH...
SUPER AWESOME SCARY AWESOME I ALSO WANT ONE OF THOSE FANS AWESOME JEALOUS AWESOME
SHUT UP!!
スパーン
SMACK
WELCOME BACK.
WE ALSO MADE PROG-RESS GOING THROUGH THE FILES!

AND WE FOUND OU SOMETHIN PRETTY AMAZING...
OH, WHO ARE WE GOING TO MAKE THE NEXT HOT SHIT?
WE NEVER DID DECIDE, DID WE?
DO YOU WANT TO JUST DRAW STRAWS?!
YEAH, THAT SOUNDS GOOD!
IT'LL KEEP US FROM FIGHTING OVER IT!
TADAA
バーン

WHAT ?!
ARE YOU SERI-OUS?!
YES... BASED ON THE TITANS IN THE FOREST, AND WHAT WE LEARNED HERE...
THE TITANS ARE REALLY—
YEAAAA

部長
I'M GOING TO BE THE NEXT HOT SHIT!!
TADAAAAAA

WHY DID YOU DRAW A STRAW?!
Heh heh...
THERE WERE LOTS OF THEM...
THE TITANS ARE REALLY WHAT?
TO BE CONTINUED !!

ONE, TWO, THREE! GOOD! THE NUMBERS MATCH UP!
MY HYPOTH-ESIS WAS CORRECT!

WHAT SHOULD WE DO WITH THEM?!
YOU CAN LET THEM GO...
SLAUGHTER THEM, YOU SAID?!
NO.
BUT TO THINK THAT WE WOULD FIGURE THIS OUT IN MY LIFETIME...
PANT
PANT
OOOOOHHHH I'M SO GLAD I WAS BORN!!
UH... UM...
PANT
PANT
PANT
PANT

WHAT DID YOU FIND OUT?!
I WANT TO KNOW, TOO...
GRAB
PANT
PANT
PANT
PANT
STICKY
WOAAHHHHH!

SURVEY CLUB
SO...
YOU'RE SURE THAT'S WHAT THE TITANS ARE?
NO MISTAKING IT. WE CAPTURED TITANS AND CHECKED.
SLOBBERRRRR
AND HERE'S THE PROOF !!
STAY AWAY FROM ME.

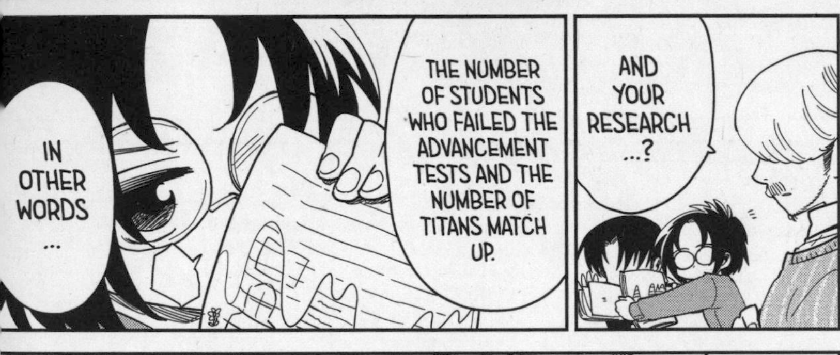

AND YOUR RESEARCH ...?
THE NUMBER OF STUDENTS WHO FAILED THE ADVANCEMENT TESTS AND THE NUMBER OF TITANS MATCH UP.
IN OTHER WORDS ...

TITANS USED TO BE HUMAN STUDENTS.
STUDENTS WHO GOT HELD BACK!!

SEVENTY-SEVENTH PERIOD: GOODBYES FOR THE FIRST-YEARS

SLAM
WHAT'S THE MEANING OF THIS?!
Assistant Principal's Office

SO YOU FINALLY FIGURED IT OUT...
HEH...
SO YOU DID KNOW ALL ALONG...

WHY DO THE STUDENTS WHO FAIL THE ADVANCE-MENT TESTS TURN INTO TITANS?!
HMM... I GUESS YOU DON'T KNOW EVERYTHING.
TO TELL YOU THE TRUTH...
I DON'T KNOW WHY, EITHER...
HEH...
HUH?

LIKE I SAID, WE DON'T ANT TO MAKE ANY MORE TITANS.
NO NEED TO GET SO TESTY.
SHEESH.
THINK ABOUT IT. IT WOULD BE ONE THING IF THEY TURNED INTO INCREDIBLY GORGEOUS WOMEN.
BUT WHY ON EARTH WOULD WE WANT TO TURN STUDENTS INTO TITANS?
I WISH THEY DID TURN INTO INCREDIBLY GORGEOUS WOMEN. I'D ENJOY COMING TO WORK EVERYDAY...
YOU KNOW I HAVE HR ON SPEED DIAL.
SO THE ADVANCEMENT TESTS ARE NOW LAUGH-OUT-LOUD EASY.
ANY FOOL CAN PASS!
PFFT
What is this?
THE FACT THAT NOT A SINGLE STUDENT HAS FAILED THE EXAM IN THIRTY YEARS IS PROOF ENOUGH.
HAHAHAHAHA
YOU'D HAVE TO BE AMAZINGLY UNLUCKY...
...OR A TITAN-LOVING WEIRDO TO FAIL.
AMAZINGLY UNLUCKY...
R A TITAN-LOVING WEIRDO...

Advancement Tests for First-Year Students
CLAMOR
CLAMOR
...OH NO...

LISTEN UP! YOU'LL NOW ENTER THESE PORT-A-POT-TY-LOOKING THINGS TO TAKE YOUR ADVANCEMENT TESTS!
THEY'RE MEANT TO PREVENT CHEATING!

WE'LL BE COLLECTING YOUR ANSWER SHEETS AFTER THE TEST. YOU ARE NOT TO TAKE THEM HOME UNDER ANY—
I HEAR THE ADVANCE-MENT TEST IS REALLY EASY.
CLAMOR
YEAH, I HEARD CONNIE BRAG HE GOT A PER-FECT 115% ON THE PRACTICE TEST.
CLAMOR
CLAMOR
SQUEEEEE
THAT MEANS YOU'LL PASS FOR SURE, FRANZ!
AND WE'LL BE TOGETH-ER HAPPILY EVER AFTER... OR UNTIL COLLEGE.

SQUEEEE"
Y BUTT...

GROAN... WE'LL TURN INTO TITANS IF WE FAIL...
OUR FACES WILL BE WEIRDLY REALISTICALLY DRAWN...!!
AND WE'LL BE NAKED, WITH NO LITTLE FELLA...
Y-YOU'RE ALL THINKING ABOUT IT TOO MUCH!
RELAX RELAX!!
IF EVEN CONNIE CAN PASS, THEN...
...WE'LL ALL PASS! UNLESS YOU'RE INCREDIBLY UNLUCKY!

UNLUCKY ENOUGH TO FORGET TO WRITE YOUR NAME ON THE ANSWER SHEET...?
AAAAAUGH!!

HOLD ME, BERTOLT! I'M SCARED!!
AAAAAUGH!!
SNAP

GLARE
QUIET OVER THERE!!
AAAAAUGH!!

DIIIING
EREN...
MM?

PASS...
!!

THIS IS...!
IT'S A CHEAT SHEET!!
SHHH! THE TEACHERS WILL HEAR, IDIOT.

I CAN'T TAKE THIS!!
DO YOU UNDERSTAND WHAT YOU'RE SAYING?!
SO, YOU THINK I WOULDN'T PASS IF I DIDN'T USE THAT?!
UH, I MEAN... YEAH?

PLUS, WHAT IF SOMETHING GOES WRONG ...
SO YOU'RE TELLING ME THAT I MIGHT BE DUMBER THAN CONNIE ?!
I'LL NEVER, EVER TURN INTO A TITAN,
YOU HEAR ME?!
GRAB

HNG

SLAM

GWONGH

EREN!!

EVERYONE TO YOUR STALLS!!

THE TEST WILL BEGIN SHORTLY!!

I WAS WRONG...
KTUNK...

WHOEVER'S LISTENING... GOD, BUDDHA, ALLAH, KRISHNA, ALEXA, SIRI, THE NSA...
TEST QUESTIONS
Don't open this until we tell you, you little monsters!

See what it says?! Keep you hands off the box until I say!

PLEASE, HEAR MY PRAYER...

FIFTEEN SECONDS

...TEN... NINE...

DON'T LET HIM FAIL...

...THREE... TWO... ONE...

START!!

FLING

TADAAA

ORIGAMI FOR KIDS

DOES EREN...
HMMM
うーん
KNOW HOW TO FOLD PAPER...?

NO, STOP... IN THE EVENT OF AN EMERGENCY, PUT YOUR OWN MASK ON BEFORE HELPING OTHERS.
WHAT'S THE QUESTION?

TEST QUESTION

THE QUESTION THAT WILL DECIDE MY WHOLE LIFE...!!

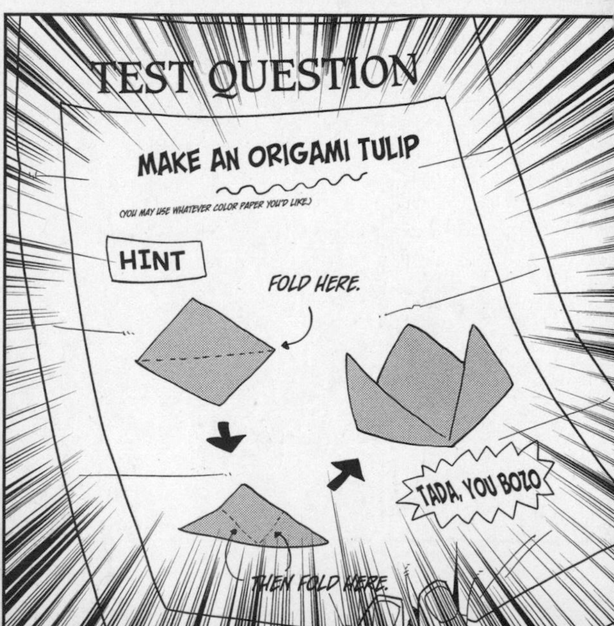

TEST QUESTION
MAKE AN ORIGAMI TULIP
(YOU MAY USE WHATEVER COLOR PAPER YOU'D LIKE.)
HINT
FOLD HERE.
THEN FOLD HERE.
TADA, YOU BOZO

Attack on short notes: Kids can make an origami tulip at about three years of age! Easy even for first-timers!! (Research by the editor)

IS THAT REALLY IT...? I'M FINISHED...?
IS THIS SCHOOL ACCREDITED...?
PENCILS DOWN!!
NO, WHAT I SHOULD REALLY BE WORRIED ABOUT NOW!..
...IS WHETHER **EREN** FINISHED...
KAKLAK...

MOOOOPE
GUYS...

SO EASY, RIGHT?!
SUPER EASY!!
I FEEL STUPID FOR GETTING NERVOUS!!
I LIKE FLOWERS!
UM...
WHAT ABOUT EREN...?
SEE?

YOU DIDN'T NEED TO WORRY ABOUT ME.
EREN!!

YOU DIDN'T GET FIFTY PAPER CUTS AND BLEED OUT?!
HUH?!
YOU DIDN'T STICK THE PAPER UP YOUR NOSE?!
HEY, I'M NOT A KID...
YOU DIDN'T MAKE A HAT AND SAY, "I'M EREN, THE PAPER HAT KING..."
LEAVE ME ALONE!!

YOU REALLY DID IT?

TSK...
IT WAS SO EASY THAT I FELL ASLEEP.
SNIFFLE...

AND SORRY ABOUT EARLIER.

I YELLED AT YOU WHEN YOU WERE JUST WORRIED ABOUT ME...

I-

IT'S FINE.

SHAKE ぶんぶん SHAKE

I WAS JUST THINKING OF YOU.

CON-GRATS, MIKASA!

LOOKS LIKE EREN WON'T TURN INTO A TITAN!

WHISTLE ピュ～ WHISTLE

IS EREN REALLY THAT DUMB? AND THIS IS ME ASKING.

AGGH JEAL-OUS!!

HUH?

L-LET'S GO BACK TO CLASS.

I'M JUST GLAD EVERY-ONE'S OKAY!

AHAHAHA あははは

I DIDN'T KNOW YOU COULD DO ORIGAMI!

OF COURSE I CAN!

SO, THEY GAVE US WAY TOO MUCH TIME FOR THE EXAM, RIGHT?
WHAT DID YOU GUYS DO?
I...
...MADE ORIGAMI THROWING STARS.
THE PAPER TASTED LIKE PURPLE.
EW.
CRUNCH CRUNCH
WHAT? IT TOOK ME THE ENTIRE TIME.
I SLEPT UNTIL THE END...
YAWN... ふぁ...
RUSTLE

IT CAN'T BE—

STOMP STOMP STOMP STOMP STOMP STOMP

UH, THERE'S BEEN A... I FORGOT TO... ER...

DASH

HERE'S MY TULIP!!

SO YOU'RE THE REASON THAT WE WERE ONE SHORT...

BUT YOU'RE TOO LATE.

HUH?!

WE'VE ALREADY FINISHED COLLECTING THE ANSWER SHEETS!!

WE CAN'T ACCEPT YOURS!!

WHA?!

EREN...

...IS GOING TO TURN INTO A TITAN...?!

SEVENTY-EIGHTH PERIOD: THE DANGEROUS MAN IN GLASSES

LAST PAGE, IN THIS BOOK YOU'RE READ-ING...
THE PROTAGONIST EREN FAILED HIS YEAR-END TEST, DOOMING HIM-SELF TO REPEAT HIS GRADE AND TURN INTO A TITAN!
WHAT WILL HAPPEN TO HIM NOW?!

YOU'RE... REALLY CALM...
HAHA, RIGHT?
I'M SUR-PRISED, TOO.

BUT WHY...?
I WAS THINKING...

I FAILED THE TEST, BUT I HAVEN'T TURNED INTO A TITAN!
IT MUST BE BECAUSE I HAVE SUCH GOOD KARMA!

...HUH?
IS THAT WHY YOU'RE SO RELAXED?
AHAHAHA
あっはっはっは
WELL, THINK ABOUT IT THIS WAY.
IF IT HASN'T HAPPENED YET, IT'S NOT GOING TO HAPPEN AT ALL!

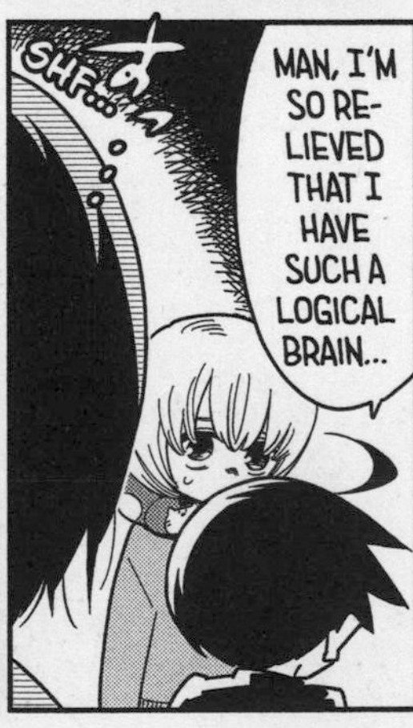
MAN, I'M SO RE-LIEVED THAT I HAVE SUCH A LOGICAL BRAIN...
SHF...

EREN, IT'S NOT FINE. IN THIS WORLD, NOTHING IS FINE.
HUH?

EVEN IF YOU DON'T TURN INTO A TITAN, YOU STILL FAILED THE TEST.

IN OTHER WORDS, YOU'LL REPEAT A YEAR OF JUNIOR HIGH...

ANOTHER YEAR OF NOT GETTING ALGEBRA
WEIRD TEENAGER BEARD WHEN NO ONE ELSE HAS HIT PUBERTY YET
CENTRAL IDAHO STATE UNIVERSITY
WORK AT THE HOG FACTORY
MEDICAL EXPERIMENTS AND HOT POCKETS FOREVER

AAAAU-UUUGH!!
SLAAAAM

WHY DID YOU HAVE TO SHAT-TER MY DELICATE FACADE OF LIES ...?!
COULDN'T YOU SEE THAT I WAS JUST BARELY KEEPING MYSELF TO-GETHER?!
WE HAVE TO DO SOME-THING...

I'M GOING TO MAKE THEM LET YOU REPEAT THE TEST!
DON'T WORRY, YOU WON'T HAVE TO LIVE IN A VAN AND BECOME A FREEGAN!

CAN YOU REALLY DO THAT...?!
I HAVE TO TRY ...!!

RIGHT ...
I'D PASS A RETEST FOR SURE ...!!

TITAN-FIGHTIN' TRIO ASSEMBLE! LET'S GO!
DASH
RIGHT!

WAIT, WHERE ARE WE GOING ?!
EREN, THIS WAY!
YAAANK

KLABLAM
HOW DARE YOU BARGE IN DURING MY PRIVATE GAZING TIME?
VICE PRINCIPAL ZACKLY!!
PLEASE LET ME TAKE THE ADVANCEMENT TEST AGAIN!
OH...
SO YOU'RE THE IDIOT WHO FAILED THAT TEST.
THAT WAS AN ACCI-DENT!!
PLEASE!
STEP...

HF!!
I DON'T NORMALLY LIKE PRO-TRACTORS, BUT I'M OUT OF TIME.
USING FORCE TO HAVE YOUR WAY...?
MIKASA !!
!
YOU KNEW ...?!
AH, YOU'RE WORRIED HE'LL TURN INTO A TITAN.
SO PLEASE !
I DON'T KNOW IF YOU KNOW...
...BUT NOW THAT EREN HAS FAILED THE ADVANCE-MENT TEST, SOMETHING TERRIBLE MIGHT HAPPEN TO HIM.

!
KA
OF COURSE.
TUG
MIKASA! YOU FELL IN A HOLE!!
UGH!
THUD
YES, HOW UNFORTUNATE FOR YOU.
TUG
THWACK
BUT IT'S YOUR OWN FAULT FOR FAILING.
I GOT INTO "EDUCATION" SO THAT I COULD TORTURE CHILDREN WITHOUT GOING TO FEDERAL PRISON.
HOW WOULD GIVING YOU A RETEST FIT IN WITH THAT?
GUH...
WH-WHAT IF WE GAVE YOU...
...SOME-THING YOU WANTED?
!

I'LL DO ANYTHING! PLEASE...
BOW
ANY-THING!!

HM. YOU'RE PER-SISTENT.
WHAT DO YOU SAY?!
IF... IF YOU'LL GIVE HIM A CHANCE ...

KNEEL...
THE SAME GOES FOR ME...!!

VICE PRINCI-PAL!
PLEASE LET ME RETAKE THE TEST!!
WHAM
PLEASE!!

Hmph...

YOU. THE DIVOT WHO COULDN'T FOLD ONE PIECE OF PAPER.
TELL ME YOUR NAME AND CLASS.

I'M EREN YEAGER, FIRST YEAR, CLASS FOUR.
YEAGER... WHAT IS YOUR BIGGEST WEAKNESS?
MY WEAKNESS? HMM... I CAN'T REALLY THINK OF ONE...
URMMMMMMM
EREN, ARE YOU FOR REAL RIGHT NOW?
WAS-SAT?

YOU START FIGHTS FASTER THAN AN ANGRY-DRUNK REALITY SHOW STAR.
YOU KEEP A "COOL GUYS" LIST AND I'M NOT ON IT.
WHAA?
YOU GET FUSSY IF YOU HAVEN'T HAD YOUR JUICE BOX.
WHEN WE PLAY UNO, YOU WON'T STOP FLICKING YOUR CARDS.
YOU CALLED YOUR MOM "POPE JERK IV" FOR A MONTH.
...
YOU BURP AND A LITTLE DROOL RUNS DOWN THE SIDE OF YOUR MOUTH.
YOU'RE NOT A NAZI BUT YOU ARE VAGUELY NAZI-ESQUE...
And...
ENOUGH! I'VE HEARD ENOUGH!

OKAY.
I'll put down "lots."
ONE MORE QUES-TION.
BWUUUH
TELL ME YOUR LEAST FAVOR-ITE...
TITANS!!

I'VE DEVOTED MY LIFE TO ERADICATING THEM, EVERY LAST ONE AND THAT'S WHY I-
OH GOD, MY EARS.

TUG
FOLLOW ME.
RUMBLE
AND DON'T MAKE THAT SCREECHING NOISE AGAIN.

YOU MEAN...?
I'VE DECIDED ON MY CONDITIONS FOR YOUR RETEST.
TH-THANK YOU, SIR!!
WELL...
DON'T THANK ME YET.
CHILL...
?

CHILL

IF YOU WANT A RE-TEST...

...SPEND A FULL DAY LIVING WITH THE TITANS IN THEIR FOREST.

THAT'S THE ONLY WAY I'LL GIVE YOU ANOTHER SHOT, TULIP BOY.

EREN!

THIS IS TOO CRUEL...
IT'S HARD ENOUGH FOR AN AVERAGE PERSON TO SPEND TIME WITH A TITAN...
EREN, MAYBE I CAN OFFER TO CUT OFF ONE OF MY FINGERS...
MIKASA--

WE ALREADY BEGGED ON OUR KNEES...
BESIDES, THERE'S NO GUARANTEE THAT CHANGING THE CONDITIONS WILL MAKE THINGS ANY BETTER ...
SO MIKASA...

HAVE FAITH IN ME!!
I'LL BE FINE, I PROMISE !!

EREN...

KTCH...
TITANS...
I'LL BE YOUR GUEST FOR A LITTLE WHILE.
LET'S GET ALONG, JUST FOR TODAY!!

EREN!!
HNG
GLORP
YOU STUPID TITAAAAANS
YEAH, THAT'S WHAT I EXPECTED...

HA... HAHA. I'M USED TO BEING COVERED IN SPIT...
TITANS... YOU JUST WAIT AND SEE...

SPLAT
ベちゃっ
EREN!!

I'M GONNA TURN INTO A TITAN...
!
...AND BEAT YOU ALL TO A PULP...!!

!!
GASP

WHAT DID I JUST SAY...?!
WHAT AM I TALKING ABOUT?! I CAN'T BECOME A TITAN! I'M THE MAIN CHARACTER!

THE SALIVA WAS MESSING WITH MY BRAIN...
HEY, EREN!
SHFF
IS IT TRUE YOU HAVE TO SPEND A WHOLE DAY HERE?
SOUNDS ROUGH, MAN!
HEY, IT'S THE OTHER, NOT-MAIN CHARACTERS!

Y-YES, YOU'RE RIGHT.

BECAUSE I FAILED THE TEST...

RIGHT, YOU'RE TURNING INTO A TITAN.

SO YOU CAME HERE FOR A PRACTICE RUN, HUH?

NO, SEE I'M NOT TURNING INTO A TITAN!

WE BROUGHT YOU SOME THINGS TO HELP!

LOOK!

GIANT TOOTH-PASTE TO PREVENT TITAN GUM DISEASE!

SMAAACK

NO, SEE...
WE BROUGHT YOU A BIG TOOTHPICK FOR THOSE HARD-TO-REACH MOUTH CAV-ERNS!

I'M...
U-UM, I WASN'T SURE WHAT TO GET YOU...
BUT I THOUGHT YOU'D NEED A PAIR OF UNDER-WEAR...

I'M NOT GONNA ...
THE OTHERS ARE BRINGING YOU SUCH LOUSY GIFTS.
WE SPLURGED ON A SAMSUNG GALAXY XXL!

WHAT I'M...
I'M TELLING YOU...
SHAKE
I'M NOT GONNA BE A TITAN...
SHAKE...

E-EREN ...
巨人用 カタヌキ
IS THAT TRUE...?

JUST LEAVE!!
AAAAAH

*Bertolt is holding something that says "cutout candy for Titans." It's a common activity at Japanese festivals. Or is it? You have no way of knowing. Not really. You are at the mercy of me, the translator, your sole conduit for understanding what your beloved characters are trying to express in a language you cannot comprehend. Tremble in awestruck wonder at my terrible power. It could say, "I'm actually in love with Reiner, not Annie." Would you like that? Would you yelp in pleasure if Bertolt expressed such a sentiment? Well, he has not. It really does say "cutout candy for Titans."

...Or does it?

GUH
THUD
EREN ?!

HUFF
HUFF

OH ...!!
EREN, YOU HAVE A FEVER!!
THAT'S... PHYSIO-LOGICALLY IMPLAUSI-BLE!
OR... COULD IT BE ...?!
WHEEZE
WHEEZE

IS THIS THE FIRST SYMPTOM OF TITANITIS?!

IT...
IT CAN'T BE...!

HMM. YOU DON'T LOOK SO GOOD.
LOOKS PAINFUL. LET ME GET A PHOTO FOR MY COLLECTION.
VICE PRINCIPAL ZACKLY ...!!

I'M... TOTALLY FINE...!!
WHEEZE...
I EXPECT YOU TO KEEP YOUR PROMISE ...!!

PLEASE ADMINISTER MY RETEST WHEN THIS IS OVER!!
AS SOON AS POSSI-BLE!!
YEAH, I SAID I WOULD, DIDN'T I?
LET'S HOPE...

...THAT YOU CAN STAY HUMAN UNTIL THEN...
EREN YEAGER.

I-I'M HUMAN...
NOT... TITAN...
I... HU...
EREN?
SNAP

AHAHA HA HA HA HA HA HA

HA

EREN, WHAT ARE YOU DOING?!
COULD IT BE...?!
UHAHE-HEHE HE-HE HE HE HE
SMACK
SMACK

THOSE WEREN'T SYMPTOMS OF TURNING INTO A TITAN!!

HE'S STILL JUST AN IDIOT!! SPENDING TIME WITH TITANS WAS TOO STRESS-FUL...

...AND NOW HIS SPIRIT IS BROKEN!!
AHA HEHAHE AHEHE HEH HAHA HE
N-NO...
WOW, I DIDN'T EVEN HAVE TO BUILD A MACHINE TO FEED YOU YOUR OWN POOP.

I GUESS WE CAN FORGET ABOUT THAT RE-TEST...
WAIT, PLEASE!!
WE'LL SPEND THE DAY HERE IN HIS PLACE.
PLEASE LET US DO THIS FOR HIM!!
YOU TWO LOOK WELL-ADJUSTED. PROBABLY HAVE GOOD HOME LIVES.
YOU'LL GET THROUGH THIS FINE, SO WHERE'S THE FUN IN THAT?
P...
PLEASE ...
WRING
YOU SHOULD CONSIDER LESS VIOLENT WAYS OF RESOLVING YOUR PROBLEMS.
FINE.
PUT ON A SHORT PERFORMANCE TO ENTERTAIN ME.
A PERFORMANCE?!
IF YOU MAKE ME LAUGH, I'LL RETEST THE DINGBAT.
YOU EACH GET ONE CHANCE.

WHAT'S SHE GOING TO DO!!?!

AAAND

"PERSON"

PERSON

SHE'S FORMED THE CHINESE CHARACTER FOR THE WORD... "PERSON!" WHY AM I EXPLAINING THIS IN SUCH A STILTED WAY?

AH...
OH...!!
THAT'S FUNNY...!!
IT'S ONE LETTER, SO I'LL GIVE YOU...
...ONE POINT.
1
TADAAA
THAT'S SUPER LOW!!

I'M SORRY, ARMIN. I WASTED ONE OF OUR PRECIOUS CHANCES...
NO, THAT TOOK COURAGE.
THANKS TO YOU...

OUT OF A HUNDRED POINTS!
DIDN'T YOU JUST SAY THAT IT WAS FUNNY?!
1

THAT WAS A SPLENDID ACT BY MIKASA.
A TITAN AND A PERSON SUPPORTING EACH OTHER TO MAKE "PERSON." THAT'S FUNNY!!

I THINK I GOT A FEEL...
... FOR THE VICE PRINCIPAL'S SENSE OF HUMOR!
REALLY ?!

HE SAID IT WAS FUNNY... BUT ONLY GAVE IT ONE POINT!
IT WASN'T QUITE HIS BRAND OF HUMOR...!!
THAT MEANS... HIS SENSE OF HUMOR IS...
1

I HAVE NO IDEA...
VICE PRINCI-PAL...

I AM GOING TO MAKE A FUNNY FACE NOW. PLEASE PREPARE TO LAUGH.

すっ…
SHF...

ぽっ
POP
JOLT

HMMM.
ONE POINT.
1

OUT OF ONE POINT.
GASP

YOU MEAN...
MY HEART IS TOO BLACK TO EXPRESS IT...
...BUT DEEP IN MY SOUL, I AM LOSING MY SHIT LAUGHING.
WE DID IT!!

ARMIN... THANK YOU!!
AHAHA... I DIDN'T THINK IT WOULD WORK!
WE DID IT, EREN!!

NOW, LET'S TAKE THE RETEST...
HUH?

EREN'S GONE?! WHOSE TURN WAS IT TO WATCH HIM?!
Oh?
STRANGE, I DIDN'T SMELL HIM LEAVE!
HE MUST HAVE WANDERED OFF...

NO...AND JUST WHEN WE GOT HIM THE RETEST...!!
WHERE COULD HE HAVE GONE?!
EREN!!
DASH

EREN, YOU IDIOT!!

パチッ PLUTCH

HUH...? HOW DID I GET HERE...?
ホー HOOT
ホー HOOT
UM... I WAS WITH MIKASA AND ARMIN...

GASP
R-RIGHT, THE RETEST!!

I'VE... I'VE GOTTA HURRY OR I'LL TURN INTO A TITAN!
うおぉぉぉぉぉぉ AAAAAAAUGH
IF THAT HAPPENS, MY DAD WILL DIS-OWN ME! AGAIN!

OH, BUT I'M FINE RIGHT NOW.
I FELT KINDA TITANIC EAR-LIER, BUT NOT ANYMORE...
KRCH...
HI THERE.

TIME FOR YOU TO BECOME A TITAN.
WHAT ...?!
GUST...

SEVENTY-NINTH PERIOD: SCARY CAMPUS TALES! HE WHO TURNS KIDS INTO TITAN

IT'S NO USE. I FINISHED GOING THROUGH ALL OF THE FILES THAT THE FIRST-YEARS BROUGHT...
I COULDN'T FIGURE OUT HOW STUDENTS TURN INTO TITANS...
SHIRY
...OR IF THERE'S ANY WAY TO PREVENT IT.
MAYBE IT'S TIME TO CONSIDER CUTTING OUR LOSSES HERE.
HE'S JUST SUCH AN IDIOT!

I SEE... THEN WE HAVE TO SEARCH FOR CLUES ELSEWHERE.
THANKFULLY, HE HASN'T TURNED INTO A TITAN YET, ONE DAY AFTER THE TEST. WE HAVE TO DO SOMETHING BEFORE IT'S TOO LATE...
BUT WHERE DO WE EVEN START...?
UM...

"Shiryo" is the Japanese word for "materials," so that's probably what's on that book up top. ...OR IS IT?

ARE YOU TALKING ABOUT...
THE MAN WHO TURNS KIDS INTO TITANS?

GWAH, WHERE'D YOU COME FR...?!
CLAMOR...
OH? YOU HAVEN'T HEARD THAT STORY?

IF YOU FAIL YOUR TEST AT ATTACK JUNIOR HIGH OR TAKE TOO MANY DEDUC- TIONS ON YOUR NEW JERSEY STATE TAXES, YOU GET KIDNAPPED BY THE MAN WHO TURNS KIDS INTO TITANS!
AND YOU GET TURNED INTO AN UGLY TITAN!
MY FATHER USED TO TELL THAT STORY ALL THE TIME.
YOU HAVE A WEIRD DAD...
Is that an urban legend?

HE TURNS KIDS INTO TITANS? BUT HOW?!
I DON'T KNOW... BUT WE SHOULD TELL EREN ABOUT THIS, TOO.
RIGHT!
OH, BUT WHERE IS HE?!
YOU REALLY DON'T KNOW THAT STORY?
NOT AT ALL...
NO WAY! COULD IT BE THAT YOUR MEMORIES HAVE BEEN ERASED...?
Really?
Huh ?!

DASH
DASH
SENSEI!!
SEMPAI!!

EREN IS...
EREN IS MISSING!!
GAH!! WHAT?!
WE WERE JUST ABOUT TO LOOK FOR HIM, TOO!!

EVERY-ONE, SET SCANNERS TO DOLT! LET'S FIND EREN!
YES, SIR!

GUST

HOOT
HOOT

WHO...
WHO ARE YOU...?!
STEP
STEP

HMM?
SHFK
I JUST TOLD YOU.
SPARKLE

FLASH

I'M THE MAN WHO TURNS KIDS INTO TITANS.

NOW DROP YOUR PANTS AND LET'S SEE THAT TUCHUS.

HUH ...?!
SO YOUR NAME IS "MAN WHO TURNS KIDS INTO TITANS"?

I DON'T WANT TO BECOME A TITAN!!
WELL, STOP IT!!

WHAT DO YOU THINK YOU'RE DOING?!
WHAT IF THAT HAD HIT ME?!
UH...
THAT'S KIND OF THE POINT, LITTLE BUDDY.

UH.
SORRY, I GUESS?
SHUF SHUF
ごそごそ

IT'S THE ONLY JOY I HAVE IN LIFE.
YOU REALLY ARE CRAZY!!
ダアッ
DASH

AAAUUUGH
うおおおおぉ
STOP
まてー
NO WAY
またーん

WHEEZE
ゼェ
WHEEZE
ゼェ
PANT
ハァ
WHEEZE
ゼェ
ハァ
PANT

HE
TIME OUT.
NO! I'M GETTING AWAY ON MY SUPPLE YOUNG LEGS!
GWUH!
WHEEZE
WHEEZE
AWW. I'M FEELING MY AGE. I GUESS IT'S ONLY NATURAL.
SIGH...
I'VE BEEN CHASING DOWN AND INJECTING JUNIOR HIGH STUDENTS FOR YEARS.
IT REALLY TAKES A TOLL...
YOU'VE BEEN DOING THIS FOR YEARS?!
HUH, YOU'RE STILL HERE.
HEH
YOU'RE A FUNNY KID, EREN.
HUH?
I LIKE KIDS LIKE YOU.
CREEP...
OKAY.
I WON'T TURN YOU INTO A TITAN!!
WHAT?! REALLY?!

MM HMM. I NEVER LIE.
HELP ME UP.
OH, ALL RIGHT.
HERE.
YANK
YOU REALLY ARE AS DUMB AS THEY SAID YOU'D BE.
GRAB
HUH?! HEY! YOU TOLD ME YOU NEVER LIE!!
I DON'T.
THAT WAS JUST AN EXAGGERA-TION.
WHAT?! THAT DOESN'T MAKE ANY SENSE!
I'M TELLING YOU, I DON'T WANT TO TURN INTO A TITAN!!

AW, COME ON, IT'S REALLY NOT SO BAD.
YOU'LL GO FROM BEING THE OPPRESSED TO THE OPPRE-SSOR.
WHAT'S WRONG WITH THAT?
THE OPPRES-SOR...?
GRAB
THAT'S WHY I DON'T WANT IT!
THEY TAKE WHAT'S IMPORTANT TO OTHER PEOPLE WITHOUT THINKING TWICE!!
I PREFER THE UNADULTER-ATED RAGE OF THE VENGEFUL, ANTI-IMPERLI-ALIST REBEL!
I HAVE TO BECOME STRONGER...
...AND ERADICATE EVERY LAST TITAN!!

YAWN...
SCRATCH
THERE WAS SOMEONE LIKE YOU BEFORE.
HE WAS RAMBLING ON ABOUT BEATING THE TITANS.
BUT HE FAILED THE ADVANCEMENT TEST JUST LIKE YOU DID...
...AND TURNED INTO A TITAN IN THE END.
GUST
GUH...
DON'T DO THIS ...!!
NO NO, DON'T STRUGGLE.
YOU DON'T WANT THIS TO HURT, DO YOU?
AAAAUUUGH

GRAB

HM?

HEY, WHAT IS THIS?
HUH?
STEP
STEP
STEP

STEP
UH, OK, THERE ARE A LOT OF YOU.

THANKS FOR TAKING CARE OF ONE OF OURS.
I WOULDN'T MIND YOU LETTING HIM GO NOW.

AW, BUT I MIND.
MR. SMITH ...!!
MR. LEVI ...!!

THWA
HNG
SPLAT
EREN!

S-SEMPAI!
THANK YUGH-!!
WHF
NINCOM-POOP!
WHACK
DO YOU KNOW HOW MUCH TROUBLE YOU CAUSED?!
YOU IDIOT! CLUTZ!
LEVI SHOULD'VE BEEN IN BED DREAMING OF MR. CLEAN HOURS AGO!!
WHACK
BOOT

AH!! YOUR WORDS AND FISTS ARE HURT-FUL!!
SHUT UP. YOU REAP WHAT YOU SOW.
NOW, WHO IS THIS...?
THUD

SCRATCH
SIGH... I'VE NEVER HAD TO WORK SO HARD TO STAB AN UNACCOMPANIED MINOR WITH A NEEDLE BEFORE.
ERWIN...
MR. SMITH!!
DON'T WORRY ABOUT ME...!!
MM HMM.
NO NEED TO WORRY.
IT'S JUST A LITTLE SHOT.
PSSHHHT
FLASH

BWOOF
WHAT THE... ?!
RUMBLE
TA-DAAA! OH MAN, YOU OUGHT TO SEE YOUR FACES
RUMBLE

HEY... HE INJECTED HIMSELF...
..AND THEN HE TURNED INTO A TITAN!
SCRATCH SCRATCH
DON'T CATCH ON QUICK, DO YA?
ZOOM
ACK!

SMACK
!
THAT HURT ...
MR. LEVI!
STEP
GET OUT OF HERE, EREN.
HUH?!
THAT HAIRY ONE IS TARGETING YOU. IN OTHER WORDS, YOU'RE THE ONLY ONE THAT NEEDS TO RUN.
WE'LL TAKE CARE OF THE REST.
NOW GO!

WHAT KIND OF A MAIN CHARACTER WOULD I BE...
...IF I SPENT THE ENTIRE STORY RUNNING AWAY?!
NOBODY CARES! NOW GET OUR WEAK ROTAGONIST ASS OUTTA HERE!
B-BUT...
YOU COULDN'T EVEN FOLD AN ORIGAMI TULIP, SO YOU'RE NOT WORTHY...
...TO WIELD THE PEAK IN PAPER ARMS...
FLICK
HESE!!
THESE PAPER FANS ARE PROOF THAT MR. LEVI THINKS WE ARE ALL SUPER SWELL AND NEATO!
WITH THEM, WE CAN FIGHT THE TITANS AND WIN!!
TADAA

YOU DON' HAVE ONE!
SNA

AND AT THIS RATE, YOU'LL REPEAT A YEAR...
...AND MAYBE TURN INTO A TITAN!
SO WHAT I'M SAYING IS...

YOU'RE A WASTE OF SPACE !!

AAAAUGH
SIGH
DASH
GOOD, OFF HE GOES.

UMMMMM
OH

AREN'T I A NICE GUY?
WAITING UNTIL YOU'RE DONE CHATTING?
OH... THANKS FOR BEING SO CONSIDERATE.

GRIP
NOW...
LET US SHOW YOU OUR APPRECIATION.

I'M REALLY WEAK...
MY SEMPAI HAD TO SAVE ME AGAIN...
DAMN IT... DAMN IT...!!
THUMP
THUMP
THUMP
I WANT TO BE STRONK...!!

I ALWAYS WANTED TO BE STRONK-ER STRONG.

I WANTED TO FEED PUNCHING SANDWICHES TO ALL THE GUYS WHO LOOKED DOWN ON ME IN JUNIOR HIGH.

AND AFTER A LOT OF HARD WORK, I FOUND A WAY TO DO IT.

IT GETS PRETTY HAIRY, BUT IT WORKS.

OH YEAH, IT ALSO MADE ME IMMORTAL.
AFTER A WHILE, MOST OF THE GUYS I WAS MAD AT DIED OF OLD AGE, AND I GOT KINDA BORED.
SOB SOB SOB SOB SOB SOB
SO I DECIDED TO START GIVING HOPELESS CHILDREN UNSOLICITED INJECTIONS.

I FAILED THE ADVANCEMENT TEST... IT'S ALL OVER...
REPEATING A YEAR IN JUNIOR HIGH...
EVERYONE AT SCHOOL IS GOING TO PICK ON ME...
I... I CAN'T...
WHO CAN TAKE A RAIN-BOW...
PSS
プスッ

FINAL PERIOD: FAREWELL, ATTACK JUNIOR HIGH!

FLASH

PSSSSST

I TURNED EVERYONE THAT FAILED THAT TEST INTO TITANS.

WOAH.

YOU'RE A BIG HONKER.

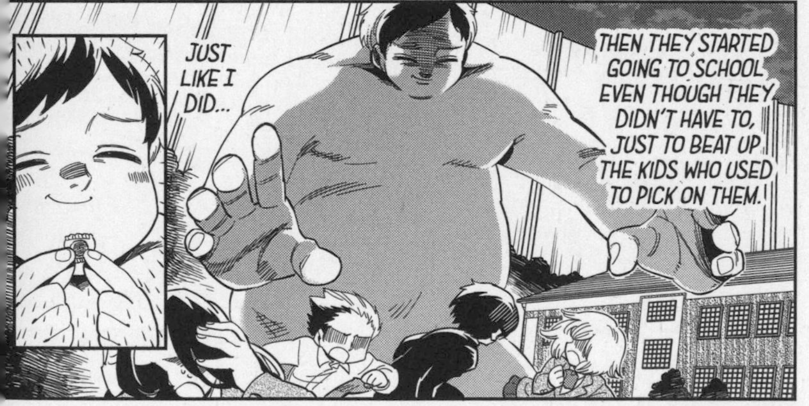

THEN THEY STARTED GOING TO SCHOOL EVEN THOUGH THEY DIDN'T HAVE TO, JUST TO BEAT UP THE KIDS WHO USED TO PICK ON THEM.
JUST LIKE I DID...

THEIR LIVES ARE SO MUCH BETTER AS TITANS...
SNIFFLE

BUT WHEREAS I CAN TURN BACK TO HUMAN FORM, THE OTHERS STAYED TITANS.

I DON'T KNOW WHY. MAYBE IT'S BECAUSE THEY WERE STILL CHIL-DREN AND THE SHOTS WERE TOO POWERFUL.
BUT DON'T WOR-RY.

I ONLY INJECTE YOUR DUMB FRIENDS ...
...WITH SEDATIVES.
GUST...
... BUT YOU GAVE ME SO MUCH TROUBLE THAT I HAD NO CHOICE BUT TO USE THEM ON YOU.
DSHHHHH
STAB
I WAS SAVING THESE TO CATCH THE LITTLE RACIST WHINER...
DANC IT...
WHEEZE
THUD

HE...
HE CAME OUT OF THE TITAN BODY...!!
SHF
SHF
SHFF
DASH
OKAY, EREN.
HERE I COME...

PANT PANT

WHERE CAN I RUN ...?
I HAVE NO PLACE TO GO BUT HERE...

I HAVE TO FIND A PLACE WHERE NO ONE WILL SEE ME...
...WHEN I GET TURNED INTO A TITAN...

AAAAAA AAAAAAA AAAUGH

SHAKE
SHAKE

WHY AM I ASSUMING I'LL GET TURNED INTO A TITAN?!
WHY AM I SUCH A PATHETIC LITTLE WIENER?!
I'VE GOT TO DO SOME-THING..

GASP
はっ
BECAUSE IF HE CATCHES ME, I HAVE NO CHANCE...
HOW LONG...
...WILL I HAVE TO STAY ON THE RUN?
WILL I NEED TO STAY ON THE LAM FOR YEARS?
RUN AWAY TO CANADA AND GROW A BEARD?
GET A JOB ON A BOAT FULL OF LUMBER-JACKS...
...UNTIL A BLONDE WOMAN NAMED CAROLYN, TOSSED AROUND BY LIFE BUT POSSESSING OF A DEEP-SEATED BEAUTY, TAKES A SHINING TO ME AND COAXES ME OUT OF MY SHELL, AND WE EMBRACE UNDER THE UNMOVING ARCTIC SUN...
HAHA...
WHAT AM I THINK-ING...?
I'M TOO WEAK TO PROTECT EVEN MYSELF. I COULD NEVER PROTECT CAROLYN.
KICH...

SOB
HIC
HIC
SOB
HIC
HNG
HIC
HIC
DROOL
NOISES
ETC.
I'M
SO...
...WEAK.
SOB!
SNIFFLE...
I WON'T...
RELY... ON
ANYONE
ANY-
MORE...
I
GUESS
THIS IS
IT...
EREN!
SNIFF

YOU'RE SAFE!
WOAH LOOK AT ALL THAT MUCUS.
YOU GUYS... HOW...?
MR. SMITH SAID HE GETS TO ASK THE ANGEL MORONI ONE QUESTION EVERY YEAR, SO HE ASKED WHERE YOU WERE.
NOT SURE WHAT HE WAS TALKING ABOUT, BUT HE WAS RIGHT.

EREN.
NO MATTER WHAT HAPPENS TO YOU, WE'LL ALWAYS BE BY YOUR SIDE.
WE'LL NEVER LET YOU TURN INTO A TITAN.
WE'LL PROTECT YOU...
...NO MATTER WHAT.
KTCH
YOU CAME HERE BECAUSE SOMEONE WAS CHASING YOU.
I'LL HANDLE HIM.
YOU—
TUG

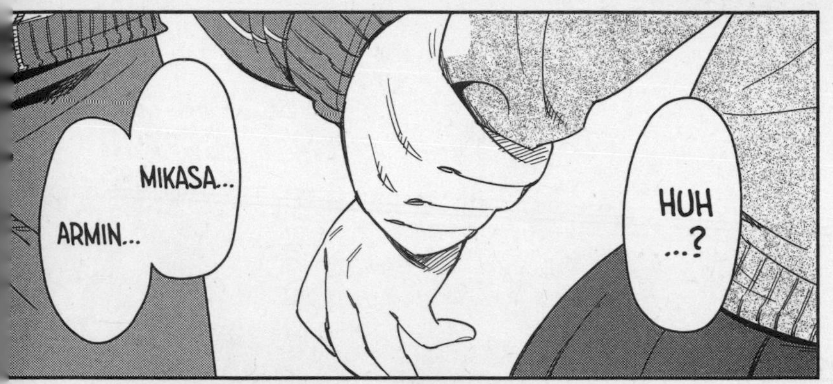
HUH ...?
MIKASA...
ARMIN...

THANKS.

TUP
TUP
OH!

YOU FINALLY GAVE UP.
KTCH...

EREN! WHY?!
GOOD.
NOW YOU CAN BE STRONG.
I'M WEAK.

I HAD TO BE PROTECTED BY OTHERS.
EVEN NOW...
MY FRIENDS AND SEMPAI PROTECT ME.
ALL BECAUSE ...

I'M WEAK.
AND WHAT'S WRONG WITH BEING WEAK?!
I...
I WANT TO PROTECT YOU BECAUSE YOU'RE YOU...!!
BUT I WANT TO BE STRONK.
HEY.
LET ME PROTECT YOU TWO...
...JUST THIS LAST TIME.
SQUEEZE
ぎゅ

LET ME GO...
I'LL TAKE CARE OF HIM...
MR. LEVI WAS NO MATCH FOR HIM.
I DON'T THINK YOU'D DO BETTER.

YOU REALLY ARE JUST LIKE HIM.
HE SAID THE SAME THING.
BUT HE TURNED INTO A TITAN THAT VERY MOMENT.
THE BIGGEST ONE I'VE SEEN YET.
WELL.
NONE OF THAT MATTERS NOW.
TUG
GOOD-BYE...
...HUMAN EREN.

HUH?

LOOOM
OH!
IT'S HIM.
HNG
WHACK
ズ
THUD
ザッ
WHAT THE ...?!

SORRY.
MY BODY SORT OF REACTED.
SHAKE SHAKE

HUH...? WHAT SORT OF EXCUSE IS THAT ...?
AW MAN, THIS IS THE LAST ONE, BUT I HAVE NO CHOICE.

JUST A LITTLE SHOT.
EEK
GET OUT OF HERE, BOTH OF YOU!!
FLASH

AW, THIS DAY IS NOT GOING MY WAY.

HEY, LET ME GO. WHAT'RE YOU DOING?

IT'S THANKS TO ME THAT YOU'RE SO BIG.

WHACK WHACK

AH!

RUSTLE
THUD
RUSTLE
RUSTLE
RUSTLE
...
HEH ...
GOOD THING I'M IMMORTAL ...
STOMP...
ALL MY BONES ARE BROKEN...
BUT ONCE I'M HEALED, I'LL SHOW THOSE BRATS AND THAT BIG ONE, TOO...
STOMP...

STOMP

AAAAUUUUUUUUGH
I DON'T KNOW ...

BEYOND THE WALLS, DEEP IN THE SCHOOL ...?
HE THREW HIM ALL THE WAY INSIDE WALL SHEENA, WHERE IT'S CRAWLING WITH TITANS!

DID THE PRINCI-PAL...
SAVE US...?

I THINK...

HE WAS JUST REPAYING HIS DEBT...
FOR EATING MY LUNCH THAT TIME...
AFTER ALL...
HISSSSSSS
...WE BOTH LOVE CHEESE MEATLOAF.
ARE WE REALLY ENDING THIS SCENE ON THAT JOKE?
HUH.
LOOKS LIKE IT.

EREN PASSED HIS RETEST WITHOUT INCIDENT.
AND THE MAN IN THE GLASSES WAS NEVER SEEN AGAIN.

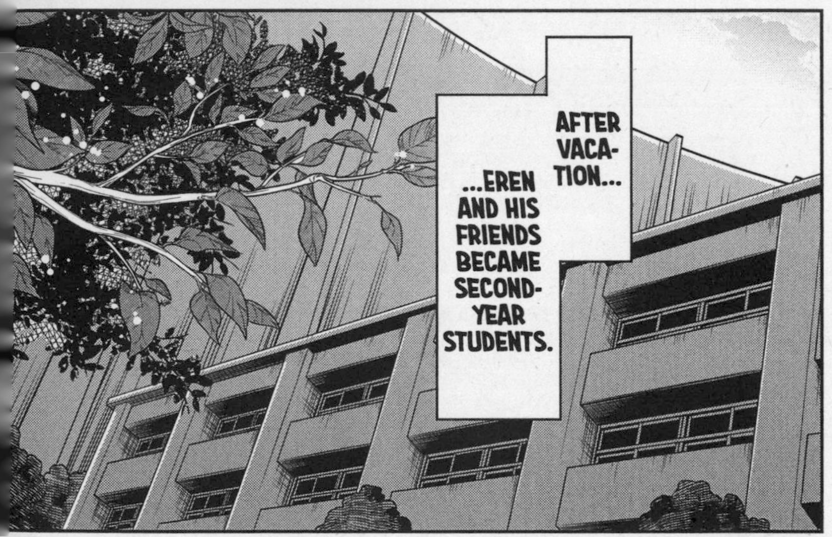
AFTER VACA-TION...
...EREN AND HIS FRIENDS BECAME SECOND-YEAR STUDENTS.

STOMP
STOMP
2ND YEAR, 3RD CLASS
STOMP
STOMP
STOMP
GOOOOD MORN-ING, PEN-CIL NECKS!
SLAAAAM

M-MORNING...
きょろきょろ
TURN TURN
OH!
MORNING, REINER!!
TSK
WOWZA!
MORNING!!
BADUMP
YES...!! I'M IN THE SAME CLASS AS KRISTA AGAIN...!!
C-CON-GRATS...
SQUEEEEEEEEE
WHAT ABOUT YOU?!
IS ANNIE HERE?!
I-I DON'T KNOW...
SHE EITHER HASN'T COME IN YET OR SHE'S IN ANOTHER CLASS...
WHISPER WHISPER
WHISPER
WHISPER
WHISPER
HUH?!

THEN WHAT'RE YOU MOPING AROUND HERE FOR?!
LET'S GO TO THE OTHER CLASSES AND CHECK!!
SLAM!!
HUH?!
DO WE REALLY HAVE TO?

HE'S RIGHT. ANNIE ISN'T HERE.
HEY, LET'S GO LOOK WITH THEM!
UGH.
FINE.

SLIDE
2ND YEAR, 4TH CLASS
THINK FAST, BLUBBER BUTTS!
IS ANNIE HERE?
OH, GOOD MORNING TO BOTH OF YOU.
YUP, SHE'S HERE.
REALLY?!

OH! SO...
...YOU GUYS ARE IN THE SAME CLASS AGAIN.
YUP. NO CHANCE OF MAKING NEW FRIENDS AND IMPROVING OUR GRADES.
ALSO!!
THEY'RE TO-GETHER, TOO.
H-HEY GUYS, NO STABBING!
FLASH
S-SO ANNIE IS IN CLASS FOUR...
NO,
SHE'S IN CLASS THREE.
HUH?!
RUMBLE
WHY ARE YOU HERE ...?
AREN'T YOU IN THE CLASS NEXT DOOR?
WHAT DO YOU CARE?
GET OUT OF MY WAY.

ARE YOU HERE FOR EREN...?
GET OUT.
No strangling either!
HE'S IN NO SHAPE TO HAVE VISITORS!!
WOMEN FIGHTING OVER HIM AGAIN...
DID SOMETHING HAPPEN TO EREN?
YOU'RE LYING, AREN'T YOU?
WHAT DO YOU MEAN, HE CAN'T HAVE VISITORS ...?
POINT
JUST LOOK!
OH--
GRRONNGH
HE REALLY IS IN NO SHAPE FOR VISITORS!!
WHAT HAPPENED TO HIM ...?
I DON'T KNOW... HE'S BEEN LIKE THIS SINCE VACATION...

ほげ
HNNNNNNG

HE'S GOT SUCH A DUMB FACE, TOO.
CHECK HIS JAW TO SEE IF RIGOR MORTIS HAS SET IN.

BOOGER SHOCK ATTACK!!
PLUNGE

WHACK
WHACK
WHOA, HE'S LIKE, SERIOUSLY DEAD, YOU GUYS.
WHACK

SAY SOME-THING!!
STREEETCH

GUYS ...?
S-SORRY...
RUMBLE
RUMBLE
RUMBLE
RUMBLE
RUMBLE

MAYBE WE CAN SELL HIS ORGANS.
HRRRRMMMM
HEY, YEAH. HOW MUCH DOES A LUNG GO FOR THESE DAYS?
HEY-OH!!

SEMPAI!
WHEEEEE
WE WERE BORED SO WE CAME TO HANG OUT!!

WHAT ABOUT HIGH SCHOOL?!
WE START TOMORR-OW.
WHAT'RE YOU ALL DOING TOGETHER?

WE ARE POKING EREN'S BODY.
WHA?

DID HE COME TO SCHOOL DURING VACATION?
I DON'T THINK SO...
OH, I KNOW WHAT'S GOING ON.
REALLY ?!

EVERYONE, OPEN THE CURTAINS!
SLIIIDE
MOVE EREN CLOSE TO THE WINDOW!
Why do I have to help?
DASH

YES, WITH-OUT A DOUBT!
WILL THIS TURN EREN BACK TO NORMAL ...?!
HNNNNG
BUT HOW...
GASP

GATUNG

SLIDE
E-
EREN...
AAAAAA
AAAAAUGH
STOMP
STOMP
STOMP
STOMP
STOMP
STOMP
COULD IT BE ...
...THAT HE WAS LETHARGIC FROM NOT SEEING TITANS IN SO LONG...?
WHERE'RE YOU GOING ?!

THE TITANS GOT HIM ALREADY

うおおおおおおお

AAAAAAUGH

TITANS!!
SOMEDAY... I'LL ERADICATE YOU!!
EVERY LAST ONE!!
HE'S STILL TALKING A GOOD GAME...
HE NEVER LEARNS, DOES HE?
HAUMPH
OH!
TOSS
AAAAUGH

AAAAAUGH
THUMP
M-MIKASA!
CATCH!
HEY, YOU'RE EMBARRASSING ME!
LET ME GO, DUMMY!
EREN--
SHWAT
WE WERE ALL WORRIED ABOUT YOU...
GAAAAAH

I GOT A LUMP BECAUSE OF YOU!!
WHACK
WE'VE ADVANCED A GRADE, BUT NOTHING'S CHANGED.
Guys, don't
SMACK
WHACK
THWACK
I DON'T KNOW WHAT'S HAPPENING BUT IT'S ALL YOUR FAULT!!
OH--
WHY, YOU!!
DASH
...
SORRY FOR MAKING YOU WORRY...
GUYS ...

I'M GLAD YOU'RE MY FRIENDS!
THE END
*...Or is it??!
No, it is.

ATTACK on TITAN
JUNIOR HIGH

YAY
THIS IS THE END OF ATTACK ON TITAN JUNIOR HI

THANK YOU SO MUCH TO ALL OF YOU WHO READ THIS MANG

AND TO EVERYONE WHO HELPED US MAKE IT!

IT'S BECAUSE OF YOU THAT WE WERE ABLE TO WORK ON "ATTACK ON TITAN JUNIOR HIGH" TO COMPLETION.

PLEASE CHEER ON THESE CHARACTERS AS THEY KEEP FIGHTING IN "ATTACK ON TITAN."

Saki Nakagawa

AKIRA

THE TIMELESS SCI-FI EPIC RETURNS LIKE NEVER BEFORE!

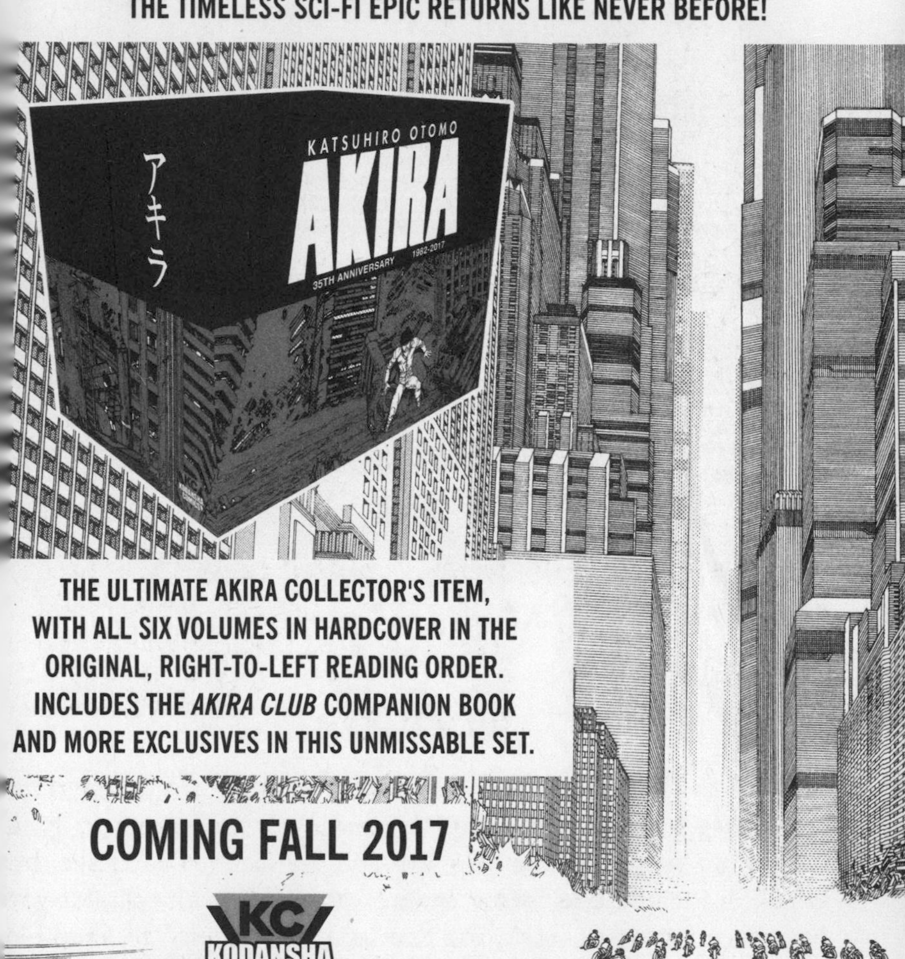

THE ULTIMATE AKIRA COLLECTOR'S ITEM, WITH ALL SIX VOLUMES IN HARDCOVER IN THE ORIGINAL, RIGHT-TO-LEFT READING ORDER. INCLUDES THE *AKIRA CLUB* COMPANION BOOK AND MORE EXCLUSIVES IN THIS UNMISSABLE SET.

COMING FALL 2017

KC KODANSHA COMICS

KC
KODANSHA COMICS
In love, there are no save points.
NOW A
ANIME!
ヲタクに恋は難しい
WOTAKOI
LOVE IS HARD FOR OTAKU
by FUJITA

Narumi has had it rough: Every boyfriend she's had dumped he once they found out she was an otaku, so she's gone to grea lengths to hide it. At her new job, she bumps into Hirotaka, he childhood friend and fellow otaku. When Hirotaka almost get her secret outed at work, she comes up with a plan to keep hi quiet. But he comes up with a counter-proposal: Why doesn't she just date him instead?

Attack on Titan: Junior High volume 5 is a work of fiction. Names, characters, places, and incidents are the products of the author's imagination or are used fictitiously. Any resemblance to actual events, locales, or persons, living or dead, is entirely coincidental.

A Kodansha Comics Trade Paperback Original

Published in the United States by Kodansha Comics, an imprint of Kodansha USA Publishing, LLC, New York.

Publication rights for this English edition arranged through Kodansha Ltd, Tokyo.

First published in Japan in 2015 and 2016 by Kodansha Ltd., Tokyo as *Shingeki! Kyojin chûgakkô*, volumes 9, 10, and 11.

ISBN 978-1-63236-410-4

Original cover design by Takashi Shimoyama/Saya Takagi (Red Rooster)

Printed in the United States of America.

www.kodanshacomics.com

9 8 7 6 5 4 3 2 1
Translation: William Flanagan, Taka Tanaka
Lettering: AndWorld Design
Editing and adaptation: Ben Applegate
Kodansha Comics edition cover design by Phil Balsman